Economic Skills in Practice

Economic Skills in Practice

PETER GOODRIDGE

YTS Co-ordinator, Business and Management Studies Division
North Warwickshire College of Technology and Art
Nuneaton

incorporating the second edition of *Daily Economics*
by Jack Nobbs and Paul Ames

McGRAW-HILL Book Company (UK) Limited

London · New York · St Louis · San Francisco · Auckland · Bogotá · Guatemala · Hamburg · Johannesburg
Lisbon · Madrid · Mexico · Montreal · New Delhi · Panama · Paris · San Juan · São Paulo · Singapore · Sydney
Tokyo · Toronto

Published by McGRAW-HILL Book Company (UK) Limited
Maidenhead · Berkshire · England

British Library Cataloguing in Publication Data

Economic skills in practice: incorporating the
   second edition of Daily economics by Jack Nobbs
   and Paul Ames. — (Skills in practice)
   1. Economics
   I. Goodridge, Peter   II. Nobbs, Jack   III. Nobbs,
   Jack. Daily economics   IV. Ames, Paul   V. Series
   330   HB171.5
   ISBN 0-07-084657-X

Library of Congress Cataloging in Publication Data

Goodridge, Peter.
   Economic skills in practice.

   1. Economics. 2. Vocational guidance.
3. Business. I. Nobbs, Jack. II. Ames, Paul.
III. Nobbs, Jack. Daily economics. IV. Title.
HB171.5.G643 1985   650.1   85–4321
ISBN 0-07-084657-X

1 2 3 4 5 WC 86543

Printed and bound in Great Britain by
William Clowes Limited, Beccles and London

Contents

Foreword vii

Preface ix

Unit 1 **Starting work** 1

Topic 1.1 Finding a job 2
    1.2 What happens at work? 9
    1.3 Your wage packet 13
    1.4 Unemployment 17

Unit 2 **You won't get all you earn** 24

Topic 2.1 Deductions from your wage packet 25
    2.2 Tax on your wages 31
    2.3 Tax on the goods you buy 37
    2.4 How the Government spends your money 42

Unit 3 **Will you join a trade union?** 46

Topic 3.1 What will the trade union do for you? 47
    3.2 Trade unions and your wages 50
    3.3 Why are trade unions criticized? 54
    3.4 Industrial relations 57

Unit 4 **Spending your wages** 61

Topic 4.1 Going shopping 62
    4.2 Shopping at home 69
    4.3 Buying goods on credit 75
    4.4 Consumer protection 82

Unit 5 **Banking your money** 87

Topic 5.1 Saving money through your bank 88
    5.2 Spending money through the bank 93
    5.3 Other financial services provided by your bank 98

Unit 6 **How goods are produced** 103

Topic 6.1 Starting a factory 104
    6.2 Mass production 109
    6.3 Automation 112
    6.4 Who provides the money? 116

Unit 7 **Advertising** 121

Topic 7.1 An advertising campaign 122
      7.2 Informing and persuading 125

Unit 8 **Insurance** 128

Topic 8.1 What is insurance? 129
      8.2 Taking out an insurance policy 133
      8.3 What should you insure against? 139
      8.4 Making a claim 142

Unit 9 **Social services** 146

Topic 9.1 The welfare state 147
      9.2 Education 153
      9.3 The National Health Service 156
      9.4 Local authorities and voluntary workers 159

Unit 10 **Population** 162

Topic 10.1 Population growth 163
      10.2 Modern trends 169

Unit 11 **Housing** 175

Topic 11.1 Renting a home 176
      11.2 Buying a house 181

Unit 12 **Communications** 186

Topic 12.1 The Post Office and British Telecom 187
      12.2 Road transport 193
      12.3 British Rail 197
      12.4 Sea and air 201

Appendix 1 **CSE Examination questions** 206

Appendix 2 **Objective test questions** 214
         Answers to Objective test questions 222

Index 223

Foreword

During the last few years there has been a continuing change in the economic world in which we have to survive. Similarly the pattern of attendance on educational courses and the examination targets set for young people have also undergone significant modification. Peter Goodridge has drawn upon his extensive experience in running courses for students in the business and retail subjects to bring this previously excellent book in line with today's needs. While retaining the well-tried pattern introduced by Jack Nobbs and Paul Ames he has modified the approach to the subject and thereby widened its appeal. It can still be considered as ideal for those studying at CSE level but *Economic Skills in Practice* will also prove invaluable for young people on YTS courses because, as its title suggests, it relates economic theory to everyday life. North Warwickshire College has been able to react effectively to the recent educational changes because of the high quality and dedication of its staff. Peter Goodridge has been in the forefront of this change in the business and retail field and has used his experience to enrich this edition.

Richard S. Angold
Principal
North Warwickshire College of Technology and Art
Hinckley Road
Nuneaton
CV11 6BH

Preface

This book is written for students preparing for their post school/college life or who are already trainees on a Youth Training Scheme taking the off-the-job element of their course in a College of Further Education.

It is based very largely on *Daily Economics,* first published in 1975, but thoroughly updated and adapted to today's conditions. It remains ideally suited to CSE course in economics and social studies and Appendix 1 contains a number of carefully selected examination questions.

A further group who would derive considerable benefit from the book are students working through City and Guilds Foundation and Vocational Preparation courses: these might be fourth, fifth or sixth year students in schools or those on such courses in colleges of further education. Mainly with Foundation and Vocational Preparation students in mind, Appendix 2 is composed of objective test questions of the multiple choice type, covering all topic areas.

The **activities** sections following each topic have received much praise from teachers and lecturers and are retained in this new book. **Data response** (comprehension/stimulus) passages are introduced; these have been extracted from topical books, journals, and press articles. These extracts will help with revision and consolidation of the text and will stimulate students to read for themselves and understand more of what they read.

Many years of teaching have convinced the authors that economics and kindred subjects can provide a course which is especially interesting to young people. It is their belief that *Economic Skills in Practice* provides such a course.

The main aims of the course are as follows:

1. To provide lively teaching situations related to young people's own experiences.
2. To engender an enthusiasm for economics as a *useful* and *living* subject.
3. To link closely with other subjects in school or college, forming a broad liberal education intended to help young people to become discriminating citizens.
4. To inculcate a sense of service to the community.
5. To tap vocational incentives without lessening the general educational value of the course.
6. To achieve a smooth transition between school or college and the world of work, and in the case of YTS trainees, to provide valuable links between work experience and off-the-job training.

Economic Skills in Practice is not just an examination course: it provides the basis for a sound educational course in its own right.

A careful examination of the contents will show that the course has a 'natural flow'. It starts with a young person 'going to work', receiving a wage packet, puzzling out the deductions (especially tax) and considering whether to join a trade union. He has choices to make; how will he spend or save his money? Savings lead to investment in factories, production and the advertising of goods. From private insurance we move to National Insurance, and from local authority services to the population as a whole — how people are housed and their means of transport and communication. As each step is taken it is merged in the student's mind with previous steps. The course structure is a dynamic arrangement of linked units providing a sequence with true progression.

The authors wish to point out that masculine pronouns and possessive adjectives have mainly been used throughout the book, for the sake of consistency and clarity of expression. No sexist bias is intended.

Jack Nobbs
Paul Ames
Peter Goodridge

Unit 1

Starting work

TOPIC 1.1 Finding a job

What type of job do you want?

Figure 1.1 gives you an idea of the main groups into which the 25 million workers in Great Britain may be divided. Which are the two largest groups? Have you older brothers and sisters, or other relatives, whose occupations fit into these groups? If you have already decided on the job you hope to do, which groups of workers will you join if you are lucky enough to find the job you want? If you look again at Fig. 1.1, you will see that there is much more chance that you will be a factory worker than a farm worker, but this will depend a lot upon the part of the country in which you live.

Jobs fall into three main categories: skilled, semi-skilled, and unskilled. Of course, skilled jobs require more training than semi-skilled or unskilled jobs. Each year, about 40 per cent of boys and 6 per cent of girls find jobs where they must attend training schemes. Why do so many girls take jobs where there is no proper training scheme?

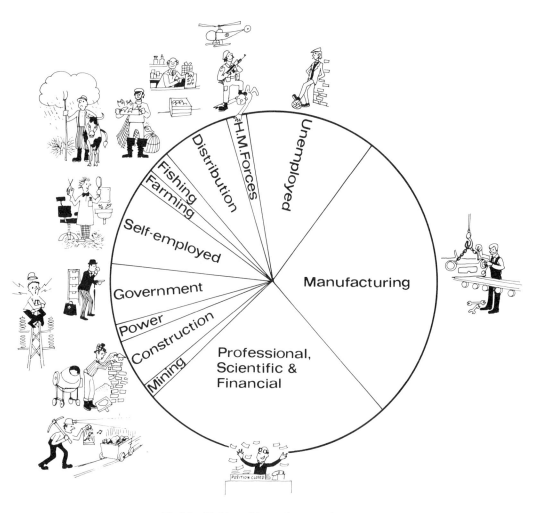

Fig 1.1   Division of the working population

How will you choose your job?

Over half a million girls and boys leave school every year and try to find the right job. Before choosing a job, you must try to find out all you can about the industries in the area in which you are most likely to work. The job you choose will depend on many things. Look at Table 1.1.

School careers department

In 1923 all Local Education Authorities became responsible for helping young people to find work. You probably have a careers teacher to advise you and a careers room where pamphlets are on display. Use them. In addition, careers lessons give valuable advice upon necessary qualifications and training as well as teaching you the best way to

Table 1.1   Things that affect your choice of a job

Factors to consider	Details
(a) The industries in your area	
(b) Types of job available	
(c) Your own special preferences	
(d) Your standard of education at 16	
(e) Your other abilities and interests	
(f) How long you are prepared to spend training	

Copy Table 1.1 and complete the right-hand column.

If you are wise, you will not take the first job that comes along. You should seek the services of people who are trained and qualified to help you choose the right job.

apply for a job. Look at the information and advice listed below. Using this try to construct a letter of application for the vacancy advertised in Fig. 1.2. Figure 1.3 is part of a job application form.

BALLY ...steps ahead

We are looking for school leavers who confidently expect to obtain four O-levels (including English and Maths) to join our Technical Department as

MANAGEMENT TRAINEES

Good comprehensive training of all aspects of the shoe industry will be provided along with further education on day release.

The company offers an attractive starting wage, 40-hour week, excellent canteen and welfare facilities and an ideal opportunity to train to be a future member of our management team

For further details contact
Gwen Skedge, Personnel Officer

Bally's Shoe Factories (Norwich) Ltd

HALL ROAD, NORWICH. Telephone 21414

Fig 1.2   Job advertisement

CONFIDENTIAL	**BALLY**	FOR OFFICE USE ONLY	
Bally Group (U.K.) Limited Wells House 79 Wells St London W1P 4JL Telephone: 01-580 3831 Telex 261105 **Return to:**	APPLICATION FOR EMPLOYMENT	Co.	
		Pos.	
		Ref.	

A. PERSONAL (PLEASE USE BLOCK CAPITALS)

SURNAME:-	CHRISTIAN NAMES:-
MR./MRS./MISS (DELETE AS APPLICABLE)	DATE OF BIRTH:-
	AGE:-
PERMANENT ADDRESS:-	NATIONALITY:-
	MARITAL STATUS:-
	No. OF CHILDREN:-
	DO YOU HOLD A VALID DRIVING LICENCE?
	HOW MANY ENDORSEMENTS?
	ARE YOU A CAR OWNER?
	ARE YOU MEDICALLY FIT?
	DATE OF LAST MEDICAL EXAMINATION:-
TELEPHONE:	REASON:-

B. EDUCATION

FULL TIME

NAME & ADDRESS OF SCHOOL	From	To	EXAMINATIONS PASSED	OFFICES HELD, SPORTS, ETC.

FURTHER EDUCATION

NAME & ADDRESS COLLEGE/UNIVERSITY	From	To	COURSE OF STUDY	EXAMINATIONS PASSED

MEMBERSHIP OF PROFESSIONAL ORGANISATIONS:-

Fig 1.3 Part of a job application form

Application for employment

Ten golden rules for your letter of application

1. Write clearly.
2. Keep your letter short and to the point.
3. State what job you are applying for.
4. Make the information you give relevant to the job, so read the advertisement carefully first.
5. Use plain writing paper and ink, not pencil.
6. Draft out what you want to say in rough first.
7. Give all the information you are asked for.
8. Check your spelling and punctuation.
9. State when you are available for interview.
10. Print your name clearly under your signature.

You may also find it useful to write out a 'curriculum vitae' on yourself. This can be submitted with any application you make and is a quick way of giving a prospective employer detailed information about yourself. It may also save you a considerable amount of time when making applications for several different jobs. Look at the example shown below. Using the headings which are given you may find it useful to construct your own 'curriculum vitae', especially if you are thinking of leaving school in the near future.

Curriculum Vitae

NAME:

ADDRESS:

TELEPHONE:

DATE OF BIRTH:

SCHOOLS ATTENDED:

   (Name and town) From . . . . . . to . . . . . . (dates)

COLLEGES ATTENDED:

   (Name and town) From . . . . . . to . . . . . . (dates)

QUALIFICATIONS:

   (Name of examinations) (subject) (grade)

(Include all school and college examinations which you have passed and any other relevant qualifications or achievements in fields like sport or music)

POSITIONS HELD:

   (If any — include any part-time or Saturday jobs)

INTERESTS AND ACTIVITIES:

   (Your hobbies, interests — anything from watching old movies to knitting blankets for Oxfam)

FUTURE EDUCATION PLANS:

   (Any subjects you are currently studying or courses you plan to take)

REFERENCES:

   (Names, addresses, phone numbers of headmasters, teachers, youth workers or ex-employers who may be approached for references)

The Careers Advisory Officer

A Careers Advisory Officer regularly visits large schools. Each officer is expected to deal with about 350 pupils who are thinking of leaving school. He has the latest information about jobs in his area and besides giving expert advice the Careers Advisory Service provides several other important functions as shown in Fig. 1.4.

Information — liaison with schools

Recent improvements in the collection of information have been the development of computer aids by the Careers Advisory Service, e.g., CASCAID (Careers Advisory Service Computer Aid) and DORS (Data and Occupational Retrieval System). Both are designed to help school leavers make the right choice of employment.

Youth Training Scheme

For a number of years now the Government has provided paid training schemes for school leavers who otherwise would not have been able to find a job. The latest of these, the Youth Training

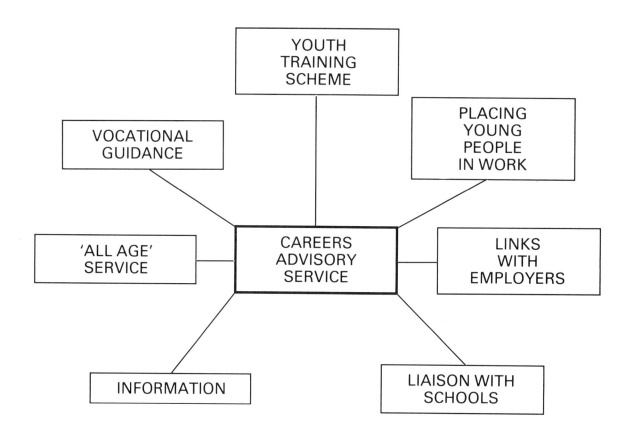

Fig 1.4   The role of the Careers Advisory Service

Scheme, replaces the earlier schemes such as the Youth Opportunities Programme and the New Training Initiative, and provides a combination of work experience and off-the-job training for one year. It is open to all 16-year-old school leavers and some 17-year-olds as well. It will be explained more fully later.

Job Centres

School leavers can also make use of their local Job Centre. This is set out like a supermarket. After walking around and looking at the vacancies advertised, the individual can then ask for more information on any jobs which may be of interest. However, many such Job Centres tend to advertise vacancies suitable for older unemployed people,

leaving the Careers Advisory Service to deal with those under the age of 18.

Conclusion

When you have found suitable vacancies and are satisfied that you can write a good letter of application it is time to think about a job interview. Think beforehand of the questions you might be asked and the answers which might get you the job. Be truthful. The employer will soon find out if you are not. If he offers you the job, you will be starting your working life which will probably last for about 40 years, although it is unlikely that you will do the same job for all that time.

TOPIC 1.1   Activities

1. Read the following extract carefully and then try to answer the questions:

Most people in an industrial society do not work for themselves. They work for the Government, for local authorities, in the nationalized industries, for private businesses large or small. Few live in the country: most in large towns. Their standard of living, by comparison with the standard of living in this country in past times or in backward countries at the present day, is high. To the politician they are voters; to the entertainer, the audience; to the trade union leader, 'my members'; to firms making consumer goods, consumers in the mass market. In fact, to a large extent, 'employees' and their families *are* industrial society and they set its tone politically, socially, and in economics.

Much of the employment offered in an industrialized society is not in itself attractive, though probably far less unattractive than most of the work offered in any other kind of society. Think how hard the labour was, until very recently, how unpleasant and often dangerous the conditions were, how dull and how ill-paid many of the jobs were, in unmechanized farming, mining, fishing, building, sailing a large ship. In any society, when opportunities real or imagined open up in industry, as they did in the 19th century England, people leave the country for the towns to seize them and no one has so far reversed the flow by more than a trickle.

Even at high levels of skill, conditions of work in the past were often unpleasant, dangerous or unhealthy. Perhaps for this reason, craftsmen of the 18th and 19th centuries were often unreliable. They preferred to work hard for short spells and then relax, probably getting drunk in the process, rather than to work steadily for a steady wage, which was one of the problems faced by James Watt and other pioneers of the Industrial Revolution.

(Source: *Business and Society* by W. J. Reader – A Unilever Educational Booklet.
Reproduced by permission of Unilever Educational Publications.)

(a) What do you think is meant by an 'industrial society'?
(b) What kind of jobs do most people have in a society of this sort?
(c) List the different roles of an employee which are mentioned.
(d) Compare the description of working life in the extract with what you know of work today.
(e) What is meant by '. . . and no one has so far reversed the flow by more than a trickle'?
(f) Why were craftsmen in the 18th and 19th centuries often unreliable, and in what ways?

2. Using Fig. 1.1, under which heading would you put these jobs?
(a) Chocolate packer.
(b) Postman.
(c) Milkman.
(d) Bus driver.
(e) Farm labourer.
(f) Teacher.
(g) Hairdresser.
(h) Motor mechanic.
(i) Bricklayer.
(j) Town clerk.

3. Draw a sketch map showing a three-mile radius of your school or college, or if you live in the country draw a map of your nearest market town. On the map, mark the major firms which usually take school leavers.

4. Make a list of as many jobs as you can think of that are available in your area. Which jobs require some special training? Tick those jobs that would require going to a technical college each week.

5. Collect 10 advertisements from the 'Situations Vacant' columns of your local newspaper. Stick these on to three separate pages, according to whether they ask for skilled, semi-skilled, or unskilled workers. Write a letter in reply to one of the advertisements you have found in the newspaper.

6. Study the following list of things which help to make up a person's work situation. Rewrite the list, placing them in the order of importance which most appeals to you:
(a) Rates of pay.
(b) Hours of work.
(c) Job satisfaction.
(d) Flexitime (variable hours).
(e) Fringe benefits.
(f) Promotion chances.
(g) Sex equality.
(h) Training facilities.
(i) Distance from home (travelling time).
(j) Holiday time.

7. You are likely to find that life at work is very different from life at school. Copy the following table into your notebook and list five important differences.

School	Work
(a)	(a)
(b)	(b)
(c)	(c)
(d)	(d)
(e)	(e)

TOPIC 1.2   What happens at work?

Your first few weeks at work

Going to work is very different from going to school. To begin with you will probably be asked to sign a form which sets out your conditions of employment with the firm you have joined (see Fig. 1.5). You will be given a copy in order to check the exact nature of your work as well as pay and holidays.

The working day is longer and you may have to obey more rules and regulations, for example, you may be expected to clock in and out (see Fig. 1.6).

Perhaps the first person to meet you will be the Personnel Manager, who will spend some time telling you various things about the firm you are working for.

Sometimes new employees spend the first two weeks learning about the firm. This may be known

BALLY

Bally Group (UK) Limited

STATEMENT OF MAIN TERMS AND CONDITIONS OF EMPLOYMENT

This statement is issued to you pursuant to Part 1, Employment Protection (Consolidation) Act 1978

These terms and conditions together with the Company's rules and procedures published in the Systems Manual and elsewhere, form the basis of the Agreement between you and the Company. The Company reserves the right to change these terms and conditions either by consultation where facilities exist, or unilaterally by letter, circular or posting notices on employee notice boards in accordance with Part 1 Employment Protection (Consolidation) Act 1978 and by amending legislation.

NAME OF EMPLOYER: ....

NAME OF EMPLOYEE: ....

HOME ADDRESS: ....

....

....

....

HOME TELEPHONE NUMBER: ....

JOB TITLE: ....

JOB CATEGORY/GRADE: ....

LOCATION: ....

HOURS OF WORK: ....
*NOTE: Your working week may change if you move to another location.

DATE OF COMMENCEMENT: ....

PREVIOUS CONTINUITY OF EMPLOYMENT: ....

BASIC WAGE/SALARY: ....
*NOTE: Your salary will be reviewed annually provided that such a review is possible under any legislation or Government Policy then applicable.

HOLIDAY ENTITLEMENT: ....

DISCOUNT ENTITLEMENT: ....

PENSION SCHEME: ....

I am in receipt of my contract of employment and having read the conditions I duly accept them.

DATE: SIGNED:

Fig 1.5   Statement of terms and conditions of employment

9

as an induction programme. This is a very useful period as it will help you to answer many of the questions that you may have been asking yourself before you started the job:

1. How big is the firm?
2. How is it organized?
3. Where does your job fit into what the firm is producing?
4. Who is in charge of you?
5. What are your prospects?

You and your boss

Your employer is the person who pays your wages, although he may not necessarily be the person who tells you what to do. This will depend upon the size of the firm and on your particular job. There are still many firms employing fewer than five workers. In the building industry, for example, there are more than 20 000 small firms like this. Can you suggest why this should be? If you worked in a firm of this size your orders would come straight from your employer. However, there are also many larger firms employing as many as 1000 people or even 5000. In these cases, instructions are given by the various heads of department and are passed on to you by an overseer, supervisor or foreman.

How will your firm be organized?

Each department within a large organization has a special responsibility, while each worker has a particular job. This method of organizing production is known as the division of labour. Most large firms organize their work in this way. If you worked in such a firm, your own particular job would help to produce goods. Goods are made by many people all doing a small part of the job. Figure 1.7 illustrates the division of labour.

Will you use machinery?

Since much of the work done in factories and other places involves the use of machines, it is likely that you will have to operate a machine of some type. Machines can perform simple tasks more quickly than man and machines never need to sleep.

In the 1980s, machines in the manufacturing and service industries are becoming increasingly complex. The use of the 'microchip' means that tasks which used to be carried out by hand can now be performed often more efficiently by a machine. This may mean eventually that fewer workers will be required but it also means that those people who do work with the machines may require extra training and specialized knowledge. Employers must make sure that all machines are safe. The 1974 Health and Safety at Work Act is intended to

Fig 1.6   Clocking in

protect all employees, as well as the general public, from industrial hazards. It gives factory inspectors the power to inspect working premises. They have the power to prevent a machine being used if they consider it to be unsafe. In a similar way all workers must obey safety regulations.

Conclusion

People rely on one another to produce all the goods that they need. Could you make a car on your own? You could possibly grow your own food, but would you have enough variety? When you start work you will join this large group of producers. You will receive a wage which will allow you to purchase the many things that you are unable to produce for yourself.

Fig 1.7   Division of labour

TOPIC 1.2   Activities

1. Read the following extract and answer the questions which follow:

CRACKDOWN ON NOISE

A crackdown on noisy workplaces by health and safety inspectors was announced recently by John Rimington, newly appointed director general of the Health and Safety Executive. The new tougher policy means that inspectors will be paying even greater attention to noisy plant and machinery and to whether hearing protection is being made available and is being worn.

The aim of the enforcement policy, which has been agreed by the HSE's inspectorates and agencies is to make sure that industry complies with existing standards. That means getting noise levels down to 90 dB(A) wherever this can reasonably be done — and better if possible — and making sure that hearing protection is worn where noise continues to exceed that level.

(Source: *Employment News,* February 1984)

(a) What Act of Parliament is enforced by the Health and Safety Executive?
(b) Why should the Inspectors be so concerned about noise in workplaces?
(c) What do you think the reference to '90 dB(A)' means?
(d) Apart from noise, list *five* possible hazards a worker in a factory needs to be aware of.
(e) Name *two* workers, other than those in a factory, who might need protection from noise.
(f)   What might a Health and Safety Inspector look for if he inspected your school or college?

2. Make a list of five firms that employ more than 1000 people. If any of these firms has a branch in your area, draw a sketch map showing its location.

3. Draw a cartoon strip to show how the division of labour might be used in the making of a cardboard box.

4. Make a survey among the members of your class using these questions:
(a) Do you have a spare-time job?
(b) Do you work more than 16 hours per week?
(c) Do you work for a firm which employs more than 20 people?
(d) How much do you earn?
(In your notebook draw a block graph to show the results of this survey.)

5. Imagine you are a Personnel Officer. Plan a two-day course which will give new employees a chance to see and find out as much as they can about the firm.

6. Make up a newspaper advertisement aimed at attracting school leavers to a particular firm.

TOPIC 1.3   Your wage packet

How will you be paid?

When you start your new job, no doubt you will think that *pay-day* is the most important day of all. You may be paid once a week, once a fortnight, or once a month. You will probably be paid in one of the following ways:

1. In *cash*: in a sealed envelope.
2. Into a *bank account*: your employer may pay your wages direct into your account.
3. By *cheque*: your employer may give you a cheque to pay into your account.

For years many workers have claimed the right to be paid in cash. There are two main reasons for this:

1. In the last century, workers were often paid in 'goods', but they were frequently robbed by their bosses because the goods were of a poor quality.
2. Workers who live from 'hand to mouth' need the cash on Friday nights in order to shop for the weekend. Many workers do not use banks. In any case, the banks close early on Fridays and may not be open on Saturday morning, though some banks now offer this facility at certain branches.

But there are snags attached to being paid in cash. Your employer has to go to the bank, draw out the right amount of money to meet his wages bill, and then have his *wages clerk* make up the individual wage packets. By paying wages by cheque or direct into a worker's bank account, an employer does not need to have large amounts of cash on the premises. Paying wages direct into the worker's bank account is a safer method of payment and is becoming more common.

Your 'take-home' pay

No matter how you are paid, you should receive a slip, which tells you how your wages are made up, and how the final total, your 'take-home' pay, is arrived at. The most important items on your wages slip are:

1. *Gross pay*: how much you have earned.
2. *Deductions*: how much has been taken out of your wages.
3. *Net pay*: how much you have to take home (or will be paid into your bank account).

Your 'take-home' pay is arrived at by doing the following simple sum:

Total Gross Pay *(money earned)*	minus	Total Deductions *(compulsory and voluntary)*	equals	Net Pay *(cash)*

How much will you earn?

On starting work, your age will be one of the most important factors in deciding your wage. In some jobs, your age will affect your pay right up until you are 21 years old or more. For example, the hourly rates paid to apprentices are far below those of a fully skilled worker. As an apprentice, you could expect to receive a pay rise each year, gradually building up to the full adult rate by the end of your apprenticeship. The full rate of pay for a job is known as the *flat rate* or *basic rate*. The basic minimum rate is usually laid down in wage agreements made between employers and trade union leaders.

Why do some workers earn more than others?

1. *Supply and demand*: Some people at work have unique talents or very specialized skills. Because there are few of them they are able to

negotiate very high rates of pay as many people demand their specialized or unique skill and service.

2. *Time spent training*: Your earnings may be relatively low when you begin work but are likely to increase when you become fully trained in a skill; often the longer a person has worked in a job the more he gets paid.

3. *Dangerous jobs*: Oil rig 'roughnecks' may not be particularly skilled but receive high wages because of the element of danger involved in their work.

4. *Responsibility*: This may mean extra hours of work, together with the worry of keeping others working efficiently. As a result more money would be expected.

5. *Extra hours*: By working extra hours an employee will be entitled to overtime which is at a higher rate than the standard amount for doing a job. The amount of overtime a person under the age of 18 is allowed to work is restricted.

6. *Anti-social hours*: Many people work while others are sleeping or enjoying their leisure time. To compensate them for this they are paid extra money.

Your hours of work and your wages

The number of hours you work will affect how much money you earn. If you are paid on an hourly basis then *time means money*. As well as paying a certain wage for a week's work (say, 40 hours), an employer may make an extra payment for *the amount of work done in a certain period of time*. By offering workers a chance to earn more, the employer expects to get more work done. Workers paid in this way are called *pieceworkers*. In a similar way, shop assistants or salespeople may receive extra money according to how much they sell. This is known as *commission* and is designed to encourage the worker to sell more goods.

If you start as an apprentice, you will probably have regular daytime hours. The maximum number of hours you are allowed to work by law while under the age of 18 is 48 hours. You can expect to work a five-day week, although you may get one day off a week to attend a technical college for a day-release course. However, some workers cannot have such regular hours. Some factories work a 24-hour day (so that their expensive machinery is never idle), while public transport has to run for longer than eight hours per day. There are many jobs where a worker's hours are not the same from week to week, but to compensate them for their irregular hours, these workers, generally known as *shift workers,* receive extra wages.

Conclusion

There are several ways in which you can earn your wages. Moreover, not all that you earn will be yours to take home. However, the crisp notes and jingling coins in your first wage packet are yours — you earned them.

TOPIC 1.3   Activities

1. Read the following extract and then answer the questions which follow it:

> Back in 1979 the four young musicians of the rock group Queen were drawing directors' emoluments ranging from £660 001 to £697 003 each from their company, Queen Productions.
>
> The Queen quartet are Freddie Mercury, Roger Taylor, Brian May and John Deacon, EMI Records considers the group's 1980 successes, such as the soundtrack for the film 'Flash Gordon', a million plus selling LP 'The Game', and an American number one single 'Another One Bites the Dust', will significantly trump the 1979 turnover of £4.5 million.
>
> Queen's accountant, Nick Lye of Thornton Baker, is quick to try to put a damper on the 'record' earnings. 'To say the highest paid director in the country is a member of Queen may technically be the case', he admits, 'They use a company as the best means of getting the most cash in their pocket'.
>
> (Source: *Observer,* February 1981)

(a) Why has the pop group described above been able to earn such large amounts of money in one year?
(b) Name six other people outside the world of pop music who would earn very large amounts of money in one year.
(c) What is the work of an 'accountant'?
(d) In 1979 the average weekly earnings of men were £98.28 while average earnings for women were £58.44. How do you account for the difference?
(e) How would you rate the value to the community of the following occupations?
   (i)   Refuse collector
   (ii) Doctor
   (iii) Police officer
   (iv) School teacher
   (v)   Disc jockey
   (vi) Footballer
Do you think the value of a job to the community should be a factor in deciding the wage for that job?

2. Copy the table and fill in the types of job which could be listed under the headings:

Salary earners (paid monthly)	Wage earners (paid weekly)	Hourly paid Workers	Pieceworkers
(a)			
(b)			
(c)			
(d)			

3. Imagine you are a wages clerk. Calculate the overtime rates in the table.

Pay rate	Amount
Basic rate per hour	£2.40
Time and one-third	
Time and one-half	
Double time	

4. Many workers are able to obtain meals in works canteens; these meals are partly paid for by their employers. Public transport workers are able to obtain cheap travel. These are 'fringe benefits'.
(a) Why are they a method of payment which is becoming increasingly popular?
(b) List five jobs which have such benefits associated with them.

5. Give reasons why agricultural labourers have always been some of the lowest paid in Britain. Do they receive any other benefits?

6. After being accepted for your job, your employer tells you that your wages will be paid into your bank account. Do you think it is a good idea? (Give your reasons.) Make a list of the advantages and disadvantages from your point of view and from your employer's point of view.

TOPIC 1.4   Unemployment

People without work

Figure 1.8 shows that it is more difficult to get work in some parts of the country. Can you find other areas on the map where there is (a) low unemployment and (b) high unemployment? Many people are out of work through no fault of their own.

In 1983 there were over 3 million of the working population unemployed. Some 300 000 people successfully apply for vacancies and a similar number are estimated to join the unemployment queue each month, so it is not always the same people who are unemployed all the time. Why do you think that such a large proportion of the working population is unemployed at any one time?

Why do people lose their jobs?

1. *Fewer exports*: The sales of goods abroad may drop, because foreigners do not wish to buy the goods we produce. Therefore production in Great Britain must be cut back so workers lose their jobs. For example Great Britain no longer sells so many shoes to other countries, so fewer people are employed in the footwear industry.
2. *Changing tasks*: Workers may lose their jobs because people in Great Britain no longer want to buy as many goods of a certain kind. Many people now buy foreign shoes and this means that there is less demand for British made shoes.

    Figure 1.9 shows the great jobs shake-out which took place in Britain between 1966 and 1980. According to a review undertaken by the Manpower Services Commission, there has been a net fall of 882 000 manual jobs between 1971 and 1979 whereas the number of white collar jobs has risen by 1.26 million. In other words, the vacancies that might be filled by unskilled and semi-skilled males are drying up.

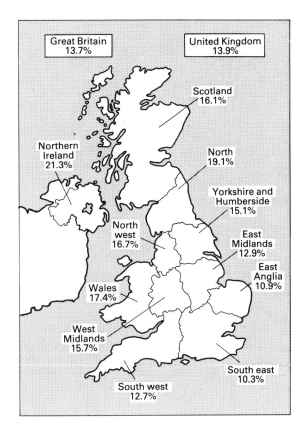

*Fig 1.8   UK unemployment by regions January 1985
(Source: Employment Gazette, February 1985)*

3. *New inventions*: New inventions have been replacing workers ever since machinery was first introduced into industry in the eighteenth century. An electronic letter sorter has replaced many post office workers who used to sort letters by hand. Computers are able to do calculations more rapidly than men. These men become *redundant*.
4. *The weather*: People whose work is outdoors are often unable to work because of bad weather. Bricklayers find it difficult to work during the winter. When they cannot carry on with their job, they may be out of work for a short time.

17

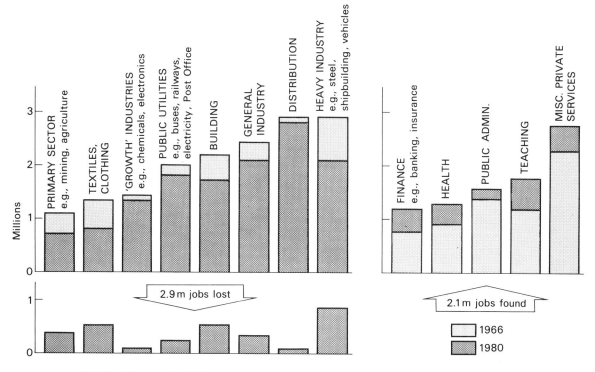

Fig 1.9   The great jobs shake-out 1966 to 1980 (Source: Sunday Times Business News, 6 July 1980)

5. *Seasonal occupations*: There are people who take jobs which last only for a short period. Fruit-pickers are only required in the summer, and snow-clearers even less often.
6. *Physical or mental illness*: There are also a number of people who are unemployed *all the time* because they are not fit enough to work. They may be physically or mentally sick and this prevents them from working. But handicapped people can often find work, especially through the government firm of **Remploy.** There are always those who prefer not to work, but those people will not have much money to live on.

Contrary to popular belief, very few of the unemployed are 'workshy' or fraud cases. Official estimates suggest that only about 135 000 people could be classified as 'unemployable'.

7. *Unsuitability*: Some workers prove unsatisfactory and get the sack. They are usually given seven days' notice but if they commit a serious offence they may be dismissed on the spot.

Unemployment benefit

Although unemployed workers do not earn wages, they receive *unemployment benefit* each week. This money is paid from the National Insurance fund. Unemployment benefit is paid by a Giro Order which is sent by post each week. As long as a worker has paid his National Insurance contributions for six months, he is able to claim unemployment benefit.

If you are under the age of 18 and become unemployed you should immediately contact your Careers Officer. After being out of work for more than *three days* you may be entitled to receive unemployment benefit, depending on why you lost your job. If you simply gave up your job, you might have to wait *six weeks* before you can claim.

An older worker who is unemployed usually goes to the local job centre at regular intervals to find out if there are any suitable jobs available. These centres are run by the Manpower Services Commission and are notified of vacancies by employers. In 1983 there were about 1000 job

18

centres in Britain, and in 1984 it is proposed to increase the provision to perhaps 1200 but with a new three-tier system. About 350 main job centres will continue to exist, giving a full service of putting employers and job-seekers in touch with each other. In addition to these, there will be perhaps 350 job shops with 3 – 9 staff and 400 – 500 job points with one or two staff: these will concentrate on self-service but with professional staff on hand to help and advise where necessary (see Fig. 1.10 and Table 1.2).

How can a worker train for another job?

Many people who lose their job may find it difficult to get similar work because fewer workers with their particular skills are needed. It is possible for people in this situation to re-train for another job.

The Training Opportunities Scheme (TOPS), which is run by the Manpower Services Commission, offers a wide range of practical courses lasting from one to twelve months at skill centres. A person can be considered for training if he is over 19 and has had at least three years away from full-time education. It is also a condition that he intends to take up employment with a new employer in the occupation for which he has been trained. Many redundant workers take the opportunity to re-train in a new skill in the hope of finding employment (see Fig. 1.11).

What happens at a job centre

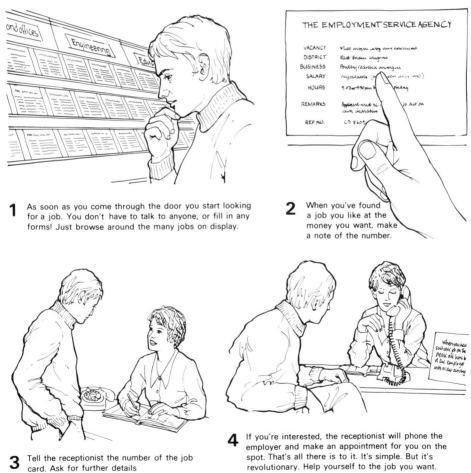

1 As soon as you come through the door you start looking for a job. You don't have to talk to anyone, or fill in any forms! Just browse around the many jobs on display.

2 When you've found a job you like at the money you want, make a note of the number.

3 Tell the receptionist the number of the job card. Ask for further details

4 If you're interested, the receptionist will phone the employer and make an appointment for you on the spot. That's all there is to it. It's simple. But it's revolutionary. Help yourself to the job you want.

Fig 1.10   You help yourself — job self-service

Table 1.2   Proposed job centre network and levels of service 1984 (Source: *Employment News,* May 1984)

Comparison between the present organization and the network planned under the development proposals.

Present Organization	Number of Staff	11+	6-10	3-5	Under 3
	Number of offices	325	198	285	187
	% of offices	33	20	28	19
	% of staff	69	17	11	3

Future network	Main job centres	job shops	job points (existing locations)	job points (new sites)
Number of offices	350	350	300	100-200
% of offices	32	32	36	

Unemployed school leavers

Increasing concern has been expressed in recent years about the large numbers of school leavers who are unable to find employment. Because these young people have no specific skill or experience the Manpower Services Commission has, over the past few years, devised various training schemes aimed at providing work experience linked with training and further education for unemployed school leavers. The latest of these schemes is the Youth Training Scheme which began in the summer of 1983 (see Fig. 1.12). It is designed for all 16-year-old school leavers and for some 17-year-olds, such as those who stay on for a year in the sixth form or attend a college of further education, or who become unemployed during their first year after leaving school. Employed 16- and 17-year-olds may also be put on the scheme by their employers. Some 460 000 young people are eligible for the scheme but experience in 1983/84 has shown that in many areas only about half of the available places have been taken up.

The scheme lasts for 52 weeks, a minimum of 13 weeks of this being 'off-the-job' training, typically in a college of further education but possibly with a private training organization or in a firm's own training department. The off-the-job training element would include communication, numeracy and social skills together with specialist training related to the trainee's employment on the scheme, with perhaps a recognized qualification, particularly if a college of further education is involved, such as a City and Guilds Foundation or Vocational Preparation certificate, or a B/TEC General Certificate.

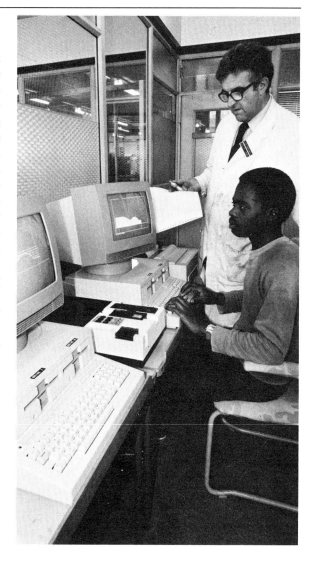

Fig 1.11   A trainee at Birmingham Skill centre uses a computer simulator (Source: Manpower Services Commission)

A TYPICAL YTS PROGRAMME

52 WEEKS WITH AT LEAST 13 WEEKS OFF THE JOB TRAINING, 35 WEEKS IN COMPANIES + 4 WEEKS HOLIDAYS

INTRODUCTION TO THE SCHEME
2 WEEKS IN A TRAINING CENTRE (OFF THE JOB)

To explain the content of the scheme + to give you the chance to get to know more about yourself + your job potential.

INTRODUCTION TO INDUSTRY
9 WEEKS IN A COMPANY (ON THE JOB)

The chance to find out for yourself what working in the hotel + catering industry is like. One day a week of this period will be spent on a course (day release).

LIVING AND WORKING AS A TEAM · PART I
1 WEEK OFF THE JOB

This includes group + individual activities that will help you to be more creative at the same time as learning new ways of working with others + developing confidence in yourself.

WORK EXPERIENCE · PART I
12 WEEKS INCLUDING DAY RELEASE + OFF THE JOB TRAINING IN-COMPANY

You will be able to try different jobs + have the chance to work in the different departments of the company.

LIVING AND WORKING AS A TEAM · PART II
3 WEEKS OFF THE JOB

Here you will have the chance to learn more about things like computers, to acquire basic office skills such as letter writing + book-keeping, + the skills of planning + analysing.

WORK EXPERIENCE · PART II
12 WEEKS IN INDUSTRY (ON THE JOB)

A chance to develop some specific job skills, taking part in interesting work projects + one day in-company courses.

PREPARATION FOR EMPLOYMENT
1 WEEK OFF THE JOB

Completing + presenting projects.

WORK EXPERIENCE · PART III
8 WEEKS IN A COMPANY

The final part, which will include one day a week back at training centre.

Fig 1.12   A typical YTS programme

Fig 1.13

The MSC has made *Managing Agents* responsible for individual programmes under YTS. A Managing Agent may be an organization such as a Chamber of Commerce or a Careers Office, while a large firm can act as its own Managing Agent. The agent is responsible for recruiting trainees, finding them suitable work experience placements and arranging for the off-the-job training. The trainee is paid a weekly allowance, currently £26.25, and is given assistance with travelling expenses. If you are leaving school shortly and wish to find out more about the Youth Training Scheme, enquire at your local Careers Office.

Similar schemes run by the MSC are organized under the Community Enterprise Programme, where work is provided on community projects and helping to improve the environment, for example, constructing a park out of a bomb-site, or restoring a disused canal. In such work the unemployed receive the local approved wage for doing the job.

Conclusion

Many workers may experience a period of unemployment during their working lifetime, and a large number of school leavers will find that they cannot find a job straight away. As a result they may have to be prepared to be trained or re-trained once or even two or three times during their careers (Fig. 1.13).

TOPIC 1.4 Activities

1. Read the following passage and then answer the questions which follow:

Jerry Tonner, 16, has just left school and was painting the Catholic church railings on the Falls Road. 'This is my first job, but it's not a real job. It's work practice, actually, from the Clowney Youth Training Programme. They haven't been offered a job by any employer in the three months I've been there. We're doing this for charity. I'm really glad of the work. I'd do any kind of work, anything I was offered.'
   'I get £23 a week unemployment benefit. I keep £8 and give the rest to my Mum. It's really hard to get work round here. I went for a packing job at Boots last week, and they wanted six O levels.'

(Source: *Observer,* 15 February 1981)

(a) Why was Jerry Tonner painting the church railings?
(b) Why was he glad of the work?
(c) How could he gain by participating in the Youth Training programme?
(d) Why does the MSC organize such schemes for unemployed youngsters?
(e) Why is Jerry's temporary job better than being unemployed?
(f)   In what ways could his work experience help him to find permanent employment at a future date?

2.
(a) How many people are unemployed in your area?
(b) List five major industries in your area.

3. Imagine you are the works manager of a large shoe factory. Write a notice explaining why you have to make 50 of your workers redundant. Remember it will have to be read and understood by these workers. (Your reasons must be sound.)

4. Make a list of:
(a) Five jobs in which people can work only during certain seasons of the year.
(b) Five jobs where workers are likely to be prevented from working when the weather is very bad. (Do not list jobs mentioned in the text.)

5. If you were the manager of the local job centre and you had to interview an unemployed person, what information would you need if you were hoping to find him another job? Write down the questions you would ask him and then conduct the interview with someone in your group.

6. List three reasons why a worker might apply to go to a skill centre; then, design a poster to encourage workers to re-train for another job.

Unit 2

You won't get all you earn

TOPIC 2.1   Deductions from your wage packet

What deductions?

When you open your first wage packet, you will find that your take-home pay is less than the amount you earned. This is because your employer has to make certain deductions from your pay. Also, you may wish certain sums to be taken from your earnings. Look at Fig. 2.1. There are four sums of money trickling through the holes at the bottom of the wage packet.

National Insurance (NIERC)

The amount of money a worker has deducted for a weekly National Insurance contribution varies according to how much has been earned (see Table 2.1). Hence the correct name for the scheme is National Insurance Earnings Related Contributions. A person who earns up to a maximum of £250 per week (1984) has to contribute 9 per cent of his wages to this scheme. In return his employer is compelled to pay 11.45 per cent of his employee's weekly earnings into the scheme. The amount which will be paid by both will vary according to how much the employee earns.

In addition to the above the employer used to pay a National Insurance surcharge of 3.5 per cent of the earnings range for each employee. In 1983 this surcharge was reduced to 1 per cent and in the March 1984 Budget it was abolished altogether.

Self-employed people have to pay both contributions amounting to £4.60 per week plus 6.3 per cent of their net profits between £3950 and £13 000 a year. However, they are not able to claim the full range of benefits from the scheme that an employed person is entitled to. A record of a self-employed person's Class 2 contributions is kept by the stamps which are purchased at a post office being stuck on the National Insurance card.

How could you benefit from the National Insurance scheme?
Sickness Benefit

If you are ill and cannot go to work, you may be entitled to claim sickness benefit (see Fig. 2.2). Under the present rules, you do not need to obtain a sick note from a doctor for the first week of your illness, but you should, of course go to see your doctor if you think that you need medical advice. If your illness lasts for more than three days you are entitled to sickness benefit provided you have made the necessary National Insurance contributions. You should then obtain, from your doctor's surgery or your local *Department of Health and Social Security* office, a self-certification sickness benfit claim form (SC1). This should be completed as instructed and sent to the DHSS office. If your illness lasts for more than a week you must see your doctor and obtain a medical certificate from him confirming that you are not fit to work. While you are ill you will receive some money through the post to help keep you at a time when you are unable to earn.

Table 2.1   National Insurance contributions (1984)

	Employee	Employer	Total
Standard rate	9%	11.45%	20.45%
Reduced rate	3.85%	11.45%	15.3%
Retired people	nil	11.45%	11.45%

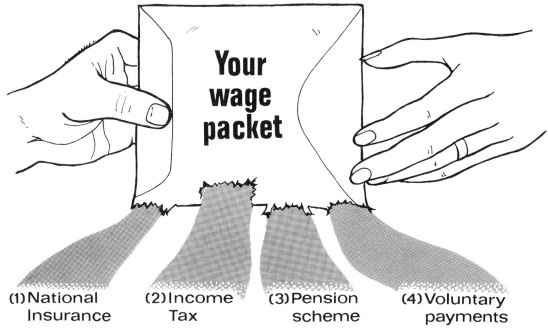

Your wage packet

(1)National Insurance (2)Income Tax (3)Pension scheme (4)Voluntary payments

Fig 2.1   Deductions from your wage packet

Unemployment pay

This is another benefit which is paid out of the National Insurance fund. As you saw in the last unit, most people without a job are able to obtain unemployment pay.

Unemployment benefit varies according to how much you earned in your last job and the number of National Insurance contributions you have paid. Unemployment pay is also paid through the post.

Industrial injuries

The National Insurance fund is also used to pay people who have an accident at work. If a worker broke his arm on a building site, it would be called an *industrial injury*. While the arm is in plaster, he would be unable to earn and would be glad of this benefit (Fig. 2.3).

National Health Service

About one-tenth of your National Insurance contribution goes towards the *National Health Service*. Everybody in this country is entitled to free medical treatment, though most people have to pay something towards such things as dental treatment and spectacles, and a charge, at present

Fig 2.2   When you are sick you are unable to earn

£2.00, is made for each item collected from a chemist on a doctor's prescription. Part of your National Insurance payment goes towards the cost of this treatment. The rest is met by taxes.

Summary

We have looked at the main benefits which are paid from the National Insurance fund. All workers who have paid sufficient contributions are entitled to claim these benefits. Other benefits which may be claimed are:

1. Maternity grant.
2. Widow's pension.
3. Guardian's allowance.
4. Family Income Supplement.
5. Death grant.

How would people manage if they didn't have all these benefits?

Fig 2.3   An industrial injury

Pension schemes

The state pension (Fig. 2.4)

Your grandparents may not go to work. But if your grandmother is over 60 and your grandfather over 65, they will probably draw some money each week from the post office. This is their *retirement pension*. With this money, they are able to buy the things which they need. This money is important to them as they are no longer able to earn a wage.

The right to draw a pension when you retire from work is one of the chief benefits of the National Insurance scheme. You are probably not very concerned about this at the moment are you? You have about 40 working years ahead of you. But old people are glad of their pension even though it is much smaller than the wage they were receiving while at work.

Private pension schemes

So that they can add to the state pension, many workers join an *occupational pension scheme* or a *superannuation scheme*. Each week they put a percentage of their earnings towards the scheme. If you join such a scheme, the more you earn the more will be deducted towards your retirement pay.

Here are two examples of private pension schemes:

1. a *teacher* contributes 6 per cent of his salary each month for about 40 years. He receives a lump sum and about half of his last year's earnings as an annual pension when he retires at 65.
2. *A bank clerk* contributes nothing, but receives similar extra pension when he retires. Contributions are paid for him by the bank where he works.

Some insurance companies provide retirement insurance schemes for small businesses. If you go to work for a small firm, your employer may pay premiums on your behalf to the insurance company, so that you will have a pension in addition to the one provided by the State when you retire. Employers do this in the hope that their employees will remain loyal to them rather than leave and go to work for another firm.

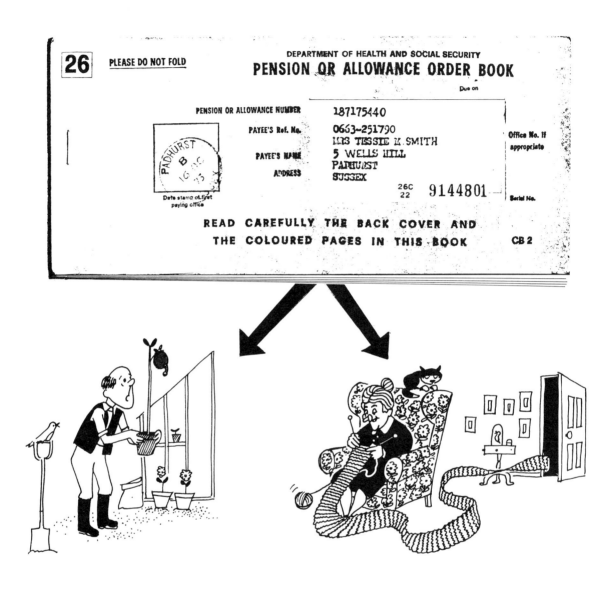

Fig 2.4   A pension book (Reproduced by permission of the Department of Health and Social Security)

Voluntary contributions

When you begin work you will have to wait at least a week before you receive any wages. This makes it difficult to buy special clothing or tools. To help with this problem, many employers allow workers to pay for special items on a weekly basis. This can be done by taking a certain sum of money from a worker's wage packet (Fig. 2.5).

In a similar way you may volunteer to pay a small sum of money each week into various other schemes. These may be organized by your employer or by the workers themselves. Here are some examples:

1. Savings scheme	£2.00
2. Trade union subscription	50p
3. Charity donation	20p
4. Works social club subscription	25p
5. Sports club subscription	10p
Total	£3.05p

Fig 2.5 Voluntary contributions for special clothing

Conclusion

Although you will not get all you earn, it is a good thing to be able to get help if you are sick, unemployed, or injured at work. One day, even you will be old and will need a pension. The State makes you save for a rainy day.

TOPIC 2.1 Activities

1. Look at the following table and then answer the questions which follow:

Dangers at work

Deaths in one year for various industries

Deep sea fishermen	28	Shop workers	17
Construction workers	128	Coal miners	42
Factory workers	124	Farm workers	24
Quarry workers	17	Seamen	81

(Source: *Annual Abstract of Statistics,* 1983)

(a) Describe how any three types of workers could be exposed to danger in their everyday occupation.
(b) What benefits could these workers expect from the National Insurance scheme if they were unable to work?
(c) How would their families be assisted if they were killed while at work?
(d) Which types of occupation may encourage attention to wander, thus increasing the risk of an industrial accident?
(e) Why is it essential to report any type of accident which happens in a place of work?
(f) Write an imaginary accident report.

2. Joe Worker, a joiner in Northwich, pushed a piece of wood through an unguarded machine and lost a finger. Give your reasons to explain who you think was to blame if:
(a) The machine had no guard attached to it.
(b) The machine had a safety guard but Joe did not use it.
(c) The safety guard was rusty and could not be moved into position.

3. Design a poster so that workers at a factory will be more aware of safety regulations.

4. Make a list of five jobs where you would expect to receive full pay if you were ill. Opposite, list five other jobs where workers get no wages if they are away from work.

5. Imagine that you will get £100 a week when you are 20. Make a list of how you would spend your money. Find out how much pension a retired married couple receives and make a list of how they might spend their money.
  Now compare your two lists. How much do you think pensioners *should* receive each week?

6. 'The fortunate many help the unfortunate few.' Describe, in your own words, how this might be true of the National Insurance scheme.

TOPIC 2.2   Tax on your wages

How much tax will be taken from your wages?

Everyone grumbles about income tax, but you would have to be earning a great deal of money before you had to pay half of it to the Government in income tax. Although this tax is another compulsory deduction from your wages, not everybody pays the same amount. The amount you pay depends on how much you earn and your allowances. Some people pay no income tax at all because they do not earn enough. If you do have to pay tax, you will only pay it on part of your income. What remains is known as your *tax-free income*. As you earn more money, you pay more tax. The tax system in this country is called 'Pay As You Earn'. Money is paid to the Government and used for the benefit of everyone. The Government is a modern Robin Hood: taking from the rich to give to the poor.

Your tax allowance

Everybody is allowed to earn a certain amount of money on which he pays no income tax. In addition, tax allowances are given in accordance with your financial responsibilities. The more responsibilities you have, the greater your tax allowances. These allowances are usually claimed annually on a special form, known as a return, sent out by the Inland Revenue, which is the Government department responsible for collecting income tax. Here are some of the main allowances for which you may be able to claim tax-free income (1984-85).

1. *Personal allowance*: This allows a *single* person to earn £2005 a year before any income tax is paid.
2. *Personal allowance for a married man*: Because a married man has greater responsibilities than a single man, he is entitled to a higher tax allowance of £3155 a year.
3. Wife's earned income allowance: If a wife has a job, she is allowed to earn £2005 a year before she pays any income tax.

There are other allowances for which a person may claim. For example, if an ageing grandmother came to live with you and had little money to pay for her keep, your father could claim a tax allowance under the title of 'Dependent Relative'. To obtain detailed information of all the allowances available, you should get the leaflet PA1 entitled *Personal Allowances* from your local Inland Revenue office. It is important to know the tax allowance to which you are entitled since you pay no tax on the total sum of your allowances. Any amount of money you earn over your total tax allowances will be taxed at a rate of 30 per cent, i.e., 30 pence in the pound will be deducted, up to the point where the higher rates of tax come into effect (see Table 2.2).

For income tax purposes, the financial year is from 6 April in any year to 5 April in the following year. The Chancellor of the Exchequer usually presents his Budget in March or April, when rates of taxes and allowances may change.

Your code number

When you have completed the form setting out all the tax allowances you wish to claim, the Inland Revenue will send you a 'Notice of Coding' (see Fig. 2.6) which will show all your tax allowances and your *code number*. This code is found by adding up all your tax allowances and taking away the last figure of the total. If you are a single man, the code number will be followed by the letter 'L'. If you are claiming a married man's allowances, it will be followed by the letter 'H'. The code number is the 'allowances given against pay' without the *last figure*, for example:

Allowances £2005 — Code 200L (Lower allowance for a single man)
Allowances £3155 — Code 315H (Higher allowance for a married man)

This code number helps the Inland Revenue, your employer, and you, to know exactly the proportion of your earnings on which you have to pay income tax (see Fig. 2.6).

Table 2.2   Rates of tax and bands of taxable income 1984/85

		£
Basic rate	30%	1 – 15 400
Higher rates	40%	15 401 – 18 200
	45%	18 201 – 23 100
	50%	23 101 – 30 600
	55%	30 601 – 38 100
	60%	Over 38 100

A form P3 (PAYE coding guide) is enclosed or was
sent to you with a previous notice of coding

How your PAYE code is calculated

Expenses ... ...
Death and Superannuation Benefits ... .
Interest payable ... ...
Personal allowance ... ...
Age allowance (estimated total Income £ ....)
Wife's earned income allowance ... ...
Additional personal allowance ... ...
Dependent relative allowance ... ...
Widow's bereavement allowance ... ...

Total allowances

Less allowances given against other income

Untaxed interest ... .
Occupational pensions ... ..
Social security benefits ... ..

Net allowances

Less adjustments for

Tax unpaid for earlier years

198 –8   £ ....
equivalent to a deduction of

198 –8   (estimated £ ....)
equivalent to a deduction of

Allowances given against pay etc.

Your code is shown overleaf

Printed in the UK for HMSO Dd 8263592 8/83 99365 4

*Fig 2.6   A notice of coding (Reproduced by permission of the
Controller of Her Majesty's Stationery Office. © Crown
copyright)*

32

If you consider that the allowances shown on the Notice of Coding are incorrect, you should obviously write and inform your tax office as soon as possible (a pre-paid envelope is usually enclosed with the notice). Otherwise, you may be paying more income tax than is necessary. At the end of the tax year your employer must give you a Form P14 showing your total pay for the year and the tax taken from it (see Fig. 2.7). This form should be kept as it is a further check that you have paid the correct amont of tax. If you change jobs, your old employer will give you a Form P45 showing your pay and tax deductions to date (see Fig. 2.8). This should be given to your new employer as soon as possible so that he can continue to deduct the correct amount of tax from your pay.

Sharing the burden

The same burden of taxation does not fall on everybody. If your total earnings in one year are below your total tax allowances, you will pay no income tax at all. However, if a person earns a very large amount indeed, some of these earnings may be taxed at the rate of 60 per cent (or 60 pence in the pound). In this way, lower paid people are helped by those who are better off.

Conclusion

You will probably pay no income tax at all when you first start work and will only start to pay when you earn more than your tax allowances. This is 'progressive taxation': as you progress, you pay more taxes. The important thing for you to know is how much you have to pay: even the Inland Revenue can make mistakes.

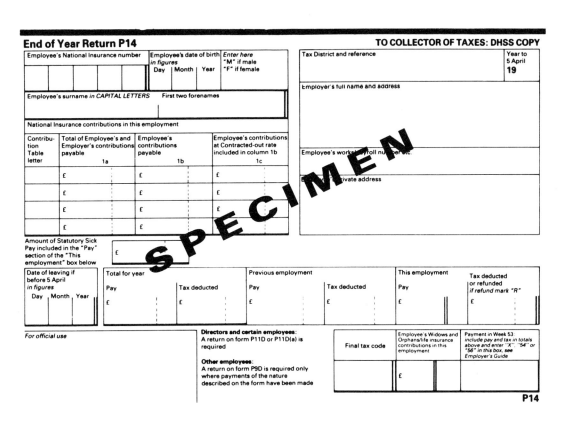

Fig 2.7 P14 form (Reproduced by permission of the Controller of Her Majesty's Stationery Office. © Crown copyright)

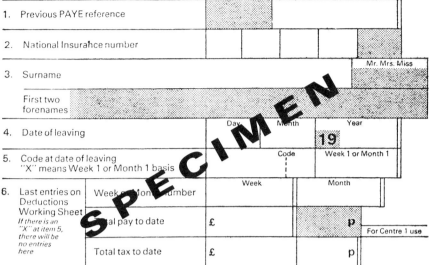

P45 EMPLOYEE LEAVING – COPY
OF EMPLOYER'S CERTIFICATE

1.	Previous PAYE reference		
2.	National Insurance number		
3.	Surname		Mr. Mrs. Miss
	First two forenames		
4.	Date of leaving	Day Month Year	19
5.	Code at date of leaving "X" means Week 1 or Month 1	Code	Week 1 or Month 1
6.	Last entries on Deductions Working Sheet	Week or Month number	Week	Month
	If there is an "X" at item 5, there will be no entries here	Total pay to date	£	p	For Centre 1 use
		Total tax to date	£	p	

EMPLOYEE – THIS FORM IS IMPORTANT. *DO NOT LOSE IT.* You cannot get a duplicate. *Do not separate the two parts.*

GOING TO A NEW JOB?

Give this form to your new employer, otherwise he will have to tax you under the emergency code. If for some special reason you do not want your new employer to know the details entered on this form send it to your Tax Office BEFORE you start your new job, and give the name and address of your new employer. The Tax Office can make special arrangements, but you may pay too much tax for a time as a result.

CLAIMING UNEMPLOYMENT BENEFIT*?

Take this form to the benefit office so that they can pay you any tax refund to which you may be entitled when your claim ends (or at 5 April if earlier).

NOT WORKING AND NOT CLAIMING UNEMPLOYMENT BENEFIT*?

If you wish to claim a tax refund, get form P50 from any Tax Office or PAYE Enquiry Office. The form tells you what to do.

(including supplementary benefit paid by reason of unemployment)

INSTRUCTIONS TO NEW EMPLOYER

● Check and complete this form and prepare a Deductions Working Sheet according to the "New Employee" instructions on the P8 (BLUE CARD).

● Detach Part 3 and send it to your Tax Office **IMMEDIATELY**. *Keep Part 2.*

P45

Fig 2.8   P45 form (Reproduced by permission of the Controller of Her Majesty's Stationery Office. © Crown copyright)

TOPIC 2.2   Activities

1. Read the following extract and answer the questions which follow:

HOW IS MY TAX WORKED OUT?
If you have not claimed unemployment benefit, your first employer will give you a PAYE code. This code will be based on the single person's allowance. If you use the coding claim form, your PAYE code may have to be changed. The tax office will work out what extra allowances or income to take into account. They will send you a new code and show you how it was worked out. They will also send your new code to your employer who will use it to tax your pay.

Your PAYE code represents your tax-free pay for the year. Your employer will use this code with 'tax tables' which spread your tax-free pay between the number of pay days in the tax year, 52 if you are paid weekly or 12 if you are paid monthly. On each pay day the tables show the right amount of tax-free pay to be subtracted from your earnings and you only pay tax on what is left.

If for any reason you are not paid for a while, the tax-free pay for those weeks builds up until it can be subtracted from your earnings on a later pay day. If your earnings are less than your tax-free pay at any time then of course you do not pay any tax.

If you claimed unemployment benefit before starting work, you will get a form P45 from your benefit office to give to your employer. More is said about this form below. It will tell your employer what code he must use for you. Until he gets it, he will have to use a special 'emergency code'.

(Source: Leaflet *'Income tax and the school leaver'*, Inland Revenue)

(a) What do the initials PAYE stand for?
(b) What happens to the money that you pay as income tax?
(c) What sort of allowances might enable you to pay less tax?
(d) Why does an employer have to use an emergency code if he has not been notified of an employee's correct code number?
(e) Your employer will give you a form at the end of the financial year, early in April. What is this form called and what information does it give?

2. Miss Suzanne Smith is a single person aged 22. Her Notice of Coding for the coming tax year shows she has been given a code number of 178L and she is earning £85 per week. Calculate:
(a) Her gross wages for the year.
(b) The amount of tax she will pay in one year.
(c) The amount of tax which will be deducted weekly from her wages.
(d) Her net weekly wage after tax.

3. If you have a job which requires you to spend a certain proportion of your salary while doing the job, you may be able to claim some of this expenditure as tax allowances. This would come under the heading of 'expenses'. List some of the items for which the following people may have to pay while doing their job:
(a) A commercial traveller.
(b) A door-to-door salesman.
(c) A self-employed builder.
(d) A managing director.

4. Using up-to-date tax allowances, how much would a married man have to pay in income tax if he was earning the following amounts:

	Sum earned	Amount paid in tax
(a)	£5000	
(b)	£3000	
(c)	£11 500	
(d)	£15 000	
(e)	£36 000	

5. Imagine your local Inland Revenue office has sent you a Notice of Coding. You check your code number against your allowances and find it to be incorrect. Write a letter back pointing out why you think your code number is wrong.

6. Would you rather pay more taxes from your wages or more on the goods you buy? Give reasons for your answer.

TOPIC 2.3   Tax on the goods you buy

You are taxed twice

You will have to pay tax on your *wages* and upon some of the *goods* you buy. All the items on the left-hand side of Fig. 2.9 have a certain amount of tax placed on them by the Government. This makes them more expensive for you to buy because the amount of tax comes on top of the cost of producing and marketing the goods. How much tax you pay depends on which goods you buy. In this respect taxes on spending are somewhat voluntary: you can avoid some taxes by not buying certain goods that are taxed.

Which goods are taxed?

You would not see the signs in Fig. 2.9 in your local shop window. Many people do not know whether some of the goods they buy have tax on them or not. As with tax on your wages, an attempt is made to see that taxes on spending fall more heavily on richer people. This is done in the following ways:

1. No tax is placed upon many goods which are considered to be 'necessities', e.g. food and children's clothes which are important in order that people may live.
2. Some goods, which are considered to be 'luxuries' and are bought mainly by people who are considered to be better-off, are taxed more heavily, e.g., there is an extra 10 per cent tax on new cars.
3. Taxes on spending may be added on as a percentage of the selling price of the article. Thus a 15 per cent tax on a pair of shoes will mean that a richer person pays £4.50 in tax on his £30 pair of shoes, whereas a less well-off person will only have to pay £2.25 on his £15 pair of shoes.

Value added tax

Many goods and services purchased by consumers are more expensive because a tax has been placed on them by the Government. This is known as value added tax (VAT) and the present standard rate for this tax is 15 per cent. It is collected by the Department of Customs and Excise.

Value added tax is an indirect tax which is collected at each stage in the production and distribution of goods. As a result, manufacturers, wholesalers, and retailers may also have to submit VAT to the Customs and Excise. Finally the individual who purchases the product or service will pay VAT on the selling price. This type of tax accumulates at each stage of production and distribution.

1. *Manufacturer* — leather buyer purchases leather for shoe production. Price £4.80 + 15% VAT (72p) = £5.52
2. *Wholesaler* — purchases shoes from the manufacturer for a price of £12.00 + 15% VAT (£1.80) = £13.80
3. *Retailer* — purchases shoes from the wholesaler for a price of £15.20 + 15% VAT (£2.28) = £17.48
4. *Consumer* — or customer buys a pair of shoes from a retail shop for a price of £20 + 15% VAT (£3) = £23.00

In this way value added tax is passed on to the Customs and Excise at each stage in the 'chain' of production and distribution. The traders involved do not actually pay any VAT because they are entitled to deduct the tax paid to their suppliers *(input tax)* from the tax collected from their customers *(output tax)*, before submitting the tax to Customs and Excise every three months. The consumer cannot reclaim any of the tax and has to pay the full amount. He is also likely to pay VAT on services which are purchased or hired.

The most important supplies which the Government considers essential to the consumer are included in the VAT system but are 'zero-rated', which means that the consumer pays no VAT on these items. This enables traders who produce or sell zero-rated goods or services to reclaim from Customs and Excise any VAT paid on supplies which they have to purchase. Examples of zero-rated items are most types of

Fig 2.9 Taxed and untaxed goods

food (except in the course of catering), public transport fares, and children's clothing and footwear. There is also an exempt category not included in the VAT system, such as doctors' and dentists' services. In this way the Government has attempted to distinguish which are necessities as far as the consumer is concerned.

A limited choice

Although you may try to avoid paying VAT by buying only those goods which are untaxed, a glance at Fig. 2.9 will soon convince you that your choice of goods would be very limited.

Many people in Great Britain today are car owners. These people are greatly affected by any increase in the tax on petrol and other items needed for motoring. Since no suitable substitute has yet been found for petrol as a motoring fuel, the motorist who wishes to continue to run his car, must be prepared to pay the increased prices, if the tax on petrol is increased. If he does not wish to pay the increase, his only alternative is to stop motoring (Fig. 2.10).

Fig 2.10 Motorists have to buy petrol even if the tax on it goes up

Conclusion

As you probably realize, we all pay tax in some form. Even if you are not old enough to earn a wage, you will pay some value added tax on some of the things you buy. Income tax and taxes on spending are two of the main ways in which the Government collects money from producers and consumers. Income tax is an example of a *direct tax,* meaning that it is paid directly to the Government. *Indirect taxes* such as VAT are passed on indirectly to the Government through a third party, for example, a shopkeeper. The money collected in the form of taxes is re-spent by the Government on various items designed to benefit the less well-off as well as the community as a whole. So you will get something in return for the taxes you pay.

TOPIC 2.3   Activities

1. Study the table below carefully, then answer the questions which follow:

	1978	1979	£ million 1980	1981	1982
Taxes on income	22 457	25 067	30 809	35 935	40 300
Taxes on expenditure	22 951	29 868	36 882	43 471	47 082
National Insurance contributions	10 107	11 531	13 944	16 003	18 069

(Source: *Annual Abstract of Statistics,* 1984)

(a) Which of the above taxes are (i) direct; (ii) indirect?
(b) On which groups of the public does each of the taxes fall?
(c) Draw a graph to illustrate the trends shown in the table. What does your graph tell you?
(d) What are the disadvantages of the Government increasing (i) taxes on income; (ii) taxes on expenditure?

2. Copy the diagram below and list five 'luxuries' and five 'necessities'. Ask your parents what items they would place in the second column. Do you think your 'necessities' are likely to change as you grow older?

Luxuries	Necessities
(a)	(a)
(b)	(b)
(c)	(c)
(d)	(d)
(e)	(e)

3. Find out the total cost of a brand new car of a popular make. Are there any advantages in buying a secondhand car which is only three months old?

4. List the ways in which you spent your last week's pocket money or wages. Find out if you paid any value added tax to the Government. Find out what your father buys in the course of a week. How much more tax does he pay on goods than you do?

5. Write down the arguments for and against the Government placing an extra 20p tax on the price of a packet of 20 cigarettes. Would people still buy cigarettes? Why?

6. Copy and complete the following table:

Price without VAT	VAT Rate	VAT	Retail Price
£3.70	15%		
£15.80	15%		
	15%	£1.86	£14.26
£180.90	15%		
£120.30	15%		
	15%	£26.79	£205.39

TOPIC 2.4 How the Government spends your money

Government expenditure

At one time it was thought that the Government should provide justice and defence, but that the rest of the things that make for people's welfare should be left for the individual to provide. These things include education, health, housing, and the putting aside of some savings to be used in the event of death, retirement, etc.

Today, however, the Government provides these things for its citizens. The national income amounts to about £201 000 million a year (1982), of which the Government spends over £118 000 million. Clearly we must be very concerned with government expenditure (Fig. 2.11), and also with government revenue because the Government must raise the money from its citizens in order to be able to spend it in the interests of the country's welfare. Until the Bill of Rights of 1689, the king had the right to raise revenue and spend it, but since that date the control of the nation's finances has passed to Parliament. Since the Parliament Act of 1911, the House of Commons has reigned supreme over money matters, although when it comes to practical politics it is the Cabinet, and the Chancellor of the Exchequer in particular, that really hold the power.

Government expenditure has increased enormously during the twentieth century. In the early nineteenth century the Government's only large social expense was the Poor Law, which rose to £8 million in 1834 but gradually declined after the harsh Poor Law Amendment Act of that year.

In 1833 the Government made its first annual grant to education of £20 000, but it was not until the Forster Act of 1870 that education became compulsory in Britain and large increases in educational expenditure began. The Liberal Government of 1906 to 1914 increased government expenditure on social services. The impact of two world wars and the extension of state activity in social and economic matters further increased the growth in government spending. The great increase in the Government's annual expenditure since 1900 can be seen in Table 2.3. Public expenditure increased as a proportion of GDP from about 15 per cent before 1914 to a peacetime peak of over 45 per cent in the 1970's.

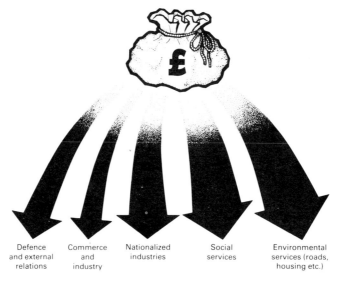

Defence and external relations   Commerce and industry   Nationalized industries   Social services   Environmental services (roads, housing etc.)

Fig 2.11   The main ways in which the Government spends your money

Table 2.3 Government expenditure 1900 – 82

Date	Expenditure (£m)
1900	134
1938	1 000
1954	5 000
1969	13 000
1974	32 000
1979	75 000
1982	118 000

The main aims of government expenditure are:

1. *Social services*: Education, health, and social security benefits.
2. *Local and environmental services*: Roads, housing, arts, law and order.
3. *Defence and external relations*: Including overseas aid and EEC payments.
4. *Commerce and industry*: Trade, industry, agriculture, fisheries, and forestry.
5. *Nationalized industries' capital expenditure*.
6. *National Debt interest*.
7. *Other services*.

Social services

People who fall upon hard times are able to obtain money to help them. This is known as social security. You saw in Topic 2.2 that many people obtain help by claiming money from the National Insurance fund. But there are many people who find that money claimed in this way is not enough for them to live on. They have to claim extra money known as supplementary benefits by applying to the local office of the Department of Health and Social Security. In providing these benefits as part of its expenditure the Government is trying to ensure that everybody in this country has a minimum standard of living. However, a report by Professor Peter Townsend in 1980 suggested there are over 14 million people in this country living on an income below the supplementary benefit level.

Education

The majority of secondary schools in this country are comprehensive and are able to offer a very wide range of subjects, as well as special facilities such as language laboratories. Many schools in the 1980s will be spending money on purchasing computers in order that pupils can be prepared for a changing industrial and technological world.

The Health Service

As we have seen, every citizen in this country has the right to free medical treatment. A small part of the cost of this comes from National Insurance contributions; the remainder is paid for by taxes. The *National Health Service* (NHS) covers many things, from a visit to your family doctor to a major operation in hospital. Dental treatment is *free* to all children of school age. The NHS helps the elderly, the mentally disordered, and the physically handicapped. In this way the Government aims to look after the welfare and medical needs of *all* its citizens.

Voluntary organizations

In spite of the large proportion of government expenditure which is allocated to those with special need, there are certain sections of the population who find they need additional help which is not or cannot be provided with government money. To fill these gaps there are thousands of voluntary organizations in this country ranging from national bodies to small individual local groups. Help may be available to those who are in need from a large organization like the National Society for the Prevention of Cruelty to Children or on an individual basis from the growing numbers of young people who participate in Community Service schemes. Both serve the purpose of providing extra help which at present is not available from the various government sponsored schemes.

Many national organizations for voluntary help have come into being through various religious groups. Examples of these include the Salvation Army, the Church of England Children's Society, the Young Men's Christian Association, the Young Women's Christian Association as well as the Jewish Welfare Board. These often were begun because there was a need for them: they continue today to supplement the basic welfare care and benefits provided by the Government.

Environmental services

Housing

The main aim of government housing policy is a home for all households at a price within their means. Although over 50 per cent of dwellings are owned by the people who live in them, nearly one-third are rented from local authorities. The Secretary of State for the Environment is in charge of housing policies and programmes. About 7 million houses are owned by local authorities and those people who wish to live in this type of accommodation often have to join a waiting list. However, not all our citizens live in reasonable houses. There are still some who sleep 'rough' without a roof over their heads and many may live in accommodation which is 'sub-standard'.

Roads

There are about 18 million vehicles licensed for use on the roads of Great Britain of which 16 million are motor cars. Motorists pay a large amount to the Government in the way of tax. In return they expect better motoring facilities. There are over 1500 miles (2400 kilometres) of motorways which are designed for high speed traffic. Together with trunk road improvements these have helped to make travelling easier and faster, particularly over long distances and between cities. These are the most important means of inland transport now that so many railways have been closed.

Law and order

Every community must have law and order if the production of goods is to take place. It is the Government's responsibility to enforce law and order. For this reason, the Government sponsors the police force from some of the money it has collected in taxes. The strength of the regular police force in Great Britain is over 124 000 (including nearly 10 000 policewomen). This represents about one officer for every 430 people. The size of the individual area forces depends on the area they serve: the Metropolitan Police Force has over 22 600 staff.

Conclusion

You have read about some of the main items on which the Government spends your money. You can probably see evidence of this spending in your local community and can probably recall when you have been glad of a free visit to the doctor. In these ways the Government is looking after *your* welfare. The Government also spends money on other things which are indirectly concerned with the people's welfare, for example, over £7000 million is spent on defence and over £2000 million on helping industry and commerce.

In all these ways the money collected by the Government by way of taxes helps you and your fellow citizens to have a more comfortable life and a higher standard of living.

TOPIC 2.4 Activities

1. Read the following passage and then answer the questions:

Housing standards are continually improving; some 93 per cent have exclusive use of a bath or shower, 97 per cent sole use of a lavatory. Most now have central heating. About 57 per cent of British households have a telephone, 57 per cent one or more cars, 90 per cent a refrigerator, 75 per cent a washing machine, 40 per cent a deep freeze and 3 per cent a dishwasher.

(a) What in your view would be sub-standard housing?
(b) Describe a typical family house of 100 years ago.
(c) In which types of accommodation would you be expected to share household facilities?
(d) What might be some of the problems if you were living in a bedsitter?
(e) How do local authorities attempt to improve older council housing?
(f) What are the economic advantages of owning a deep freeze?

2. The Government spends a lot of money on your education. Try to add up the total cost of all the textbooks you use at school.

3. Draw a graph to show the number of visits each member of your group has made to the doctor in the last year. If the doctor charged a consultation fee of £5, how much would your group have spent on medical attention in a year?

4. Draw a diagram showing some of the road improvements which have been carried out in your area in the last 12 months. How have these improvements helped motorists?

5. More cars bring problems to people.
(a) List some of the problems which the motor car has brought to your area.
(b) Can you think of some solutions to overcome the problems you have listed?

Unit 3

Will you join a trade union?

TOPIC 3.1 What will the trade union do for you?

Why have trade unions?

Your father may be a member of a trade union. Altogether in Great Britain, trade unions have about 13 million members; this is about 45 per cent of the total working population. Trade unions grew during the Industrial Revolution when factory workers realized that by joining together they stood a better chance of getting higher wages and better conditions of work. Today, trade unions still work for these two basic things, but the range of benefits that they offer has expanded (see Fig. 3.1).

Soon after starting work, you will have to decide whether or not you wish to join a trade union. In most cases, membership of a union is voluntary, although if you join you will have to pay a subscription which will probably be deducted from your wage packet each week. What will you get in return? First, you will be entitled to the benefits the union is able to offer to its members as shown in Fig. 3.1. In addition, you will be able to participate in a small way in the activities of your union.

There are different unions for different jobs. If you were a lorry driver you might wish to join the Transport and General Workers' Union (TGWU) which is the biggest union. If you intend to be a coalminer you will be asked to join the National Union of Mineworkers (NUM).

Fig 3.1   Benefits available to members of a trade union

How do unions work?

If you become a member of a trade union at your place of work, you will join a branch or lodge of the union. As a member, you have the right to attend branch meetings and take part in discussions. You have a say in union policy. Although Fig. 3.2 shows you as a member at the bottom of the scale, your opinions, if accepted by most people in your branch, will be passed up the scale and could eventually become the policy of the executive committee. It is the members on the National Executive who take part in discussions with employers, on behalf of every member of the union.

Fig 3.2   The organization of a trade union

As a member you will have the right to vote for members to represent you on the district and executive committees of your union. The executive committee members are full-time union workers, paid from union funds. Nearly all trade unions are members of the Trades Union Congress which meets annually. Decisions taken at the TUC are important to the whole country; after all, the TUC represents millions of workers.

What else will you get in return for your subscription?

Better working conditions

If your working conditions become very bad, for example, the temperature in the factory suddenly shoots up, you want immediate action. As a trade union member, you can complain to your *shop steward* who will discuss the conditions with your employers. The role of a shop steward is to represent union members at their place of work. Without him, a worker might have to wait until the next branch meeting before drawing attention to a grievance (see Fig. 3.3).

Money benefits

Trade unions often offer help to members in times of hardship. For instance, if you have a long illness you may lose your income through being unable to work. Your union may support you out of union funds during this period. In this way, your subscription may be looked on as a form of 'insurance' against loss of earnings while you are ill. For this reason, you may think it well worth while to become a union member.

Education

The TUC and many individual unions run educational courses and lectures; Ruskin College is organized by trade unions. Members attending the college are encouraged to study such subjects as economics and industrial relations.

Conclusion

Very often the work of trade unions is concerned with human relations, the relations between employees and their employers. The trade union aims to protect its members in many aspects of their working lives. As a member, the union will be concerned about you. Membership of a trade union gives you many advantages during your years at work.

Fig 3.3

TOPIC 3.1 Activities

1. Read the following and answer the questions:

THE SHOP STEWARD'S OPINION
Imagine you are a shop steward. The factory manager wants to discipline one of your union members for lateness and absenteeism. The worker's record is bad. You have a duty to defend your member but also honour the disciplinary agreement signed with the management.

(a) What line would you take?
(b) What, in your opinion, are adequate and inadequate reasons for absenteeism?
(c) In 1983 about 5.3 million working days were lost in British industry because of strikes, how do you think this figure is calculated?
(d) Explain how absenteeism on the shop floor could affect your workmates.
(e) Explain the term disciplinary agreement.

2. Copy the table below. List five complaints which a shop steward might hear in the course of his work. What action is he likely to take?

	Complaint	Likely action
(a)		
(b)		
(c)		
(d)		
(e)		

3. Read the following rule issued by a firm in 1852.

> A stove is provided for the benefit of the clerical staff. Coal and wood must be kept in the locker. It is recommended that each member of the clerical staff brings four pounds of coal each day during the cold weather.

As a trade union official, write a letter to the firm complaining about this rule and giving reasons why you think it should be changed.

4. Collect as many newspapers as you can which describe different trade union activities. Using these cuttings, write a letter to your local paper saying why you think that trade unions are *either* (a) doing a good job, *or* (b) ought to be banned by law.

5. As a shop steward, make out an *accident report* concerning a member of your union. Describe in detail why and how the accident happened and then point out why you consider it to be the employer's fault.

6. Write a letter to the local branch of your trade union claiming sickness benefit to which you think you are entitled as a member of the trade union.

TOPIC 3.2 Trade unions and your wages

Collective bargaining

When you begin work, it is likely that you will accept the wages offered to you. However, it is also likely that your wage has been decided for you and your fellow workers by discussions between trade unions and employers. Many employers have now joined employers' associations in order to be in a stronger position when negotiating with the unions. These negotiations often affect entire industries rather than individual firms. When employers discuss with workers anything that is going to change working conditions or wages, it is called *joint consultation* or *collective bargaining*. Many large firms have regular meetings between trade union representatives and management to discuss these matters; the smooth running of any organization depends on good human relations (Fig. 3.4).

Fig 3.4 Wage bargaining

Wage negotiations

The first stage in determining the wage for a certain job takes the form of discussions between trade unions and employers. On these occasions, trade unionists and employers face each other across the negotiating table, as shown in Fig. 3.5. The two sides bargain and try to reach some sort of agreement. These discussions are based on *demands* made by the union and *offers* made by the employers. The agreement eventually reached may be a compromise between the union's demands and the employers' offers. Both sides may have to 'give a little'.

The following is an example of the stages through which the discussions might progress:

Fig 3.5 Employers and trade unionists face each other across the negotiation table

1. The trade union demands a 10 per cent per week pay increase for all members.
2. The employers offer 5 per cent per week.
3. Further bargaining takes place between the two sides.
4. Both the trade union and the employers agree to a 7½ per cent per week pay increase.

Points about conditions of work may be included in such an agreement. The employer may wish to see an increase in production as a result of paying the extra weekly wage, while the trade union may try to secure some extra holiday time for its members.

Rail chief warns strikers

5000 LOSE JOBS IN PAY ROW

Fig 3.6   Pay talks break down

If they fail to agree

Not all discussions on wages are easy or successful. Agreement may not be reached between the two sides. We often see newspaper headlines such as the ones shown in Fig. 3.6. Both sides may be keen to reach an agreement, but find it impossible to do so by just talking among themselves. A gap remains between the union's demands and the employers' offers (Fig. 3.7). However there are some other ways which may assist the bargaining, and help both sides reach a satisfactory agreement.

Conciliation

If employers and unions fail to agree then conciliators from the Advisory, Conciliation, and Arbitration Service (ACAS) may be asked to help. ACAS is run by a council consisting of a chairman and nine members — three nominated by the Confederation of British Industry (CBI), three by the Trades Union Congress (TUC), and three independent members. All 10 members are experienced in industrial relations and provide an independent third party which attempts to help both sides involved in collective bargaining to reach an agreement. However, ACAS has no legal powers and cannot force the two sides to reach agreement. It can only attempt to assist if requested to do so. ACAS also deals with complaints under the Equal Pay Act of 1970, the Sex Discrimination Act 1975, and the Race Relations Act 1976.

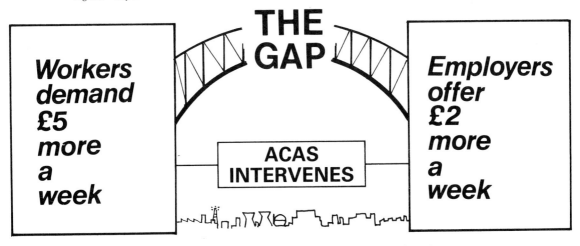

Fig 3.7   The gap between wage demands and the employers' offer

Arbitration

A Board of Arbitration is an independent body appointed by ACAS which looks into *the reasons why* the trade unions are demanding 10 per cent and the employers are offering only 5 per cent. The Board only sits when all other steps to bring about an agreement have failed. After listening to the arguments put forward by both sides, the Board recommends the amount which it feels should be awarded. Its recommendation cannot be enforced by law, although often both the unions and the employers accept it. This is because the Board is impartial, i.e., not on the side of either the unions or the employers.

Conclusion

Of course it is possible that even after all these discussions, the two sides still fail to 'bridge the gap' and the trade union may have to take further action. But the Government may try to help them reach an agreement. The process by which your wages have been determined is summarized in Fig. 3.8.

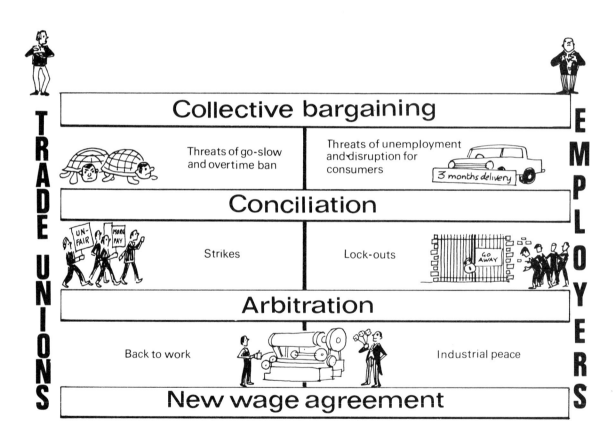

Fig 3.8   Reaching a wage agreement

TOPIC 3.2   Activities

1. Read the passage and answer the questions:

A service without formalities
There is no formality in obtaining ACAS assistance which will be given readily; this assistance is confidential. Requests for help may come from employers, employers' associations, trade unions or perhaps other related parties; sometimes requests are made jointly by both employers and employee representatives. Advice is available on matters such as:
- Disciplinary, dismissal, and redundancy procedures.
- Procedures for settling disputes and grievances.
- Manpower planning, labour turnover, and absenteeism.
- Payment systems and job evaluation.
- Equal pay and anti-discrimination legislation.
        (Source: ACAS publication *Advice on Personnel Management and Industrial Relations Practice*)

Explain what you understand by the following mentioned in the above extract:
(a) Employers' associations.
(b) Labour turnover.
(c) Job evaluation.
(d) Redundancy and dismissal procedures.
(e) Payment systems.
(f) Anti-discrimination legislation.

2. Collect newspaper cuttings which report discussions between trade unions and employers. Stick them in your notebook and underneath list the main points which were discussed.

3. Nearly 80 per cent of the workers in Great Britain have their wages set by collective bargaining. In which occupations are wages *not* determined in this way?

4. Trade unions bargain on behalf of their members. Do you think it is fair that members and non-members should receive higher wages gained by the trade unions? Give reasons for your answer.

5. List five reasons why agricultural workers are among the lower paid.

6. What is the 'Index of Retail Prices'? How might this help trade unionists when they press claims for higher wages?

7. 'One man's wage increase is another man's price increase.' Explain what you think this quotation means.

TOPIC 3.3   Why are trade unions criticized?

Industrial action

When trade unions and employers fail to reach an agreement in their discussions, union members on the advice of their leaders may take industrial action, usually in the form of a strike. Such actions may cause the general public inconvenience if they are not supplied with particular goods or services produced by workers who are taking the industrial action. Table 3.1 will give you an idea of how many working days may be lost in a year because of industrial action.

Other forms of industrial action taken when trade unionists cannot agree to a settlement with employers may slow down production; these are known as restrictive practices. In 1981 civil servants withdrew their labour and almost immediately consumers were faced with the prospect of disrupted services, and in 1984 coalminers were in extensive dispute with the Government in protest against pit closures. By early 1985 the coal strike was still in progress and coal faces and equipment worth many millions of pounds had been lost through neglect. If industrial action continues for some time, it can cost the country a great deal of money in lost production.

Strikes

If discussions fail to bring trade unions the increase they want, their members may come out on strike. As a result, much production may be lost, while the union members lose their wages. An *official strike* is one which has the backing of the trade union, whereas an *unofficial strike* takes place against the recommendations of the union. In 1983 about 5.3 million working days were lost through strike action, compared with an average of nearly 13 million days per annum in the 1970s. This represented a 67 per cent reduction in days lost. When a strike takes place, trade union members withdraw their labour, but non-union members may continue to work, although they may be very unpopular with union members. Pickets are often posted at the factory gates to dissuade non-union members from going to work.

Demarcation disputes

Disputes may take place when one person does another's job. If a carpenter fills in a hole in a wall, the union may be displeased because it is a plasterer's job. Because there are different rates of pay for different jobs, trade unions try to protect the jobs and wage rates of individual members. *Who does what?* disputes make trade unions unpopular because they slow down production (Fig. 3.9).

Go slows

By this method, trade union members slow down production without withdrawing their labour or stopping production altogether. If trade union members work strictly to the rules of employment set out by their employers, this may slow down production. Such action is known as *working to rule*. If train drivers are not happy with wage discussions, they may refuse to take out a train with a faulty speedometer. By working to rule, they do not lose money as they would if they were on strike, but such actions are likely to bring many complaints from passengers.

Overtime bans

Nobody is bound to work overtime: it is merely extra hours worked for extra money. If a trade union tells its members not to work any extra hours, it can upset production. Many employers rely upon overtime to reach their production target. For instance, an urgent order from a customer may require workers to do a great deal of overtime if it is to be finished on time. If overtime is banned, the order will be delayed and the customer may cancel it.

Conclusion

All of the actions described may mean that trade unions and their members are criticized by the Government, employers, and members of the

Table 3.1 Working days lost as a result of stoppages

	1972	1973	1974	1975	1976	*Thousands* 1977	1978	1979	1980	1981	1982
Working days lost through the stoppages which began in the year[2]	23 923	7 145	14 845	5 914	3 509	10 378	9 391	29 051	11 965	4 244	5 276
Analysis by workers involved:											
Under 100 workers	406	378	440	374	293	377	390	302	184	175	148
100 and under 250 workers	591	598	668	579	399	662	695	603	252	241	236
250 and under 500 workers	890	648	887	671	570	873	679	779	316	375	312
500 and under 1 000 workers	1 151	738	1 071	834	563	1 205	1 139	1 089	466	536	426
1 000 and under 2 500 workers	1 897	1 248	1 604	1 092	773	1 473	1 312	1 497	734	589	511
2 500 and under 5 000 workers	2 155	879	1 054	1 272	426	1 944	1 196	1 486	317	250	303
5 000 workers and over	16 834	2 654	9 121	1 094	485	3 843	3 980	23 295	9 696	2 078	3 340
Working days lost each year through all stoppages in progress[3]											
Analysis by industry[1]											
All industries and services	23 909	7 197	14 750	6 012	3 284	10 142	9 405	29 474	11 964	4 266	5 313
Mining and quarrying	10 800	91	5 628	56	78	97	201	128	166	237	374
Metals, engineering, shipbuilding and vehicles	6 636	4 800	5 837	3 932	1 977	6 133	5 985	20 390	10 155	1 731	1 457
Textiles	236	140	236	257	39	208	131	72	36	20	45
Clothing and footwear	38	53	19	93	26	56	47	38	8	19	21
Construction	4 188	176	252	247	570	297	416	834	281	86	44
Transport and communication	876	331	705	422	132	301	360	1 419	253	359	1 675
All other industries and services	1 135	1 608	2 072	1 006	461	3 050	2 264	6 594	1 065	1 814	1 697

[1] Figures are based on the Standard Industrial Classification 1968.

[2] The figures for working days lost include days lost in subsequent years where the stoppages extended into the following calendar year.

[3] This analysis shows the total working days lost *within* each year as a result of stoppages in progress in that year whether beginning in that or an earlier year.

(Source: *Annual Abstract of Statistics*, 1984)

public. They may cause hardship, but there comes a time when unions think that it is the only way by which they can get higher wages or better conditions. They may seem to take a selfish point of view without considering others. For example, a power workers' strike could mean that many old age pensioners are without heat or light. However, trade unionists argue that this is sometimes the only way in which they can get their employers to take notice of their demands. In the process, they often receive a great deal of criticism from the general public who are inconvenienced.

Fig 3.9

TOPIC 3.3 Activities

1. Read the following extract and answer the questions:

The myths of work and strikes

Britain's workers were exploding the persistent myths about our industrial performance by striking less and working better than at any time in the last three years, Employment Secretary Tom King said recently.

The first myth was that the British workers were 'always out on strike' and he pointed out that figures for the year so far had shown a massive reduction of days lost.

He said that in the 1970s Britain lost an annual average of 13 million working days and last year's [1983] figures were down to 5.3 million.

Another myth was that the British worker was a shirker. But the latest figures showed that the amount produced per worker in industry had risen by more than 15 per cent over the last three years to record levels.

The third myth was that British labour costs would always rise too fast. But recent figures for unit wage costs in manufacturing industry showed a rise of only 2.8 per cent over the past year — the lowest increase since the 1960s.

(Source: *Employment News,* December 1983)

(a) Explain the first sentence of the extract in your own words.
(b) Give some reasons why the figure for working days lost in 1983 was so much lower than the average figure for the 1970s.
(c) Express the reduction in working days lost as a percentage.
(d) Why, according to the extract, is it a myth that the British worker is a shirker? Answer in your own words.
(e) What is meant by the term 'labour costs'?
(f) Is the United Kingdom strike record relatively good or bad?

2. Imagine you are a trade unionist on strike being interviewed by a radio reporter. State your case and explain to the public why you are on strike. (If possible put the interview on tape.)

3. As a shop steward you have to report to your employers and tell them that the union members have decided to strike. Write out what you would say. Remember that you will have to give reasons for your workmates' actions.

4. Suggest some ways in which people in the following occupations might 'work to rule':
(a) Caretaker.
(b) Dustman.
(c) Postman.
(d) Schoolteacher.
(e) Shop assistant.

5. Draw a graph to show the number of hours worked as overtime by the parents of your class. How many work regular overtime? What sort of jobs do they do?

6. Make a list of five occupations which you think would cause greatest inconvenience if the workers went on strike. Opposite each occupation suggest ways in which our everyday life might be made more difficult.

7. What actions by trade unions are least likely to be successful in obtaining higher wages and better working conditions? Suggest why this should be so.

TOPIC 3.4   Industrial relations

Industrial relations in Great Britain have been established mainly on a voluntary basis. Most trade unionists take strike action only as a last resort. Such actions will result in a loss of wages for trade unionists, lost production for employers, and concern by the Government because of disruption caused to the economy. Generally all three parties are keen to maintain good industrial relations and at times may participate in tripartite talks in an attempt to achieve this end.

You will see in Fig. 3.10 that, in these discussions with the Government, the unions and the employers represented by their own organizations, and although they may have disagreements they can come together to agree on certain points.

Confederation of British Industry

The Confederation of British Industry is an association of business organizations. Such organizations may be divided into the following groups:

1. *Industrial* — companies in productive or manufacturing industries.
2. *Commercial* — companies in trading or service industries.
3. *Public sector* — public corporations and nationalized industries.
4. *Employers' organizations and trade associations* — representing individual manufacturing industries.
5. *Commercial associations* with members in finance and commerce.

As the CBI represents such a wide range of employers it is influential and often consulted by the Government. It has a membership of nearly 12 000 companies and over 200 trade and employers' associations. Both the CBI, TUC and Government may be interested in similar things such as wages, pensions, and safety at work. The employers' and employees' organizations have links through their membership of the Manpower Services Commission and the Advisory, Conciliation, and Arbitration Service. The two organizations also meet through the joint CBI/TUC Committee. As they represent different groups they often disagree, but it is to be hoped that they will often find 'common-ground' in an attempt to preserve good industrial relations.

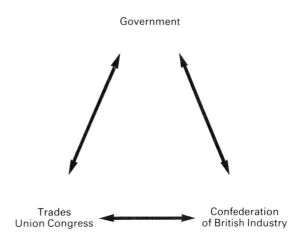

Fig 3.10   Tripartite talks may bring everyone closer together.

Trades Union Congress

By joining together, trade union members are able to exercise more power. The TUC represents nearly 11 million affiliated workers. Such a large organization attempts to persuade and influence the affiliated unions to follow its general policy guidelines.

The TUC usually meets at the beginning of September for one week, at a seaside resort. This is convenient, because the holiday makers are departing, so the hotels and assembly halls are available. Each union is allowed to send one delegate for every 5000 members. Delegates discuss motions which have been put forward by affiliated unions. These discussion points are adopted or rejected by means of a card or block vote by union delegates. This allows the large unions to cast millions of votes on behalf of their members (Fig. 3.11).

With such voting powers, the larger unions are obviously the most influential in deciding TUC policy for the coming year. The four largest unions are:

1. Transport and General Workers Union.
2. Amalgamated Union of Engineering Workers.
3. General and Municipal Workers.
4. National Association of Local Government Officers.

In a similar way to the CBI, the TUC has a full-time general secretary. The day-to-day organization is divided into five departments.

1. *Organization and Industrial Relations* — responsible for union matters and trade union legislation.
2. *Education* — responsible for educational work relating to trade unions. Ruskin College is an education establishment for trade unionists.
3. *International* — responsible for relations with trade union organizations outside this country. The TUC is a member of the International Labour Organization, which coordinates trade union affairs on a world-wide scale.
4. *Economic* — responsible for the finance of the organization and economic matters concerning trade unions in this country.
5. *Social Insurance and Industrial Welfare* — responsible for such matters as social security, health and safety.

A full-time staff works throughout the year to help trade unionists, even though the Congress itself only lasts for a week. The TUC elects delegates to the General Council and to the departments, listed above. Therefore, in any participation in tripartite talks dealing with industrial relations, the TUC is speaking on behalf of millions of workers and tries to secure the best possible working conditions for them.

Fig 3.11   A card vote at the Trades Union Congress

The Government

The Government can also affect the lives of workers and their general standard of living through its policies on housing and social security, as well as by passing laws which may affect pay and working conditions. During the past 15 years, governments have adopted prices and incomes policies in an attempt to limit price increases and large pay increases. Such policies affect both the CBI and the TUC. Although the present Conservative Government has had no prices and incomes policy it has issued 'guidelines' saying that pay increases in the public sector should not be in excess of a certain percentage. However, many groups of workers thought they were a special case and negotiated higher percentage pay increases than the Government would have liked.

The Government may also pass new laws which affect trade union activities. They see these laws as a way of securing improved industrial relations although the trade unions may not agree. Recent laws passed by Government have included the following:

1. *Industrial Relations Act 1971*: Unfortunately this Act did not work well mainly because many big trade unions refused to recognize the National Industrial Relations Court which had been set up under the Act. The trade unions also believed that good industrial relations were more likely to come about if the Government did not interfere in the free collective bargaining between unions and employers. As a result of these objections the number of working days lost in 1972 increased to 24 million — the highest number since the General Strike of 1926. The Labour Government elected in 1974 repealed this Act and restored the privileges of trade unions by passing the Trade Union and Labour Relations Act 1974 (and Amendment Act 1976).

2. *Employment Protection Act 1975*: This Act of Parliament set up the Advisory, Conciliation, and Arbitration Service and established an Employment Appeal Tribunal to hear appeals by trade unions that felt they had been unfairly dealt with. Again, this Act showed that the Government was more committed to intervene in trade union affairs and free collective bargaining in the interests of attempting to secure good industrial relations.

3. *Employment Act 1980*: This Act was passed by the Conservative Government in order to restrict what was considered to be the excessive powers of trade unions. The main points included in the Act are:
   (a) Restricting 'secondary picketing' — trade unionists may only picket their own workplace.
   (b) Encouraging the use of secret ballots for deciding on strike action.
   (c) Providing greater protection for an individual where a closed shop is established.
   (d) Giving the Secretary of State for Employment authority to publish codes of practice, particularly on the closed shop and picketing.

Conclusion

There will always be some workers who feel that they are unfairly treated, or that they are not getting enough pay, or that their conditions of work are very bad. So there must be ways in which their problems can get a speedy and fair hearing. The Government does not want production slowed down or stopped by industrial disputes. Employers do not want to lose profits. Consumers want to be able to buy goods. Peaceful industrial relations are vital to us all.

TOPIC 3.4   Activities

1. Read the following passage and answer the questions:

The Industrial Tribunal
Suzanne worked as a departmental manager for a large firm that owned shops throughout the country. She derived a great deal of satisfaction from her work until she discovered that Ben, a departmental manager at another of the firm's shops, was being paid more money for doing exactly the same job. Suzanne contacted her local trade union official and was advised to put her case to her employers to see if she could be given the same wages as Ben. She became further disgruntled when she found that some of the assistants in her department were earning more money than she was because of the commission they received on sales.

Suzanne went straight along from that interview to the job centre to complain. She was given an application form for an appeal to an industrial tribunal.

(a) Why did Suzanne become dissatisfied with her job?
(b) What is the purpose of an industrial tribunal?
(c) An industrial tribunal is made up of three people, one being an independent chairman. Who do you think the other two would represent?
(d) What do you think the finding of the industrial tribunal would be? Give reasons for your answer.
(e) Which law might have been infringed in the above case?
(f) Write another example of a complaint which might be heard by an industrial tribunal.

2. Find out who is the:
(a) Secretary of State for Employment.
(b) General Secretary of the TUC.
(c) Chairman of the CBI.
(d) General Secretary of the TGWU.

3. A. Jones is *unfairly* dismissed. How can he claim compensation?

4. Do you think workers on strike should receive social security benefits? Give reasons for your answer.

5. List five rights that trade unions enjoy under the law.

6. Collect newspaper cuttings concerning:
(a) Your local Trades Council.
(b) Your local Chamber of Commerce.

Unit 4

Spending your wages

TOPIC 4.1 Going shopping

Retailing

When goods are sold to you, this is known as 'retailing'. Retailing is an ancient trade, as shown by the shop signs in Fig. 4.1. If you had to go to the manufacturer to buy a packet of soap powder, this would be expensive in both time and money. It would also be unlikely that the manufacturer would bother to sell you just one packet. However, people do not wish to buy 100 packets of soap powder; they probably would have nowhere to store them. The word retail, however, means to 'split up'. When you purchase things from a shop, the retailer has split his bulk order from the wholesaler or manufacturer in order to sell you the single item that you want.

In today's highly competitive world, the retailer needs more than a simple sign in order to attract you to his shop. He needs a good location like the one shown in Fig. 4.2. This shows London Street, Norwich, a modern shopping precinct from which cars are banned. The retailer must also offer a wide choice of goods, attractively displayed. An attractive window display is an important way of attracting customers to a shop. For this reason, many stores employ specialist window dressers.

Fig 4.2 A modern shopping centre (Reproduced by permission of Eastern Evening News)

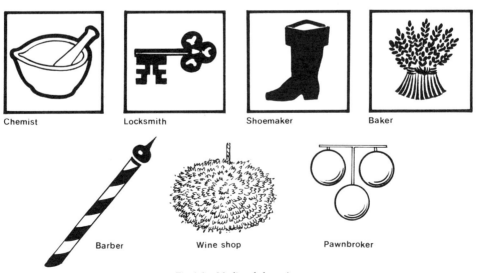

Chemist   Locksmith   Shoemaker   Baker

Barber   Wine shop   Pawnbroker

Fig 4.1 Medieval shop signs

62

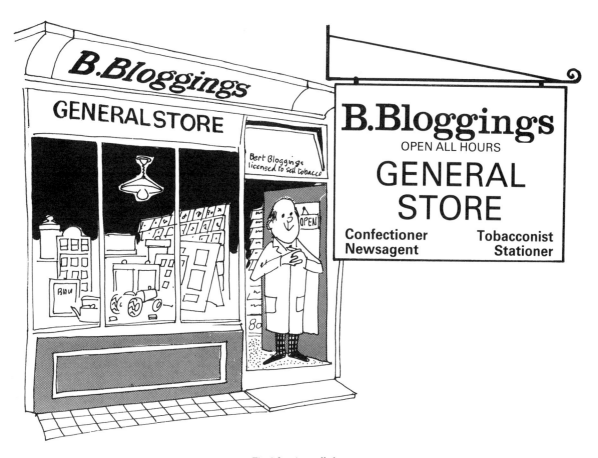

Fig 4.3   A small shop

The unit retailer

You have seen plenty of shop signs similar to the one shown in Fig. 4.3. As the sign shows, the shop is owned by *one person*. It would probably be Mr Bloggings himself who served you if you went into his shop since a unit shop is generally a one-man business. The shop is usually small and is very often situated close to the homes of the people who use it. Is there one of these small retail shops close to your home? In 1981 there were more than 250 000 unit retail shops in Great Britain, although in recent years their numbers appear to be declining.

Sometimes the owners have to take another job in order to achieve a reasonable income. The unit retailer has the advantage of knowing his customers and can, therefore, give them personal service and advice. He may also offer credit to those customers whom he knows well. They can obtain goods from him throughout the week and pay for them at the end of the week when they have been paid themselves. These services help to keep the small shopkeeper in business although his goods may be more expensive than those in the supermarket. Price competition has led to a decline in the number of small shops in recent years; people have found it cheaper to shop elsewhere.

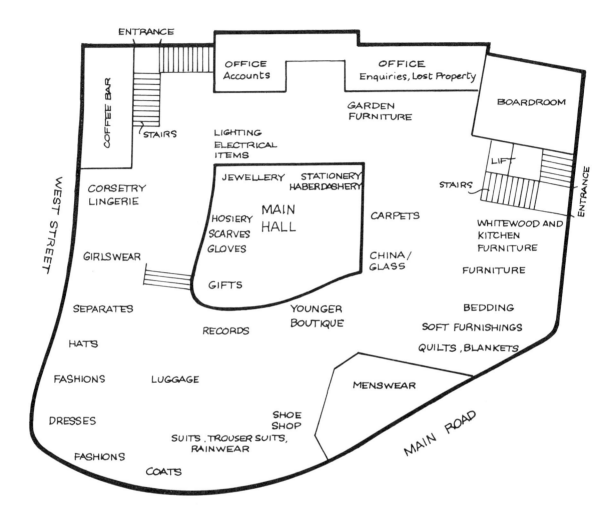

Fig 4.4   The arrangement of a department store (Reproduced by Permission of Bonds of Norwich)

Department stores

You may see a plan similar to the one shown in Fig. 4.4 on the window or door of one of the larger shops in your nearest town or city. As the name department store suggests, the shop is divided into certain sections, each selling a particular range of goods. These stores offer the buyer the advantage of *one-store shopping*. The store may also offer shoppers useful services such as lifts, escalators, toilets, car parks, and a restaurant. All these are provided to make shopping easier and more comfortable. Each department is under a Head Buyer who often chooses and buys the goods for the shop to sell. The success of the department is her or his responsibility. The main advantage which the department store has to offer its customers is a wide variety of goods in one building.

Fig 4.5   Inside a Tesco supermarket (Source: Tesco PLC)

Variety chain stores

As the name suggests, these stores have branches in many towns and, like the department stores, sell a wide variety of goods. Unlike the department stores, however, they are not divided up into self-contained sections. The merchandise is usually sold by the self-selection method whereby the customer selects goods from the fixtures and pays for them at one of the cash-and-wrap points located around the store. Woolworths, British Home Stores, and Littlewoods are all well-known examples of variety chain stores.

Multiple stores

You are probably familiar with shops such as C and A, WH Smith's, Halford's, and Curry's. They are *multiple stores* and are widely known because they have branches in most large towns. They are large concerns and have a national reputation, selling large quantities of similar goods. Because there are so many shops in one chain, they are able to buy in large quantities and offer cheaper goods. If one line does not sell well in one area, it can be sent to another branch in a different area where there may be more demand for it. The customer has the advantage of knowing that whichever branch of a multiple store he goes into, the quality of the goods will be the same. The reputation of such stores throughout the country is very important. There are those who criticize multiple stores because they do not offer a personal service. They may not deliver goods or arrange credit, and the manager may be strictly controlled by head office so that he does not have the same freedom in his shop as the independent retailer. However, these multiples still attract customers in very large numbers and over 1½ million people work in this type of store.

Supermarkets

A supermarket is a very large self-service store, usually with a floor area of more than 2000 square feet, although many are now much larger. There are more than 6000 supermarkets in Great Britain selling over £5000 million pounds worth of goods per annum. About 53 per cent of all grocery sales are from supermarkets such as the one pictured in Fig. 4.5.

Supermarkets sell mainly foodstuffs although many now sell a wide variety of other items. The choice of foodstuffs which a supermarket is able to offer is probably greater than any other shop except, perhaps, a hypermarket. There are often as many as 5000 different products available. If you have taken a basket or trolley round a large supermarket, you will know how much quicker it is to buy goods by the self-service method. How long do you think the unit retailer would take to serve you with 50 items? Because they are large, and often have many branches, supermarkets are able to buy in bulk and offer cheaper goods to the shopper. This advantage has made them very popular in recent years, especially for groceries.

Hypermarkets

These are even larger than supermarkets. They are usually situated away from the centre of town, and sell goods on an even larger scale. They, too, use the self-service method of selling. Two of the earliest hypermarkets in Britain were opened at Telford by Carrefour and Sainsbury's. The Sainsbury hypermarket has 26 000 square feet of trading area with 90 per cent of it used for foodstuffs, whereas the Carrefour hypermarket is nearly double that size with 30 per cent of the floor area being used to sell foodstuffs (see Fig. 4.6).

Some customers may not like shopping at a supermarket or hypermarket. They do not receive personal service and may be tempted into 'impulse buying'. This may mean that the supermarket enjoys higher profits and a speedy turnover, but shoppers spend more than they can really afford. What is the danger of shopping in a supermarket at lunchtime when you may be feeling hungry?

For the owners of a supermarket or hypermarket, shop-lifting may be a problem and undoubtedly some people are tempted to take goods without 'declaring' them at the checkout, in spite of 'one-way mirror' devices and store detectives. What chances are there of an innocent person being accused of 'stealing' in one of these types of shop?

Co-operative societies

The original idea behind the 'co-op' was that they were owned by the people who spent their money in them. Every six months a member received a *dividend* (a sum of money) according to how much he had spent in the store. In most co-ops today, however, members receive dividend stamps with every purchase. When they have collected a complete book worth £1, it can be exchanged for cash or put towards the purchase of another article in the store. So if you spend money in your local co-op, you have the advantage of knowing that eventually you will get something back.

Another change in recent years is that co-operative societies have joined together to form large efficient shop units. This means there are now considerably fewer co-operative outlets. Twenty years ago there were over 1000 societies but today there are fewer than 250.

Discount stores

In times of rising prices discount stores have become popular with many shoppers. Discount stores offer little to the customer in the way of store amenities or customer service, but they aim to sell goods cheaper than other shops in the area. They have expanded their sales in recent years especially in such items as electrical goods, furniture, and do-it-yourself supplies.

Conclusion

As far as shopping is concerned, the trend in recent years has been for more and more to be sold by large firms, e.g., the share of trade by multiple stores has increased while there has been a sharp fall in the number of small independent retailers. Also, many shoppers now have cars and there has been a growth in shopping centres outside large town centres. However, the small corner shop is still important to many shoppers from the point of view of convenience.

You have probably used all the types of shops described. You may be able to think of ways of buying goods without using shops at all. Wherever you spend your money, you will have a *choice*. The amount of money you have and the goods available will help you to make up your mind.

Fig 4.6   Checkout point at a Carrefour hypermarket (Source: Carrefour)

TOPIC 4.1   Activities

1. Read the following passage and answer the questions:

Look who's trying on those blue jeans
Menswear has had a bleak winter, and jeans sales have shrunk. Burton, Hepworth, and John Collier have been impressed by their staying power, and are flexing their muscles, making ready to jump into jeans in a big way.

Burton going strong
They will join Marks and Spencer, our biggest jeans retailer, in adding acceptability to a business which scares off many middle-aged customers before they can squeeze through the trendy swinging boutique doors to squeeze into the jeans themselves.

Burton have been there for three or four years, and say jeans are going from strength to strength. All of their 300 shops sell them, but Burton think they are just scratching the surface. In April, Burton will be on TV in many parts of the country, promoting 100 of their shops which will stock Vanderbilt jeans for men. These will only be sold by Burton, and will cost more than your average jeans.

Hepworth are hacking a way through the tweeds and pinstripes to make room for jeans. After a trial in 15 shops, they will appear in all 360 Hepworth branches soon.

The revolution is reaching John Collier, the UDS menswear group, more slowly. They plan to have Levi's shops inside 50 of their shops by the end of the year, and may do a similar deal with Wrangler.

Their menswear managing director David Hall says: 'This year we will have jeans in our windows for the first time, showing people we sell more than just suits'.

(Source: *Daily Mail,* 14 March 1981)

(a)   Which type of retail organizations are planning to sell jeans on a large scale?
(b)   Which is the biggest jean retailer in this country? What type of shop is it?
(c)   How does Burton plan to promote the sale of a new range of jeans this year?
(d)   Why is Hepworth's planning on selling more jeans to its customers?
(e)   What is the 'revolution' mentioned in the passage?
(f)   Why do you think jeans are such a big seller (55 million pairs were sold in Great Britain in one year)?

2. Draw a plan of the main shopping area in your nearest town. Put in the names of the shops and underneath write what types of shops they are.

3. You can buy goods without using a shop. Write down five ways in which you can do this. Beside each one describe how such methods of retailing work.

4. List 10 items of groceries which your mother has to buy each week. Make a survey and find out their prices in:
(a)   A small shop
(b)   A multiple
(c)   A supermarket
(Remember that you must compare the same brands.)

5. BOB stands for bulk organized buying. By joining together in such organizations, unit retailers can enjoy the economies of bulk buying.
(a)   Find out the names of three other organizations similar to BOB.
(b)   How many of the small retailers in your nearest town belong to one of these wholesale organizations?

6. Imagine you were left a small retail shop in your uncle's will.
(a)   What type of goods would you sell? (Give reasons for your choice.)
(b)   How would you lay out and organize this small shop (e.g., displays, storage of goods, counters, etc.)?

TOPIC 4.2   Shopping at home

Mail order firms

It has already been suggested that you can buy goods without visiting shops. You need not even leave your own home. Figure 4.7 illustrates one method of doing this.

The catalogue

Some of the firms who sell by mail order do not own shops. They use a glossy, colourful book as their shop window. Sometimes large department stores have their own mail order department and their own mail order catalogue.

The agent

The catalogues, showing the goods for sale, are sent out to agents throughout the country. Almost anybody can become an agent by filling in an application form. Most agents are housewives who do it as a spare time job. You possibly know of someone who acts as an agent.

Fig 4.7   Shopping with a mail order catalogue (Reproduced by permission of Littlewoods)

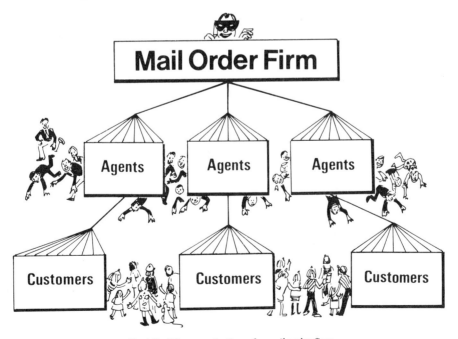

Fig 4.8   The organization of a mail order firm

BULER

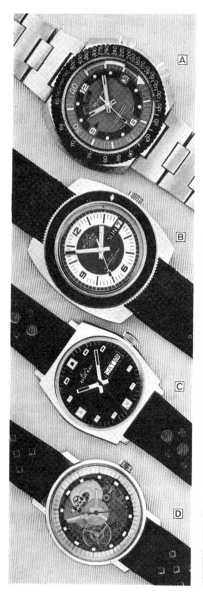

A BULER Gent's Calendar Wrist **WATCH** with shock protected Swiss 17-jewel pin lever movement. Metal case front with steel back. Centre fastening steel bracelet.
JL 9928 £12·50, 40 weeks at 32p

B Gent's BULER Automatic self-winding **WATCH** with Swiss 17-jewel pin lever movement. Day/Date device and metal dial with luminous zone. Metal case front with steel screw back. Fitted with plastic diver s strap.
JR 9941 £12·75, 40 weeks at 32p

C Day/Date **WATCH** by BULER with Swiss 17-jewel pin lever movement. Metal case front with steel back. Leather strap.
JJ 9946 £7·27 weekly 35p

D BULER "Astrolon" Wrist **WATCH** incorporating a plastic movement and a chrome finished metal bezel. Leather strap. Made in Switzerland.
JP 9950 £8·67 weekly 45p

E Ladies' BULER Wrist **WATCH** with Swiss 17-jewel pin lever movement. Metal case front with steel back. Chromed bracelet with centre fastening.
JL 9952
£9·35 weekly 45p

F BULER Ladies' Wrist **WATCH** with Swiss 17-jewel pin lever movement. Gold plated case with steel back. Complete with milanese type bracelet.
JK 9953
£6·97 weekly 35p

G Ladies' BULER Wrist **WATCH** with Swiss 17-jewel pin lever movement. Metal case front with steel back. Fitted with Leather strap.
JJ 9954
£8·75 weekly 45p

H Gent's BULER Day/Date **WATCH** with Swiss 21-jewel pin lever movement. Metal case with steel screw back. Complete with rally type strap.
JH 9955
£9·35 weekly 45p

J Gent's BULER Wrist **WATCH** with Swiss 1-jewel pin lever movement. Metal case and metal back. Fitted with expanding bracelet.
JG 9956 £5·25 weekly 25p

K Gent's BULER Calendar Automatic self-winding Bracelet **WATCH** with 25-jewel pin lever movement. Gold plated front and steel screw back. Bark finish bracelet with centre expanding links. Made in Switzerland.
JL 9936 £11·00 weekly 55p

L Gent's Alarm Wrist **WATCH** by BULER with Swiss 17-jewel pin lever movement. Chrome case front and steel back. Complete with Leather strap.
JF 9957 £9·15 weekly 45p

M Gent's BULER Automatic self-winding Wrist **WATCH**. Shock resistant Swiss 25-jewel pin lever movement. Yellow metal case front with steel screw back. Calendar device and centre seconds hand. Leather rally type strap.
JA 9896 £11·00 weekly 55p

Fig 4.9 A page from a mail order catalogue (Reproduced by permission of Empire Stores PLC)

Empire Stores PLC

18 Canal Rd, Bradford, Yorkshire BD99 4XB

Registered in England No. 110433

Order for all items except where special order form required

If heavy goods are to be sent direct to your customer please use a separate form and attach a completed Customer Label 25

Date _____

If agency address has changed since your last order, please tick ➡

Agency Number
Agent's Name
Full Postal Address BLOCK LETTERS PLEASE

Description	Colour	Colour No.	Catalogue No.	Size	Price each £ p.	How many (state if rolls, packs, yards etc.)	Office use

Do not forget to re-order stationery, patterns and special forms.

Just mark an **X** against the items you require ▷

Order forms	11	Ring size gauge		21
Wines and Spirits order	12			22
Customer label 25	13	Car insurance form		23
Envelopes	14	Wallpaper pattern book		24
Collecting book	15	Gent's made-to-measure suit patterns		25
Payment cards	16	Gent's made-to-measure suit forms		26
Commission forms	17	Car carpet forms		27
Returns forms	18	Sales reports		28
Returns label	19			
Correspondence form	20			

Fig 4.10 An agent's mail order form (Reproduced by permission of Empire Stores PLC)

71

The agent shows the catalogue to her friends and customers hoping to attract orders (see Fig. 4.8). The harder the agent works, the more custom she is likely to attract. The more goods she sells, the more commission she receives. The agent may get commission on sales at the rate of 10p in the pound. This means that if a customer buys an article for £5, the agent receives 50p for getting the order and collecting the payments.

The customer

As you can see from Fig. 4.9, the goods are attractively displayed in the catalogue. This probably encourages people to buy. Another attraction of this method of buying is that the customer does not have to pay the full cost of the article at once. Generally, payment is made by instalments over 20 weeks. The agent is responsible for collecting the weekly instalments and sending them to the company. The customer pays no interest on the money she owes and often receives the article before the first instalment is paid.

The order

When the customer has selected the article, she tells the agent its number and page number in the catalogue. The agent then fills out an order form similar to the one shown in Fig. 4.10.

The agent mails the order to the firm's headquarters. The article required is taken from the warehouse, carefully packed, and dispatched by post to the agent. She then passes it on to her customer who will then begin to pay for it. The total sales of mail order firms have increased greatly in the last few years. This method of selling is very popular in the USA, where people often live hundreds of miles from the nearest large town.

Newspapers and magazines

Goods may be advertised in a newspaper or magazine (see Fig. 4.11). If the firm has a good name, people will be willing to buy the article without seeing it. However, it is often possible to see the goods before purchasing them if you are able to visit the firm. Some firms offer a money back guarantee if the customer is not satisfied with the goods when he sees them.

Most articles advertised in this way state the price '+ P&P'. This stands for 'postage and packing'; the buyer pays towards the cost of safe packing and sending the article through the post. (This extra charge is not usually made for goods sold by means of a mail order catalogue.) Direct selling through the newspaper has the advantage that no shops or agents have to be paid, so the article may be cheaper.

However, you must be very careful when buying by this method. There are about 30 pages of mail order advertisements in national newspapers every weekend. Beware of buying unusual things such as magic stitchers which are unsatisfactory substitutes for sewing machines. When the magazine *Which?* carried out a survey, it found that about half the advertisements tended to overstate the case for the product.

Conclusion

Shopping at home is a great advantage to those people who cannot, or do not wish to, walk round lots of shops. On the other hand, people may have to wait while the goods are dispatched and this may be inconvenient. The mail order firms offer you the convenience of 20 weeks in which to pay for what you have purchased. Their increased sales show how many people are attracted by the glossy catalogues and the easy method of payment.

MILITARY SOFA BED ORDER FORM

Send to : New Dimension Military Sofa Bed Offer (CMS 237), Manor Road, West Ealing, London, W.13.

Send me ☐ Sofa Bed(s) at £39 each, plus £1.68 p&p each.
Please insert quantity required in box.

I enclose crossed cheque/P.O. No. .... Total inc. p&p £..

NAME (block letters please) ....

ADDRESS...

....

5 Exciting Shopping Centres with <u>immediate</u> take-away service.
See this week's offer and many others at your nearest centre – pay us a visit!

● **EALING :** Manor Rd, West Ealing, London, W13. Tel : 01-998 2900.
● **ISLINGTON :** 52 Essex Rd, Islington, London N1. Tel : 01-359 1762.
● **SEVENOAKS :** 74 London Rd, Riverhead, Sevenoaks, Kent. Tel : Sevenoaks 59630.
● **CROYDON :** 1a Church Rd, West Croydon, Surrey. Tel : 01-688 1416.
● **ASHBY-DE-LA-ZOUCH :** Tamworth Rd, Measham, Leics. Tel : Measham 70327.

Open Mon-Sat inclusive
9.30 a.m.–5.30 p.m.
* Also – Sunday viewing
at Ealing and Measham.
10.00 a.m. – 5.30 p.m.
(these 2 early closing
Wednesday).

Send me details of your other offers available (please tick).

☐ wall storage systems   ☐ desks, Hi-Fi and bedside tables   ☐ sofas, chairs and unit chairs   ☐ dining/
kitchen table and chairs   ☐ pine furniture and chrome furniture   ☐ occasional tables   ☐ lighting.

New Dimension Limited,
Regd. No. 1006530, England.
Regd. Office, Manor Road,
West Ealing, London, W.13
Contract Enquiries :
Apply Contracts Director at
Ealing address.

New Dimension
-where good furniture costs <u>much</u> less

Fig 4.11   Shopping by post (Reproduced by permission of New Dimension)

TOPIC 4.2   Activities

1. Read the following advertisement and answer the questions:

English Made with English Material   Ladies & Men's Styles

DUFFEL COATS
Naval pattern in superb thick 70% WOOL cloth
'Jacafleece' Simulated Sheepskin Lined
Only £23.95   2 for £46.00   Post each £1.20p.
End of Season SALE!
70% wool, 30% other fibres Lined Acrylic fur

A superb garment by any standard — smart free styling and ideal alike for business or leisure wear — in Town or country and very very comfortable — always. Built to give double snug protection in all weathers. Fashioned from a high grade close weave 70% wool cloth and lined in thermal 'Jacafleece' simulated sheepskin (not to be confused with cheaper imported check back cloth); not forgetting, of course, its cosy fitted hood — also lined in 'Jacafleece', 2 capacious pockets and fastened by smart frogged loops and handsome toggles. IN AIR FORCE BLUE or FAWN. Chest sizes 36, 38, 40 or 42in. Also sizes 44 or 46in. Only £2 extra. Sizes 48 to 50in. Only £4 extra. Money back guarantee.

Or any order sent COD (Pay postman 50p extra)

Dept. DM603, 69-71 Westow Hill,
Crystal Palace, London SE19
Also 135 High Holborn WC1

JACATEX

(Source: *Daily Mail,* 14 March 1981 (adapted))

(a)   Is there any disadvantage in purchasing a coat as described in the above advertisement?
(b)   How much money would have to be sent through the post for a coat?
(c)   What is COD?
(d)   Is the advertisement confusing in any way?
(e)   What are the good points about the coats advertised?
(f)   What would be the best methods to send money by post for one of the coats?

2. Work out the payments, over a 20 week period, for goods in a mail order catalogue at the following prices:
(a)   £19.25
(b)   £4.75
(c)   £1.10
(d)   £59.65
(e)   £10.75

3. List 10 things which *cannot* be bought from a mail order firm.

4. Design a whole page display for a mail order catalogue to try to encourage people to buy coats. Remember displays must be as attractive as possible.

5. Where would you advertise if you wished to try to sell the following goods *direct* to the public?
(a)   Clothing.
(b)   Furniture.
(c)   Garden sheds.
(d)   Sports equipment.
(e)   Watches.

6. What is the most expensive article sold by means of a typical mail order catalogue? What is the cheapest article sold? Why do you think such a catalogue does not offer expensive articles, e.g., a £5000 diamond ring? Why does it not sell something which is very cheap, e.g., a 5p packet of pins?

TOPIC 4.3 Buying goods on credit

Hire purchase (Fig. 4.12)

You have probably seen, in a shop window, a notice similar to the one shown in Fig. 4.13. The buyer is offered two ways of paying for the motor cycle:

1. Handing over £495 cash.
2. Paying on a weekly basis over a period of two years.

The second method of payment is known as *hire purchase*. The buyer must make an initial payment of a small *deposit*. Thus, he has the advantage of being able to use his motor bike before he has paid for it.

If you buy on HP, you are really *hiring* the goods. You do not legally own the motor cycle until the final payment has been made. It is against the law for you to resell the motor cycle during this period.

Hire purchase is usually only available for fairly expensive items (see Fig. 4.14), which some people might never be able to afford without HP. Sometimes people are persuaded by eager salesmen into buying goods they cannot really afford. They then find it difficult to keep up the payments. To protect such people, Parliament has passed a number of Hire Purchase Acts, the last one in 1964.

Fig 4.13   Cash or hire purchase?

Fig 4.12   Have the goods now and pay later

Fig 4.14   The types of goods sold on hire purchase

75

The hire purchase agreement

The 1964 Hire Purchase Act covers all goods costing up to £2000.

The agreement, as shown in Fig. 4.15, must state:

1. The cash price of the goods.
2. The hire purchase price of the goods.
3. The amount of each instalment.
4. When the cash instalments fall due.
5. The hirer's right to end the agreement, i.e., *Right of Cancellation*.
6. Details restricting the seller's right to recover the goods if he wishes.

ORIGINAL

Hire-Purchase Agreement

(See overleaf for Terms of Agreement)

The Copyright of this document is reserved

PARTICULARS OF HIRER (IN BLOCK LETTERS) | Br. No. | Office use only—Agmt. No. 0 | **HP/ST 1** (Amd. 7)

Full Trading Style or Surname

Forenames

Address

County Postcode

(a) Delete as appropriate

(a) Owner/Tenant (a) Married/Single Age Telephone No.

(b) If resident for less than 3 years also state previous address.

How long occupied Mortgaged (a) Yes/No Monthly payments £

(b) Previous address

(c) No enquiries made.

Occupation How long with present employers

Employers name and address (c)

Banker's name and address

Details of current credit transactions

Details of Insurance
(*See clause 2g overleaf*)
Name and address of Company/Broker

Policy or cover note No.

Expiry date of Policy

THE SCHEDULE

(d) Delete as appropriate. See also note 'k'.

PARTICULARS OF GOODS:— (d) New/Secondhand

MOTOR VEHICLES/CARAVANS (d) New/Secondhand

First Reg.	Make and Model (state if G.T. or modified)	Regn. No.
C.C.		Ch. or S. No.
		Eng. No.

Accessories

(e) Delete if inappropriate. See also note 'j'.

(e) Defects (if any)

PERIOD OF HIRE AND DETAILS OF PAYMENTS

	Exclusive of VAT	VAT at ....%	Inclusive of VAT	
Period of hire [ ] months				
Cash price	£	£	£	(A)
Less: First payment made up of Cash £ Allowances £	—	—	£	
			£	
Add: Hire charges	£	—	£	(B)
Balance of hire			£	
payable by [ ] monthly rentals of £				
commencing 19				
Purchase fee	£ 2.00	—	£ 2.00	(C)
Amount payable exclusive of VAT	£			
VAT payable [Bowmaker (Commercial) Limited VAT registration No. 186 2283 46]		£		

Hire-purchase price (A+B+C) £

Mark selected method of payment with X: through post [ ] over bank counter [ ] by direct debit order [ ]

Fig 4.15 A hire purchase agreement (Reproduced by permission of Bowmaker (Commercial))

STATUTORY NOTICE

RIGHT OF HIRER TO TERMINATE AGREEMENT

1. The hirer may put an end to this agreement by giving notice of termination in writing to any person who is entitled to collect or receive the hire-rent.

(f) Insert half the hire-purchase price plus the cost of installation (if any).

2. He must then pay any instalments which are in arrear at the time when he gives notice. If, when he has paid those instalments, the total amount which he has paid under the agreement is less than (f) £........ he must also pay enough to make up that sum, unless the court determines that a smaller sum would be equal to the owner's loss.

3. If the goods have been damaged owing to the hirer having failed to take reasonable care of them, the owner may sue him for the amount of the damage unless that amount can be agreed between the hirer and the owner.

(g) Insert the address at which the hirer signs—which must be either the dealer's premises or Finance Company's office.

4. The hirer should see whether this agreement contains provisions allowing him to put an end to the agreement on terms more favourable to him than those just mentioned. If it does, he may put an end to the agreement on those terms.

RESTRICTION OF OWNER'S RIGHT TO RECOVER GOODS

(h) Insert one-third the hire-purchase price plus the cost of installation (If any).

5. After (h) £........ has been paid, then, unless the hirer has himself put an end to the agreement, the owner of the goods cannot take them back from the hirer without the hirer's consent unless the owner obtains an order of the court.

6. If the owner applies to the court for such an order, the court may, if the court thinks it just to do so, allow the hirer to keep either:—

(a) the whole of the goods, on condition that the hirer pays the balance of the price in the manner ordered by the court; or

(b) a fair proportion of the goods having regard to what the hirer has already paid.

This document contains the terms of a hire-purchase agreement. Sign it only if you want to be legally bound by them.

Signature of hirer ....

The goods will not become your property until you have made all the payments. You must not sell them before then.

Signed by the Hirer at (g) ....

in the presence of

Witness ....

Address ....

Occupation ....

Signature for and on behalf of Bowmaker (Commercial) Limited

.... Date ....

HIRER'S DECLARATION

(1) I warrant that the details given in the "Particulars of Hirer" Section above are correct in all respects.

(j) Delete if no defects are listed in Schedule.

(2) Before I signed the above Agreement:—

(A) I saw a written statement of the cash price of the goods otherwise than in this agreement which corresponded exactly with that shown above.

(B) My attention was drawn to the provisions of Clause 8 overleaf and I understand

(i) that the clause excludes any condition of fitness of the goods for any particular purpose. It is important that I should satisfy myself as to this before signing the agreement since the owner cannot subsequently be held liable for any lack of fitness for a particular purpose.

(k) Delete if goods are new.

(k) (ii) that the goods are being let as secondhand and are so described in the schedule. The clause excludes any condition of merchantable quality in regard to such goods. This means that the owner cannot subsequently be held liable for any defects in the goods.

(j) (iii) that the goods are let subject to the defects specified in the schedule (which I have read). The clause excludes the condition of merchantable quality in regard to the defects listed there and the effect of this is that the owner is not in any event under liability with regard to those defects.

(C) I carefully examined the goods and they are in every respect satisfactory to me, and where the goods are stated to be new goods my examination did not reveal any defects other than those shown above (if any).

(3) Immediately after I signed the above Agreement I was handed an exact copy thereof.

Signature of Hirer........

Fig 4.15 (cont.)

The Consumer Credit Act of 1974 protects consumers who enter into any credit transactions including hire purchase, credit cards, and personal loans. The seller must reveal the full cost of the credit in terms of (a) cash, and (b) interest paid per year (APR or annual percentage rate). All organizations dealing with credit sales are supervised by the Director General of Fair Trading and it is an offence to mislead people by advertisements that are not clear or omit important information.

If you decide, when you are over the age of 18, to enter into an HP agreement, you should read the document very carefully and make sure you understand *all* the conditions which it sets out. As the hirer, you should receive a copy of the agreement after the salesman has signed it. The print must be black or dark grey on white paper; small print is forbidden. As the hirer, you will have to sign in a special box (see Fig. 4.15).

If you buy something on HP from a door-to-door salesman, you still have the right to change your mind. If you fill in a special section of the agreement (known as 'Right of Cancellation'), you will be able to cancel the HP agreement as long as you do so within a certain period (Fig. 4.16).

Other ways of buying goods on credit

Credit sales

Again, payment is made by weekly or monthly instalments. But credit sales differ from hire purchase because the goods belong to the buyer as soon as he makes the first payment. The credit sales agreement is usually for a shorter period, say 36 weeks or 9 months.

An account

Many large stores encourage customers to open an account. A person with an account can go into the store, purchase goods, and merely have them debited to his account. Each month a statement is sent to the customer. He may either pay all or part of what he owes.

By paying £5 a month into a *budget account,* a customer may be allowed to spend six or even eight times that amount in the store.

Fig 4.16   Thinking it over

Credit cards

Credit cards, like the ones shown in Fig. 4.17 are issued by banks so that a customer can shop without using money. This card allows him to take goods home after the seller has noted the details of the card.

Are there any disadvantages of buying now and paying later?

Buying goods by any of the methods described in this unit is certainly useful in order to obtain and use them before the cash is available, but there are some disadvantages which should be considered.

1. Paying cash is usually the cheapest way of buying goods. Any organization lending money charges interest on the loan.
2. You must be sure that you do not commit yourself to more than you can afford. The goods may appear attractive, especially with small regular payments, but you must be prepared to keep these up until the goods have been paid for. Avoid impulse buying.
3. You must be prepared to read all credit arrangements very carefully and have some knowledge of the law on the subject.
4. You cannot, by law, sign an HP agreement under the age of 18 — an adult over that age must sign to guarantee you will keep up the payments. If you do not, the adult signing is liable for your debts.

Conclusion

All these methods allow a shopper to purchase goods without paying the full cash price at the time. Without HP, a person may have to wait a long time before he has the full cash price for a colour television, but hire purchase allows him to have one straightaway. In return, he must be prepared to make regular payments over a lengthy period. Throughout this period the television is depreciating in value.

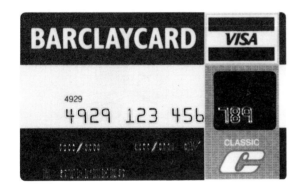

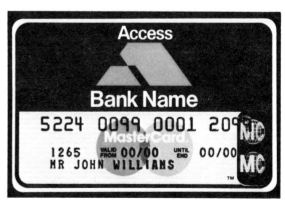

Fig 4.17   Credit cards (Barclaycard reproduced by permission of Barclays Bank PLC; Access card by permission of Access. The Joint Credit Card Company Limited)

TOPIC 4.3 Activities

1. Read the passage and answer the questions:

Comparing credit
Confusing and misleading credit and hire advertisements should be a thing of the past as a result of new regulations recently introduced by Mrs Sally Oppenheim, Minister for Consumer Affairs. The Advertisements and Quotations Regulations, made under the Consumer Credit Act 1974, require that the total charge for credit expressed as an annual percentage rate will have to be included in credit quotations and many credit advertisements. This will assist consumers in comparing one credit offer with another without much difficulty.

   Two booklets on the subject have been produced primarily for traders and advertisers. The booklets, *Advertisements and Quotations* and *Credit Charges,* are available free from: Office of Fair Trading, Government Building, Bromyard Avenue, Acton, London W3 7BB.

(Source: *Consumer News* No. 7, 1981)

(a) What do you think are some of the responsibilities of the Minister for Consumer Affairs?
(b) How could credit and hire advertisements be misleading to the consumer?
(c) What are the main terms of the Consumer Credit Act of 1974?
(d) How is the consumer to be assisted under the new regulations introduced by the Minister?
(e) What is the purpose of the Office of Fair Trading?

2. Draw the following table in your notebook and fill in the gaps.

Hire purchase

Advantages	Disadvantages
(a)	(a)
(b)	(b)
(c)	(c)
(d)	(d)
(e)	(e)

3. Make a list of five things you would like but cannot afford. Opposite each write down the cash price. Find out if these items could be bought by hire purchase and how much extra this would cost you.

4. List what you think are the five most popular items bought on HP by the parents of your class or group. Add up the totals of the list.

5. A friend is considering buying a car on hire purchase. What advice would you give him and why?

6. Some people cannot afford to pay cash for expensive items. There are also some people who should not enter into a hire purchase agreement. Write down five kinds of people who you think should not commit themselves to paying weekly instalments.

7. Conduct a survey to find out how many parents of people in your class:

(a) Use credit cards.

(b) Have an account at a large store.

Is there evidence to suggest that these methods of shopping are becoming more popular?

8. List five goods which would deteriorate quickly while you were paying for them by hire purchase. Then list five which might increase in value.

TOPIC 4.4　Consumer protection

Who protects you?

If you buy a gallon of petrol or a kilogram of sugar, how can you be certain that you are getting the correct measure or the exact weight? You may have bought something, such as a clock, with which you received a guarantee similar to the one shown in Fig. 4.18. The makers may offer to repair the clock for you free of charge if it goes wrong within the first year. But you should read the guarantee very carefully. It may state that the clock will be repaired only if the manufacturer considers that it was not mishandled or damaged by accident. This may be difficult to prove. In what ways are you protected against buying things that are under weight or of poor quality?

Weights and measures

Weights and measures, such as a gallon of petrol or a kilogram of sugar, are controlled by Trading Standards Officers who check the accuracy of weighing and measuring devices. Shopkeepers' scales and petrol pumps ought not to vary in their measurements. Regular checks are made to ensure that the customer gets an exact measure for his money. The 1963 Weights and Measures Act requires that the quantity of all pre-packed food should be stated on the package — this is particularly important with the increase in the number of self-service shops. The law also requires that certain commodities must be sold in particular quantities. For example, packets of coffee must contain 500 grams or 1 kilo and not odd amounts which might deceive the customers and make it difficult for them to calculate the price per gram. Under the Weights and Measures Act 1963, if you are given short weight or short measure, you can report this to your local Trading Standards Department which will, if necessary, prosecute on your behalf. Further advice on a local scale may be provided by the Citizens' Advice Bureau.

GUARANTEE

This Smiths Alarm Clock is hereby guaranteed for a period of 12 months from the date of purchase. The best materials and workmanship have been employed throughout, and every clock is thoroughly tested and timed before leaving our works. This guarantee covers all defects in material and manufacture, but excludes damage caused by accident or misuse.

This SMITH ALARM should give you many years of satisfactory service but in the rare event of it developing a defect within 12 months from date of purchase, the clock will be repaired or replaced at our option.

The clock, with this form and a crossed Postal Order for 25p to cover part cost of handling, packing and return postage, should be sent *carriage paid* to :—

**SMITHS CLOCK SERVICE DEPARTMENT
WISHAW, LANARKSHIRE, ML2 0RN**

Reason for return
A charge will be made for repairing a clock after the expiry of the 12 months' guarantee period and for repairs necessary through reasons beyond our control. CLOCKS BOUGHT OUTSIDE THE UNITED KINGDOM should be returned to the retailer, from whom purchased, who will make the necessary service arrangements.

Fig 4.18　A guarantee (Reproduced by permission of Smiths Clocks)

Kellogg's SPECIAL K

Ingredients
Rice, Wheat Gluten, Defatted Wheat Germ, Nonfat Dry Milk Solids, Sugar, Salt and Malt flavouring, Iron, Niacin, Riboflavin (B$_2$) and Thiamine (B$_1$).

Nutrients per ounce

Protein (N×6·25)	5·3 grams
Fats	0·14 grams
Carbohydrates	22·0 grams
Iron	4·0 mg.
Niacin	5·5 mg.
Riboflavin	0.5 mg.
Thiamine	0·4 mg.
Crude Fibre	0·23 grams

One ounce of *Special K* provides one third of the recommended daily intake of Iron, Niacin, Riboflavin and Thiamine for the average adult.

Fig 4.19   The contents of Kelloggs Special K (Reproduced by permission of Kelloggs)

Environmental Health Officers

The Environmental Health Officer sees that certain standards of hygiene are kept in places where food is either sold or prepared for cooking. Many products have labels on which the contents of the packet, jar, or can are shown (see Fig. 4.19). The *Public Analyst* may check the contents of a jar to make sure that it contains the correct proportions as stated on the label. For example, fish paste must contain at least 70 per cent fish, while salmon paste must contain at least 70 per cent salmon. In 1981, nearly 10 000 visits were made to food premises by the Officers. In this way, the food we eat is checked to make sure it is fit for human consumption. Inspectors have the backing of the law. The Food and Drugs Act 1955 states that food must be fit for human consumption. It is an offence to sell food which is not up to this standard. Again, this must be reported as individual consumers cannot get compensation under the Act.

The British Standards Institution

The British Standards Institution (BSI) tests goods and approves those which meet its standard of quality and safety. Such goods carry the kitemark label as shown in Fig. 4.20. The BSI also aims at standardizing certain products to simplify production and distribution. For example, a motorist who buys a 'standard' sparking plug can be sure it will fit almost any make of vehicle.

The Consumers' Association

This is an organization to which anybody can belong by paying the annual subscription. It has become one of the most effective organizations in checking the standards of quality and performance of many products. The Consumers' Association carries out tests on chosen products. It publishes the results of these tests in a monthly magazine called *Which?* Members are thus able to compare the performance of various branded goods and select the one which the Consumers' Association recommends as 'the best buy' so far as price and quality are concerned. In this way, members are encouraged to shop carefully.

In a similar way the Consumers' Association may test services and make certain recommendations to more than 60 000 consumers who are members of the Association. It also issues special supplements such as *Motoring Which?* and *Money Which?*

Fig 4.20   The BSI Kitemark (Reproduced by permission of the British Standards Institution)

Acts of Parliament

Food and Drugs Act 1955

This Act prohibits advertisements which are misleading, with particular reference to food and drugs. Advertisers must not claim that a drug *will* cure but that it *may* 'alleviate pain'.

Trade Descriptions Act 1968

This Act tries to stop misleading descriptions of goods and prevents consumers from being misled by deliberately badly or vaguely worded advertisements or labels. The cardigan advertised in Fig. 4.21 must be 100 per cent wool. If it is not, the buyer has the right to complain to the Trading Standards Officers about the misleading description.

Fair Trading Act 1973

This Act protects the consumer by the appointment of a Director General of Fair Trading to keep under review trade practices and commercial activity. He investigates complaints from the courts, Trading Standards Officers, and consumers.

The Supply of Goods (Implied Terms) Act 1973

Under this Act it is illegal for a shop or manufacturer to take away any of your legal rights. If you bought a car which broke down 100 yards from the garage after you collected it, the seller cannot claim it was your fault and no longer his responsibility. Before this Act, sellers sometimes asked buyers to sign contracts or guarantees which tended to exclude the seller from all responsibility as soon as the goods left his possession.

In a similar way the Unfair Contract Terms Act of 1977 provides consumers with protection for services they may have purchased — again assuring that the buyer does not sign away his legal rights.

Fig 4.21   An advertisement for cardigans showing the Woolmark (Woolmark reproduced by permission of The International Wool Secretariat)

The Consumer Credit Act 1974

This Act compels all businesses offering credit to have a licence and thus ensure that they act in a responsible and fair way towards consumers. Anyone who applies for credit and is refused has the right to know the reason why his application has not been granted.

Consumer Safety Act 1978

This Act attempts to protect the consumer from unsafe goods. The Department of Prices and Consumer Protection now publishes regulations governing the safety of certain types of goods. Such things as electric blankets and carrycots must conform to certain safety regulations. Children's nightdresses must be made of flame-resistant materials. Again, it is the responsibility of the local Trading Standards Department to carry out regular checks to ensure that certain types of goods sold by retailers conform to the regulations laid down by this Act.

Conclusion

In recent years buyers have been offered greater protection by the law and by advice from various organizations. Radio, television, and newspapers now frequently offer consumer advice from experts. As a result the consumers' rights when purchasing goods receive more publicity and the 'shoddy' sellers are often exposed.

You may buy something with which you are not satisfied. Only if you know your 'rights' as a shopper will you be able to take steps to put things right. As a sensible shopper, you should look for such things as the BSI kitemark as a test of quality and safety. Tests on goods reported in *Which?* may help you to make the best selection from the many brands available.

TOPIC 4.4   Activities

1. Read the following extract and answer the questions:

Is it safe to use?
The *Consumer Protection Acts of 1961 and 1971* and the *Consumer Safety Act 1978* lay down rules to ensure the safety of a wide range of consumer goods. The Trading Standards Department can prosecute sellers of goods which do not comply with these rules. Goods covered are as follows:

aerosols	crash helmets	paraffin heaters
babies' dummies	electrical goods	pedal cycles
* balloon kits	fabrics	pens and pencils
carrycots	fireguards	prams and pushchairs
chemicals	* glitter lamps	* stink bombs
ceramic and enamel ware	medicines	* tear gas capsules
children's anoraks	motor cars and bikes	textiles
children's furniture	nightdresses	toys
cosmetics	oil lamps	upholstered furniture

* partially or completely banned from sale

If a particular product is found to be unsafe, the Government has the power to ban it completely, or make the trader publish a warning about it. The Trading Standards Department can also prosecute a trader for selling a car which is unroadworthy, that is, too dangerous to drive on the road.

(Source: 'Talking Shop' Education Pack — Warwickshire County Council Trading Standards Department)

(a) Why is it necessary for Parliament to introduce laws like those mentioned in the extract?
(b) Why do you think the items marked with an asterisk have been partially or completely banned from sale?
(c) Select three articles from the list and describe how each might be unsafe.
(d) Describe an article bought by you or a member of your family which was, or could have been, dangerous.
(e) Find out where your local Trading Standards Office is, visit it and ask for a selection of consumer protection leaflets.

2. Conduct your own *Which?* test in groups of four. Obtain various brand names of ballpoint pens. Make up five questions as a basis for the test, e.g., 'Does the pen write without trouble straight away?' Write in your notebooks a report of the test you carried out.

3. Rewrite and re-design the advertisement shown in Fig. 4.21. Imagine the cardigan is made partly of nylon, orlon, courtelle, or acrilan, as well as wool. Your advertisement must comply with the Trade Descriptions Act.

4. Collect some food labels on which the contents of the packages are stated. Stick them in your notebook. Do any of these packages contain artificial additives?

5. What safety regulations do you think should be enforced in public meeting places such as cinemas and soccer grounds? Name *three* products to which safety regulations have to be applied by law.

Unit 5

Banking your money

TOPIC 5.1 Saving money through your bank

How much you save will depend upon how much you earn, your day to day expenses, and what you are saving for (see Fig. 5.1). When you start work, you may want to buy a motor cycle and decide to save £5 towards it every week, or you may not have an immediate aim but decide to save what you have left from your week's wages. There are various places you can save your money; you must make up your mind which is best suited to *your* needs.

National Savings Bank

This bank, which is part of the Post Office, is very popular with smaller savers. You can open an account with as little as 25p. In return, you will be issued with a bank book which is a record of your savings and withdrawals. One advantage of saving with the National Savings Bank is that there are well over 22 000 post offices in Great Britain. By producing your bank book at any one of these, you will be able to draw up £50 on demand, assuming you have that much in your account. The National Savings Bank offers two accounts for your savings:

1. *An ordinary account*: You would receive interest of about 5 per cent on this account.
2. *An investment account*: You receive a higher rate of interest on this account, but you are expected to leave your money in the bank for a longer period.

Trustee Savings Bank

The Trustee Savings Bank offers similar facilities to those of the National Savings Bank. It was established over 150 years ago especially to help small savers: £50 can be withdrawn on demand at any Trustee Savings Bank branch. The TSB has

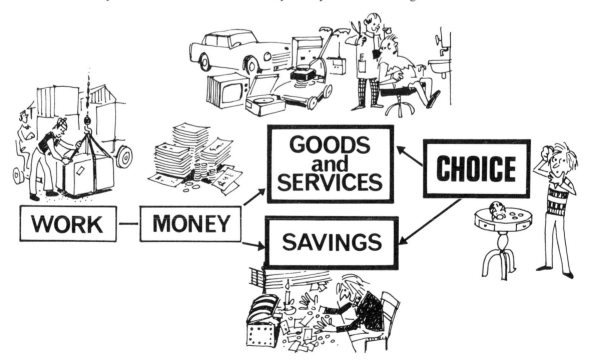

Fig 5.1   The money you earn can be spent or saved; the choice is yours

more than 8 million customers who have almost 14 million accounts. The two main types of accounts for saving money are:

1. *An ordinary account*: Money can be saved with interest at about 4 per cent and savings can be withdrawn on demand.
2. *A special investment department account*: This can be opened when £50 has been saved in an ordinary account; it offers the advantage of a higher rate of interest. Although withdrawals are subject to one month's notice, they are usually paid on demand.

Trustee Savings Banks now offer many of the services that a commercial bank makes available to its customers. These are such things as customers' cheque accounts, foreign currency, special accounts for students and school leavers, and unit trust and insurance schemes. The TSBs have recently started offering mortgages and bridging loans for customers who are buying a house or moving house. They have introduced a pilot scheme offering small-scale commercial loans. TSBs also offer free banking for school leavers as long as they stay in credit!

Commercial banks

Banks offer their customers two types of account: a current account on which no interest is paid and a deposit account on which interest is paid. The interest rate is higher than that offered by either the National Savings Bank or the Trustee Savings Bank. For very large amounts, seven days' notice of withdrawal may be required.

Table 5.1   Savings table

Savings	What they pay (interest % gross unless net stated)	Withdrawal (how much notice)	Minimum sum
Building societies			
ordinary	8.93	None	£1
high income bonds	11.07	None (but 3 months interest lost)	£1000
subscription	10.71	None	£500
Banks			
deposits	5.75	7 days	None
investment	9.25	3 months	£2000
investment	9.5	6 months	£2000
Local authorities			
3–5 year bonds	8.5	3–7 years	£1000
National Savings			
ordinary	6 (net)	None for £100	£1
investment	6.75 (net)	1 month	£1
27th Issue Certs	5.28–9.37 (net)	8 days	£25
Index-linked Certs	Same as inflation	8 days	£10
Income bonds	10	3 months	£2000
Save-As-You-Earn	Same as inflation	14 days	£4 monthly
TSB			
investment	5.75	7 days to a month	None
term	8.5–9	1 year	£500
savings	4	None	None
National Girobank	6	None	£1

Building societies

Many people who save money with a building society do so for a special reason — to save enough for a deposit to put towards the purchase of a house. You may not need to save with this aim in view until you are thinking of getting married. However, people who are not thinking of buying a house still deposit their money in a building society account because of the attractive interest rates which are offered. Building societies are also able to offer two different types of accounts for the investor:

1. *A share account*: This offers the standard rate of interest paid by the building society.
2. *A subscription share account*: This offers a higher rate of interest because you guarantee to save a regular amount each month. You would be expected to save in multiples of £1.

Save As You Earn

This is another regular savings scheme available to everybody over the age of 16. The scheme enables savings to be made in fixed regular monthly amounts over five years, with a minimum of £4 and a maximum of £50, by means of deductions from pay or by other regular payments. The interest on these schemes is often index linked. With a Save-As-You-Earn scheme it is best to leave your money for a period of five years and, if possible, an additional two years when you will qualify for an even higher percentage interest. However, if you decide on this method of saving you must be prepared to have your money tied up for a long period of time to gain maximum advantage of the interest rates offered.

Unit Trusts

If you 'save' money with a unit trust, your money will be invested in a wide range of stocks and shares. The amount of interest or dividend you receive will depend on how well the money is invested by the trust. Some unit trusts have made better investments than others in the past and have been able to offer better dividends to the people who save with them. Such savings become very attractive when tied to life insurance policies because they qualify for an income tax allowance.

Conclusion

There are many ways in which you can save your money. But generally the amount of interest you receive on your money depends upon how much money you save, the length of time your money is tied up, and the risk involved in the investment. You must be prepared not to spend too much if you are to have some savings on which you can draw.

TOPIC 5.1   Activities

1. Read the following extract and answer the questions:

A nest egg for the future
For relations, friends of the family, grandparents or godparents who would like to put away some money now to benefit the child later on, the National Savings Bank Investment Account could be the perfect answer. What better way to celebrate a birth or christening?

Money invested now and left to grow with interest over the years — and maybe topped up from time to time — may give the child a helping hand just when it will be most needed.

An Investment Account is also a good way for a child to learn how to manage money to the best advantage, as well as providing a way of saving for special wants like a bicycle or stereo. And if you prefer it, there can be two accounts in a child's name — one, perhaps, for long term growth, and the other for management by the child.

Because interest is paid in full on this account, with no tax deducted at source it is a sensible way of saving for children, few of whom are taxpayers. But if deposits in the account are a gift from the parents (as opposed to any other source) any interest exceeding £5 is aggregated with their income for tax purposes.

Children aged seven or over can open an Investment Account for themselves. A parent, relative or friend can open an account for a child below this age and as withdrawals are not normally allowed until the child is seven, can be sure that the money will stay safely and profitably invested.

Investment Accounts can be opened with as little as £1. A month's notice is needed for a withdrawal, so this is an ideal method of encouraging children to plan ahead before they spend.

The rate of interest paid on the Investment Account is kept competitive; for the current rate, please check at your local post office.

(Source: *'National Savings for the Young'*, Department for National Savings)

(a) List the advantages of opening an Investment Account (i) for the child; (ii) for the parents.
(b) What does the phrase 'with no tax deducted at source' mean?
(c) Name a disadvantage to the parents regarding income tax.
(d) What are the advantages of the Ordinary Account over the Investment Account? What is the main disadvantage?
(e) If you had a National Savings Investment Account with £1000 in it, how would you spend the money?

2. Imagine you are able to save the sum of £20 per month. In what type of savings account would you deposit it? Give reasons for your choice.

3. Conduct a survey to answer the following questions. Within three miles of your house:
(a) How many post offices are there?
(b) How many commercial banks?
(c) How many building societies?
(d) How many Trustee Savings Banks?

4. Describe how the survey which you have conducted could influence you when it came to choosing an account for your savings.

5. Imagine that you are going to buy some premium bonds. Find out:
(a) The smallest amount you can save in this way.
(b) The smallest *number* of premium bonds that you can buy.
(c) How long you have to wait before you stand a chance of winning a prize.
(d) The smallest tax-free prize that you could win.

(e) The largest prize you could win.
(f) How often the prizes are distributed.

6. Arrange the following forms of saving according to how much *risk* is involved:
(a) Units of a unit trust.
(b) National Savings Certificates.
(c) Building society deposits.
(d) Blue-chip shares.
(e) Gilt-edged securities.

TOPIC 5.2 Spending money through the bank

Using a current account

Not all the money which is deposited in banks is there for the purpose of saving. You may decide to have your weekly wages or monthly salary paid directly into a bank account at the branch of a commercial bank (see Fig. 5.2). You will then have a choice of either saving your money or saving some and spending some. However, much of the money paid into your bank account will be needed for everyday purposes, e.g., to pay for food, rent, and clothing (see Fig. 5.3). Both commercial banks and Trustee Savings Banks make it possible for you to pay for these items without having to go to the bank and draw out cash. When you open a current account at a bank, you will receive a cheque book. You can pay for things, such as clothes, by simply writing out a cheque. Of course, you must be sure to have enough money in your bank account to cover the cheque.

The *National Giro system* is a *current account* banking service organized by the Post Office. Giro customers write cheques for the payment of bills. So you could, if you wished, use the National Savings Bank for saving and the Giro system for the payment of bills. In both cases you would be using a Post Office service.

What is a cheque?

A cheque is simply an instruction written out by someone with a *current bank account* to his bank to pay a sum of money to another person. Most people use a book of cheques for this purpose (see Fig. 5.4), but cheques may be written on almost anything so long as they bear a signature. There is even a case of somebody who is supposed to have written a cheque on an egg. Cheque books are used a great deal today because more people have a current bank account and find that it saves them the trouble of carrying large sums of money in cash.

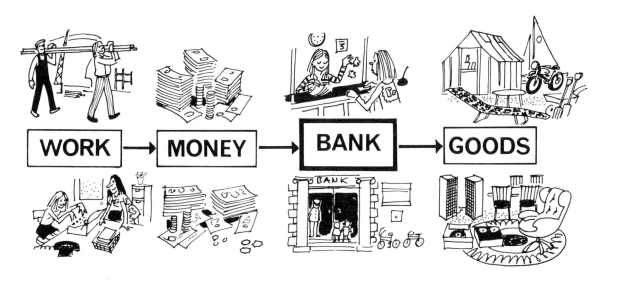

Fig 5.2   Using your bank

Making out a cheque

Study the cheque in Fig. 5.4. Answer the following questions:

1. Who wrote the cheque?
2. Whom does he want to pay?
3. Who filled in the cheque stub on the left-hand side of the cheque and why?

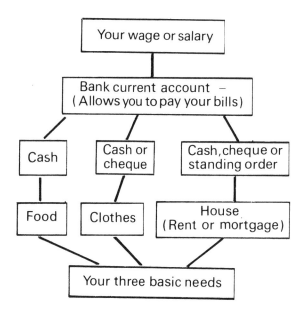

Fig 5.3   Paying for your three basic needs

You probably found these questions very easy. Now check your answers:

1. The cheque has been written or drawn by J. M. England *the drawer.*
2. J. M. England wants to pay John Burton the sum of £2.37. John Burton is the person who is to receive the money and is known as the *payee.*
3. The *drawer* fills in the cheque stub for his own records.

The completed cheque gives some other important information:

(a) *The amount*: The amount of money to be paid is written in both words and figures. This is to prevent anyone altering the amount. If these two do not agree, the payee will not receive his money. Any alteration made on a cheque must be initialled by the drawer.

(b) *The date*: All cheques must have the date written on them. Most banks will refuse payment on any cheques which are more than six months old.

(c) *Name of the account holder*: This is printed above the space where the drawer signs his name. This helps the bank to recognize on which account the cheque has been drawn: some people's signatures are very difficult to read.

(d) *Coded information*: The strange looking figures which are printed at the bottom of a cheque are in magnetic ink. This is so that the cheques can be sorted automatically by machines which recognize the magnetic figures.

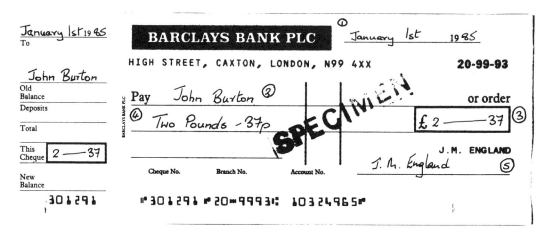

Fig 5.4   Making out a cheque (Source: Barclays Bank PLC)

Bank charges

Using a current account will cost you money, unless you keep a fairly substantial balance on current account. Your bank charges will vary according to the number of cheques you write, the amount of your current account balance, and the other services the bank provides for you. These charges will be shown on a *bank statement* which will tell you how you have spent your money and how much you have left. This will be sent to you at regular intervals or when you request it.

Conclusion

If your wages are paid directly into your bank account, you may find a cheque book very convenient. It will save you the time and trouble of going to your bank every time you want to buy something which is fairly expensive. Of course, you will always need some cash, but with a cheque book you will have a substitute for cash, provided of course you have some money in your current account.

TOPIC 5.2 Activities

1. Read the passage and answer the questions:

How can I avoid bank charges?
Over 95% of our personal cheque account customers who keep their accounts in credit will not pay any bank charges at all. This is how. All your cheques, credits, statements and standing orders will be free if you keep a minimum of £50 in your personal cheque account at all times during the quarterly charges period.

Even if your balance does drop below £50, you may not pay any charges at all. This is because we make an allowance based on your credit balance and this is offset against your charges. This allowance is calculated at 1% below Barclays seven day deposit rate. The current allowance is 14% p.a.

Often it will cancel your bank charges altogether.

If I do have to pay, what does it cost?
The cost of each entry during the whole quarterly charges period is 13p. Each cheque, standing order or other debit to your account is counted as one entry.

All credit items (money paid in) and statements are still free. If the total charge comes to less than 25p in the quarter we ignore it anyway.

This is how it works:

Example 1		Example 2	
Minimum Balance		Minimum Balance	
The smallest amount of money kept on your account during the quarterly charges period	£20	The smallest amount of money kept on your account during the quarterly charges period	£20
Average Credit Balance		Average Credit Balance	
The average of the money kept on your account during the quarterly charges period	£90	The average of the money kept on your account during the quarterly charges period	£75
25 entries on your account at 13p each	£3.25	50 entries on your account at 13p each	£6.50
Allowance made on the average credit balance on your account at 14% p.a. (i.e. 14% p.a. on £90 for 3 months)	£3.15	Allowance made on the average credit balance on your account at 14% p.a. (i.e. 14% p.a. on £75 for 3 months)	£2.63
BANK CHARGES	FREE	BANK CHARGES	£3.87

(Source: Barclays leaflet on Bank Charges — and how to avoid them)

(a) What credit balance do you need to maintain in order to avoid paying bank charges?
(b) What is the cost of each debit item shown on your bank statement?
(c) Give reasons why (i) the person in example 1 pays no bank charges and (ii) the person in example 2 pays £3.87.
(d) Why is Barclays able to offer free banking if your credit balance stays over a certain amount?

2. In your notebook draw and make out a cheque showing the following details:
(a) Payee R.G. Gibbs.
(b) Crossed.
(c) Drawer A. Smith Barclays Bank.
(d) Amount £20.75.
(e) Today's date.

3. In your notebook draw a bank statement which shows the following details:
(a) A salary credit of £200.
(b) Bank charges of £3.
(c) An overdraft of £100.
(d) A standing order of £20 from your account to a building society.
(e) A cheque drawn for £3.75.
(f) The balance of the account.

4. Make a list of the advantages and disadvantages of having bank accounts at:
(a) A commercial bank.
(b) The National Savings Bank.

5. Make a list of five articles which you could buy using a cheque and five for which you would have to pay cash.

6. Tape a mock interview between a bank manager and a customer who wishes to open a current account:
(a) What information would the bank manager want?
(b) What questions would he ask the customer?

TOPIC 5.3 Other financial services provided by your bank

How can a bank help you?

A bank will take care of your money

By opening a bank account, you will be sure that your money is looked after safely and will be available when you require it. If you leave money at home, you run the risk of losing your money or having it stolen. The bank is the place where your money will be safe. (Fig. 5.5 shows a commercial bank.)

A bank may lend you money

The idea of being able to borrow money when you are 'hard up' will no doubt appeal to you, but banks will not lend money to everybody who opens an account. It is unlikely that the bank would lend anyone £1000 to finance a holiday. However, the bank would probably lend money to someone who wished to improve his home. Can you explain this? It is possible to borrow money from a bank in three different ways:

1. *An overdraft*: If you were granted an overdraft you would be allowed to draw out more money than you had in your bank account *up to a limited amount* fixed by your local bank manager. Your debt to the bank would be shown in *red figures* or by the letters DR on your bank statement.
2. *A loan*: Your bank manager may grant you a loan of a fixed sum of money for a limited period. He may ask you to pay back part of the loan each month over a period of two years.

Fig 5.5   *A commercial bank provides many services for its customers (Reproduced by permission of Barclays Bank PLC)*

You will have to make an extra payment known as *interest*. Interest has to be paid on the full amount of the loan. (On an overdraft, you only have to pay interest on the amount of money you own to the bank.)

3. *Credit cards*: Banks also issue credit cards, such as 'Access' or 'Barclaycard', which allow customers short-term credit. They can buy goods immediately and pay for them later. For many customers these credit cards provide them with a permanent overdraft facility, but as with all borrowing they will be required to pay interest on their outstanding debt, though if the customer pays in cash when he receives the bill, no interest is payable. Barclaycard also serves as a cheque guarantee card.

General financial services

Standing orders

Your father may instruct his bank to deduct his mortgage payment from his account on a certain date every month and credit it to a building society's account. This is known as a *standing order*. Standing orders enable you to forget bills which have to be paid annually or monthly so long as the amount to be paid is the same each time, e.g., life assurance premiums.

Direct debit

With direct debit the system is reversed. Instead of the account holder instructing the bank to pay money from his account, the creditor (the person or firm to whom the money is owed) claims the debt from the debtor's account. This means that irregular amounts of money can be claimed, which is not possible with standing orders, though direct debit is becoming more widely used even for regular payments, for example, many householders now pay their rates to the local authority in 10 equal monthly instalments by direct debit. The account holder must give his bank permission for direct debit claims to be made on his account.

Foreign currency and travellers' cheques

If you decided to spend your summer holiday in Spain, your bank would help you by exchanging your English pounds for Spanish pesetas. You are then able to start spending your money as soon as you arrive in Spain. Alternatively, your bank will issue travellers' cheques to the amount you require (see Fig. 5.6). These cheques can be cashed for pesetas at any bank in Spain, as long as they are signed by you. Travellers' cheques can only be cashed by the person to whom they were issued, so if you lose them they cannot be cashed by anyone else.

Fig 5.6   Travellers' cheques (Source: Barclays Bank PLC)

Storing valuables

If a rich uncle left you a valuable gold watch, you might not wish to wear it or leave it at home for fear of losing it. Your bank would store it for you in its vault where you could be sure it would be safe. While the bank, it may even increase in value.

Paying interest

If you borrow money from your bank in the form of a loan or an overdraft, you will have to pay for the privilege. But if you put your money in a *deposit account,* the bank will pay you interest in return for the use of your money.

Bank giro

The bank giro system allows payments to be made without using cheques. A commercial bank will transfer a payment to the account of a payee, at *any branch of any commercial bank* in Great Britain. Even those who do not have bank accounts can pay in bank giro credits at any bank branch. When there are many payments to be made at the same time, the bank giro system is cheaper and easier than sending cheques.

Conclusion

We have discussed some of the main services a bank may be able to offer if you open an account (see Fig. 5.7). You may not use them all, but they are provided for your benefit as a customer. However, the more of these financial services you use, the more you are likely to have to pay in bank charges.

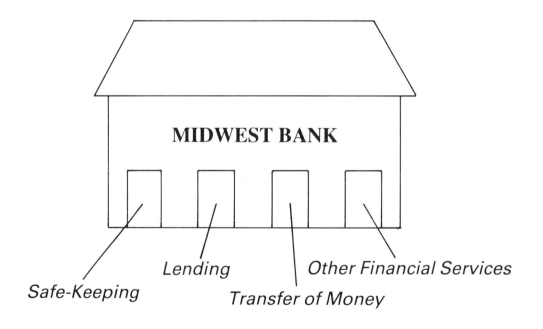

Fig 5.7   Banking services

TOPIC 5.3 Activities

1. Read the passage and answer the questions:

'The Survival Kit'
Barclaybank
With a Barclaybank card, there's less need to rush between lectures just to get to your branch in banking hours. Instead go at any time with your card to the nearest Barclaybank machine. They're usually positioned in town centres. Useful on a Saturday afternoon shopping trip, or after the late night cinema. You can draw up to £50 a day, order a statement and find out the balance on your account from any Barclaybank machine 24 hours a day, 7 days a week.
You'll get a full list of locations with your card.
Budget planner
We've designed this to help you budget as accurately as possible. On it you can set out your grant and essential expenses for each item and then calculate how much 'pocket money' you'll have left. While it won't actually stop you overspending, it can give you an early warning of when your resources are likely to be stretched, so that you can talk to your Student Business Officer in good time.
Barclaycard
As we've said earlier, a Barclaycard will guarantee cheques you write up to £50 and also let you draw cash from your bank account up to £50 a day at almost any bank in the UK. It's also a credit card which can be used instead of cash or cheques at any one of nearly 130 000 shops, stores, restaurants, and garages in Britain.

(Source: Barclay leaflet 'Our survival kit for students')

(a) What is the advantage of Barclaybank?
(b) How could the Student Business Officer at Barclays help a student plan his expenditure over an extended period of time?
(c) Why might a shop wish a customer to guarantee a cheque by showing a Barclaycard?
(d) Give *two* other advantages of a Barclaycard mentioned in the passage.
(e) Write a list of as many 'substitutes' for money as you can think of. Why do you think these methods of payment are increasing in popularity?

2. Copy the following into your notebook. Put a 'T' in the box where you think the statement is true, and an 'F' if you think it is false. A bank manager is likely to grant a loan for a fixed sum if you want money:
(a) To buy bulbs for your garden. ☐
(b) To build a sun-room on to your house. ☐
(c) To buy a new car. ☐
(d) To buy a new suit. ☐
(e) To buy a different house (assume you own a house already). ☐
(f)   To extend your business. ☐
Explain your answers.

3. Make a list of five bills which you think it would be advisable for your bank to remember for you and pay by standing order.

4. Make a list of five valuable items which you might consider storing for safe keeping with your bank. Why do you think that these items may increase in value?

5. Find out the present interest rates given to savers by the following:
(a) A commercial bank.
(b) National Savings Bank.
(c) Building societies.
(d) Trustee Savings Bank.

6. What is the name and present exchange rates for the following currencies? Copy and complete the table.

	Country	Unit of currency	Present exchange rate for £1
(a)	France		
(b)	Italy		
(c)	Greece		
(d)	Switzerland		
(e)	Austria		

Unit 6

How goods are produced

TOPIC 6.1 Starting a factory

The site

The site of a factory is very important in relation to the goods which are produced there. It might be inconvenient to site a large factory, using bulky raw materials, in the centre of a busy city or town. It would probably be difficult to get the raw materials to the factory and to transport the finished goods away from it. Figure 6.1 shows the type of site the organizer of such a factory might choose. Although the railway and the river are important ways of moving bulky materials, today roads provide one of the main means of transport for almost all goods. So it is likely that the organizer will want to be sure that his factory is situated on the outskirts of the town or city, so that lorries coming to and from the factory avoid traffic congestion in the town centre.

The workers

The organizer must consider where he is going to obtain the workforce for his factory. If the workers have to travel by bus or car to reach the factory, they will have to spend money before they begin earning their wage. To attract workers, the organizer may even have to offer to pay these extra costs. If the factory is sited close to a large city, there will be people to work in the factory as well as people to buy the finished products.

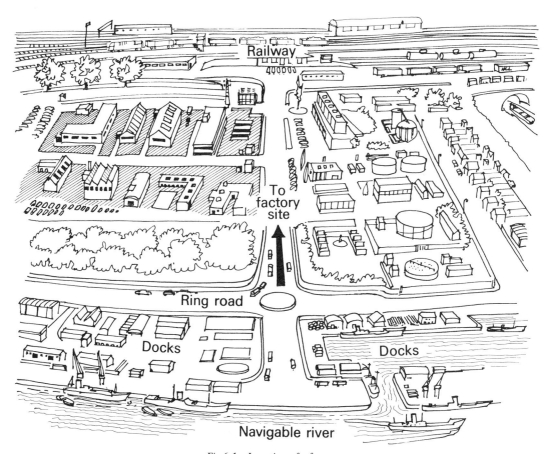

Fig 6.1   Location of a factory

Help for the organizer

The Government will give the organizer of a factory some financial assistance if he is willing to site his factory in certain areas. Some parts of Great Britain have large numbers of people unemployed because older industries have declined and no longer require many workers. These regions of the country are often called 'problem regions' because when large numbers of the workforce in an area are unemployed this may cause problems to many others who live around them. A problem region is likely to have the following characteristics:

1. High unemployment — the percentage of the workforce unemployed is above the national average figure.
2. Fewer industries and consequently fewer job opportunities than more prosperous areas.
3. The surroundings or infrastructure (such as roads, houses, factory buildings) may be old and underdeveloped; this might deter new firms coming to the area.
4. The workforce may be trained in traditional skills which may no longer be required, e.g., steel workers in Corby.
5. Many workers, especially the young, may take the opportunity to leave the area because of a lack of job opportunities — this is likely to hasten the decline of the region.

The Government divides areas which may have some of these problems into three main categories:

1. Special development areas, where the need for jobs is the most pressing.
2. Development areas.
3. Intermediate areas.

All of these areas are suffering from the types of problems outlined earlier but to varying degrees. To help industry the Government offers incentives to firms who are willing to begin production in these areas and to provide work for the unemployed. There are grants to pay for factory buildings as well as for expensive machinery. Manufacturers can also apply for regional employment premiums which are payments made to the firm for every person employed, and concessions with rates and taxes may also be given. Because of such help government policy is often referred to as one which takes 'work to the workers'.

In 1980, the Government announced the establishment of *enterprise zones* in an attempt to solve the problems of derelict land and buildings in our inner cities.

Areas where grants are available

Figure 6.2 shows the areas where government aid is available. Do you live in one of these areas?

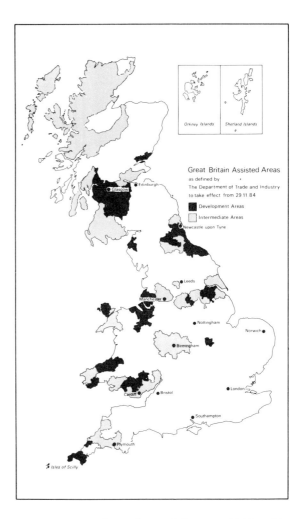

Fig 6.2   The assisted areas (Source: Information Division of the Treasury)

105

Problems facing the organizer

1. *The Organization of production*: Once the problem of where the factory is to be sited is settled, the organizer must decide how production is to be arranged (see Fig. 6.3). Let us consider two industries which provide examples of different internal organization:

   (a) In the iron and steel industry, a large firm may own everything including mines, blast furnaces, and rolling mills, right up to the factories producing the final product.

   (b) In the textile industry, the opposite is true and an individual firm is likely to specialize in one process such as spinning or weaving.

2. *Money*: The organizer must think carefully about the amount of money needed to begin production. He may have to borrow money because he has to pay for the production of the goods *before* they are sold. There is not even any certainty that the goods will be bought once they have been produced.

3. *The management of the factory*: The organizer will want particular people to be responsible for certain aspects of production at the factory. It would be impossible for one person to be in charge of everything. The organizer must decide who does what job.

4. *Selling the final product*: The organizer must be sure that he is making something that people will buy. The finished article must be sold to pay workers' wages and to pay for raw materials, rent, rates, electricity, gas, etc. He may have to pay off money borrowed when production began, plus the interest on that money. So the organizer must aim to sell his product at a profit. He may do this by selling through shops or by using direct selling methods. The *marketing* of the product is the final important decision which has to be taken.

Conclusion

You will see from this topic that the organizer has to make many decisions before he is able to start producing goods. Such decisions are very important if the factory is to make a profit. In turn, the profit is the reward to the organizer for taking the risk and beginning production.

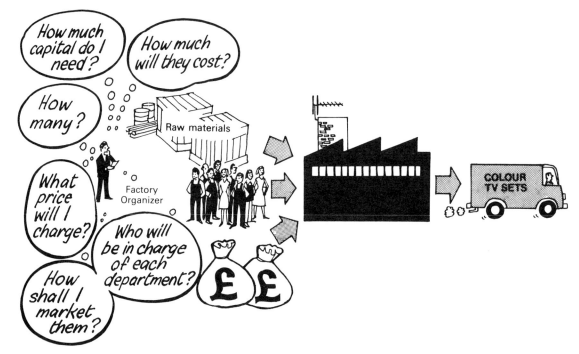

Fig 6.3 Decisions, decisions, decisions, for the factory organizer

TOPIC 6.1 Activities

1. Read the following extract and answer the questions:

Tom's Liquid Asset
A Northumberland couple are tapping the natural resources at their remote smallholding in the Pennines, by going into the bottled water business.

Tom and Cath McGoldrick came up with the idea of bottling and selling the water from the spring that rises in a small wood near their home.

Soon Allendale Spring Water from Low Turney Shield, Carrshield, West Allendale will be competing with household names in the multi-million pound mineral water industry.

Tom, aged 42, has been able to start up the business through the Manpower Services Commission's new Enterprise Allowance Scheme. He will receive the allowance of £40 a week for up to 52 weeks while the business is being established.

The scheme is designed to help unemployed people who want to set up their own business but are deterred by the fact that they would lose their entitlement to unemployment or supplementary benefit.

Tom, a former auctioneer, raised the £1000 cash necessary to qualify for the allowance and which is to be invested in the business from friends.

He and his 31-year-old wife moved to the 16-acre traditional dales smallholding eight years ago from Newcastle. The 17th century cottage and adjoining barn were derelict and there was neither electricity nor running water.

Since then they have renovated the property and eked out a living from the land for themselves and their children, Helen aged 5, and Michael, 3.

The couple considered the idea of bottling their own spring water after so many friends arrived with bottles to take some away.

They hope to start production within a month. An ultra-violet purifier will be installed to comply with health regulations and modern underground piping will bring the water up to their barn where it will be bottled.

They plan to start off with four to five hundred bottles a week and hope to increase production to around 3000 bottles a week.

'We could possibly become an employer and put some money back into the land,' said Tom.

(Source: *Employment News,* September 1983)

(a) Explain in your own words how the MSC's Enterprise Allowance Scheme works.
(b) Briefly describe the McGoldricks' business venture.
(c) Find out the names of three 'household names' with which Tom and Cath would be competing.
(d) If they were able to sell 3000 bottles per week at 25p per bottle, what would be their gross profit?
(e) If you could qualify for the Enterprise Allowance Scheme what sort of business would you set up?

2. Select three factories close to your school. Draw diagrams of their individual sites. What are the advantages of the factory being sited in that particular position?

3. What sort of things would the following be responsible for in the management of a large factory?
(a) Personnel officer.
(b) Chief accountant.
(c) Marketing manager.
(d) Purchasing manager.
(e) Transport manager.

4. Write down the names of five large firms in your area. Find out:
(a) The raw materials they require.
(b) The number of people they employ.
(c) The size of the sites.
(d) The finished products.

5. Plan an advertisement for a local newspaper aimed to attract workers to a new factory about to begin production.

TOPIC 6.2 Mass production

What is mass production?

When you begin work it is most unlikely that you will produce one complete article (see Topic 1.2). You will probably play only a small part in making the article. Your contribution is part of the process of *mass production*.

Look at Fig. 6.4. You have probably worked out that 10 people working together can produce more shirts than one person by himself. In a similar way, 100 workers produce far more per head than 10 workers. This is because each one of the 100 workers concentrates on some small part of the production of a shirt. In this way, the division of labour speeds production.

Advantages of the division of labour

Increased production

If you look once more at Fig. 6.4, you will see that one of the most obvious advantages of the division of labour is that far more goods can be produced. Simple tasks can be done quickly as the worker moves from one article to the next without having to change his tools.

Greater confidence in the job

Because the tasks are so simple, they can be learned quickly. As the worker repeats the same

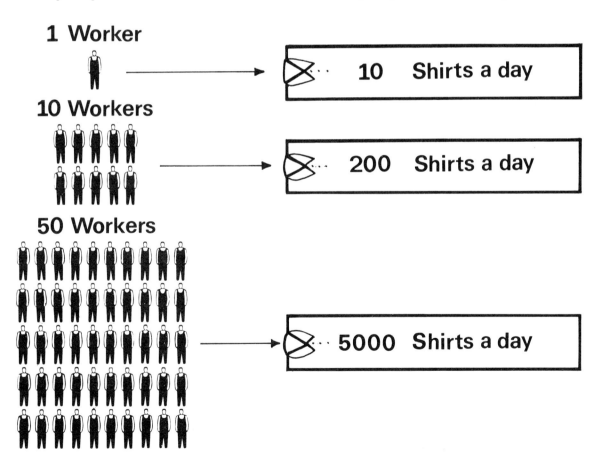

Fig 6.4   *Mass production*

process again and again, the job becomes easy. He soon feels that he is good at his job.

On the job training

One benefit to the employer is that he may not have to employ specialists to train new workers. Training may be carried out on the job by almost any worker. However, there are some jobs, even within a system of division of labour, which require training. All workers are expected to work carefully and accurately.

Added incentives

Another advantage is that workers who repeat simple tasks all day can be offered *piecework rates*. This means that the workers receive more money if they work harder and produce more. This encourages them to get on with their work. Often workers paid by this system are able to earn higher wages than if paid a fixed hourly or weekly rate.

Using machines

Yet another advantage to the organizer of the factory is that he may be able to use a machine instead of employing several men to do simple tasks. Often machines can work much faster than men and they do not require food and sleep.

Disadvantages of the division of labour

Repetition can become boring

Some people prefer to work at a job in which they do not have to think, but others find this type of job very boring. Repeating the same task day after day, for year after year, may mean that many people become fed-up with their work. With jobs of this nature, some employers try to give their workers a change every so often by setting them to different tasks. Often these feelings of dissatisfaction affect the workers' lives outside the factory.

Lack of personal involvement

The division of labour does not encourage craftsmanship or let the worker take much pride in his work. Too often, he may only want to get his part of the job finished, especially if speed means money. This may lead to a lowering of standards.

Machines may lead to redundancies

When jobs are very simple, workers run the risk of being replaced by machines which can repeat these tasks more rapidly. This leads to unemployment. It may be difficult for the redundant workers to get another job because their skills are limited.

Standardization of products

Goods produced by the division of labour are all exactly the same. Designs may change very little especially if the production process is made up of very simple operations. Some people prefer to buy goods which are individually produced and which have some 'character' about them.

Conclusion

The organization of a factory is most important if goods are to be produced efficiently. In our modern world, efficiency is usually achieved through the division of labour. Such specialization is advantageous to *all* of us because of the greater number and variety of goods which can be produced, but it may be disadvantageous to the people directly involved.

TOPIC 6.2   Activities

1. Read the following passage and answer the questions:

'We go in at seven-thirty. To get to our shop you go down a flight of stairs, and at the top of them someone has written HAPPY VALLEY. It is part of an enormous factory with a population of eight thousand. We start working on our line at about eight o'clock, after we have had a drink of tea and a look at the paper.

There are nine benches down the line, a man standing at each. We make all the tractor parts in our shop. On our line we panel-beat the hoods, each man doing his part of the work and then manhandling it on to the next man, and so on, until it gets to me. We do two hundred and sixty hoods a day, and it only takes me two minutes to do my bit of it, though I was timed for ten minutes by the time-study man.

The worst kind of foreman you can have is the one who has worked himself up from the bench, because he knows all the dodges, yet if it was a few years since he worked himself up there are a few up-to-date dodges he does not know. And anyway it's strange how soon he forgets them when he's no longer one of us. We work on our own time at a piecework rate.

(Source: Bryan Slater, 'On the line' (adapted) in *Work* ed. Ronald Fraser)

(a) How many people worked in the factory?
(b) What is meant by 'on our line'?
(c) What did they make in their shop?
(d) What particular work was done on the man's line?
(e) What is a time-study man?
(f) Why would a worker pretend that a two minute job took ten minutes?
(g) What is the worst kind of foreman? Why?
(h) Explain 'piecework rate'.

2. Write down some of the main stages in the production of an article which is made at a local factory.

3. Make a list of five articles which could *not* be produced using a system of division of labour. Give your reasons.

4. List five jobs which require at least one year's training before they can be fully mastered. Now write down five other jobs which require no training.

5. The following are piecework rates:
(a) 500–600 units = 5p per unit.
(b) 600–700 units = 10p per unit.
(c) 700–800 units = 15p per unit.
(d) 800–900 units = 20p per unit.
(e) 900 plus units = 25p per unit.
(i) Why do you think a worker does not go on to the 'piece' rates until he has produced 500 units?
(ii) How much extra would a worker earn if in one week he produced 650 units? (His basic wage is £40 per week.)
(iii) How much would he earn if he produced 990 units?

6. Conduct a survey around your school and write down all the things you can find which are standardized as a result of mass production.

7. Make up a job advertisement which tries to make a simple job in a factory seem attractive.

TOPIC 6.3   Automation

Machines are designed to help you

If you go to work in a large factory, you will soon become familiar with machines. It is possible that some of these machines will be 'automatic' and require very few people to control them (see Fig. 6.5). There are few articles in your home which have been made without the help of large machines. In the future, there will be a big increase in the use of automated machinery. Workers will need to have a specialized knowledge of automated methods of production.

Advantages of automated production

Wider range of goods

Machinery is an aid to production and one of the main advantages it brings is to allow a wider range of goods to be made. Goods can be produced much faster, leaving more time to make a wider variety. This benefits us all because we have a wider *choice* when spending our money.

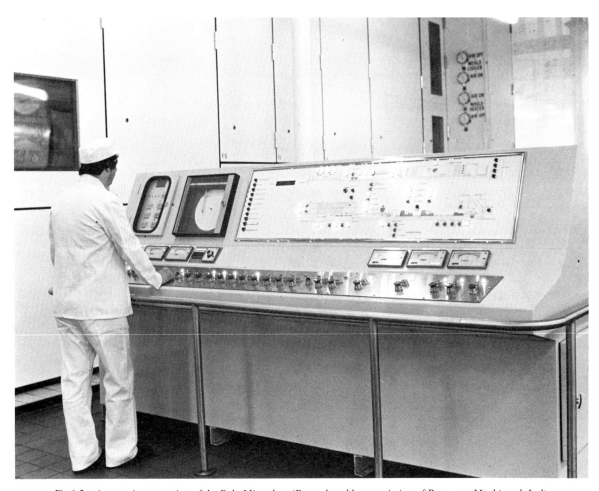

Fig 6.5   Automation: a section of the Polo Mint plant (Reproduced by permission of Rowntree-Mackintosh Ltd)

Relieves workers of the more boring tasks

Many people dislike working at monotonous jobs. Automated machinery relieves workers of many boring jobs. Housework is much easier than it was 50 years ago because of such machines as vacuum cleaners. How much better off your mother would be if she had a fully automated house-cleaner.

Shorter working week

Table 6.1 shows how the average number of hours worked each week has decreased in the twentieth century. Machines mean faster production and hence more leisure for workers. Most workers today have both Saturday and Sunday off. In the future, you may work a three-day week with four days of leisure. Do you think that more time at school should be spent in learning how to use leisure time?

Table 6.1 The working week

Year	Hours per week
1900	60
1920	50
1960	45
1970	40
2000	20(?)

Earlier retirement

These days most men retire at the age of 65 and receive a pension. Women can receive a pension at the age of 60. Is this fair? By the end of the century, it is possible that a man may have completed his working life by the time he is 50.

Automation presents us with problems

Unwanted workers

Do you know anyone who has been made redundant? If so, this may be because the job he was doing is now being done by an automatic machine. Finding another job may be difficult. People may have to be re-trained for other work. There are some jobs where it is impossible to replace men with machines. It would be an advantage for redundant workers to be re-trained for these jobs. Do you know of any such jobs?

Many workers fear redundancy through the increase in automation. When this happens, trade unions find it difficult to protect their members' wages and conditions. Some changes in working conditions cannot be prevented. In the interests of efficiency, men will continue to be replaced by machines. This has happened ever since machines were first introduced into industry.

Too much leisure (fig. 6.6)

You may think it is a very good idea to have as much time off as you want. But could you really say exactly how you would spend *four* free days *every* week? Many people may have problems if their leisure time is increased, especially if they do not have an interesting hobby or pastime to occupy them. Perhaps workers will have to be taught how they can usefully use their leisure time.

Fig 6.6 Too much leisure?

Unequal distribution of wealth

Although more goods can be produced in automated factories, we must see that the benefits are fairly distributed. If high profits and incomes are gained by the small proportion of people engaged in automation, an even wider gap may be created between rich and poor.

Machines break down

Machines sometimes break down. This can prove expensive if production has to be stopped for any length of time. We must use automation but not depend solely upon it. There will probably always be a need for skilful workers especially for the programming, control, and running of complex machinery.

In what ways has automation been used?

1. *Retailing*: Some modern supermarkets offer punch card shopping. A sample of each of the items on sale is displayed with a supply of punched cards. These cards are collected instead of the goods and handed to an assistant for processing through a tabulator. A detailed invoice is produced by the machine and this is fed into a stockroom for the order to be made up by assistants. Meanwhile, the customer is handed a second piece of paper showing the amount to be paid. A few minutes after handing her cards to the shop assistant she collects the carrier bags containing the items ordered. Other developments in retailing include electronic point of sale techniques and teleshopping. Many products now have *bar codes* on their packaging and, if the store has suitable equipment at the check-out, the bar code can be passed over a laser scanner which not only records the price of the item on the customer's till receipt but also updates the stock records. With teleshopping, the customer will be able to order goods at home by using the Teletext system in conjunction with a home computer, arranging for delivery, and payment from his bank or building society account, at the same time. Already, in 1984, there are a number of teleshopping pilot schemes operating in various parts of the country.
2. *Transport*: Computers are already being used to control the running of trains. It is possible to travel to and from work in San Francisco on an automated train. During the rush hour trains leave every 90 seconds, serving a network of 75 miles. Computers decide on the frequency of the service depending on the number of passengers. Each train carries a driver whose only job is to stop the train in an emergency.
3. *Hospitals*: Computers are used in hospitals to keep patients' records as well as to diagnose what may be wrong with them. In the future it may be possible to use robots to carry out many of the routine hospital tasks.
4. *Manufacturing*: Cars 'hand-built by robots' are now commonplace in the motor industry and automated production is spreading to many other industries. For example in paper making it is necessary to make rapid calculations so that adjustments can be made to operating conditions — this work can be efficiently carried out by a computer, so human error is eliminated.
5. *Office work*: Much clerical and general office work can be performed by computers. All banks, and most building societies, now have their own computer systems which handle customers' accounts very rapidly. The National Giro Centre at Bootle and the Department of the Environment's Driver and Vehicle Licensing Centre at Swansea are examples of computerized office developments.

Conclusion

Automation is already with us and offers many advantages in all sections of industry. However, changes in the method of production have always brought problems since the eighteenth century when simple machines were first introduced into factories. It is important to try to overcome these problems and use the automated machines of the twentieth century to the best advantage. Such machines may enable us to give more attention to those members of society whom we have somewhat neglected in the past, e.g., old age pensioners and the mentally and physically handicapped. If automation brings faster production and shorter hours of work, it can help us all.

TOPIC 6.3   Activities

1. Read the passage and answer the questions:

£250 million Robot Programme urged
British industry must invest £250m in robots over the next 10 years if it is to compete with foreign industries already benefiting from a much higher level of robot installation.

A Government-commissioned report today warns that unless robots are used to improve production reliability, the consequences will be a failure to survive not simply a decline in profitability.

The Intersoll report estimates that 7000 programmable robots are being used worldwide, only 150 of them in the UK. It recommends investment in robot applications rather than making robots.

A £250m investment programme, comprising 12 000 robots at £20 000-plus each (mid-1979 prices), is necessary. Another £20 to £25m needs to be spent on research and development to carry out the programme.

(Source: *Financial Times*, 14 July 1980, based on *Industrial Robots,* report commissioned by the Department of Industry)

(a) Why must British industry invest £250 million in robots over the next 10 years?
(b) What do you understand by a 'decline in profitability'?
(c) What percentage of programmable robots is in use in the UK?
(d) What do you understand by the term 'investments in robot application rather than making robots'?
(e) How many robots are considered necessary if Britain is to compete in the world?
(f) Suggest some of the ways in which robots might be used in the future.

2. Machines have many advantages over people. In turn, people have some advantages over machines. Copy and complete the table.

Advantages of machines	Advantages of people
(a)	(a)
(b)	(b)
(c)	(c)
(d)	(d)
(e)	(e)

3. Make a list of at least five jobs where you think it would be difficult to replace a person with a machine.

4. List five machines which you think have made your life more pleasant and comfortable. Give reasons for your choice.

5. Make a survey of the leisure facilities in your area for people between 16 and 18.

6. What extra activities would be needed for people with three or four days a week of leisure time?

7. List some people who would be grateful for extra help if the community as a whole had more time and energy to devote to them.

TOPIC 6.4   Who provides the money?

Who owns your firm?

The four signs shown in Fig. 6.7 are used by different forms of business organizations. Some businesses are owned by just one person, while others may have hundreds of 'owners'. Who provided the money to found the firm where you hope to work?

Sole proprietorship

In this case the money comes from one man, the owner. Mr Bloggings in Fig. 4.3 is a sole proprietor who has put all his savings into the business. If the business goes well and makes a profit, it will all be for him. If it makes a loss, he must bear it. Can you think of any one-man businesses? They are usually small concerns.

Partnership

Wilson and Brown, as the sign in Fig. 6.7 suggests, are partners. They have both put money into the business and share all the risks and all the profits. If a sole proprietor wanted to expand his business, it is likely that he would look for a partner who would be prepared to put some money into the firm and probably work in the business as well. In this way, the owner has more money for expansion as well as having another interested person to help run the business.

You can probably think of examples of partnerships in your area. In an ordinary partnership the number of partners can vary from two to twenty. If you are ever asked to join a partnership, make sure that you sign a *deed of partnership* which sets out all the conditions involved in the partnership. Without such a deed, one partner may find himself responsible for the debts of the other.

Private joint-stock company

As the number of people in a partnership is limited to 20, the money available is also limited. If a partnership needed more money to expand a private joint-stock company might be formed such

Fig 6.7   *Signs depicting types of business organizations*

as T. C. Andrews and Co. Ltd. (see Fig. 6.7). All the investors have what is known as *limited liability*. This means that should the company find itself bankrupt, each investor will only lose the amount he had put into the company. His investment is 'limited'. Before limited liability was made legal in 1855/56, an investor might have had to sell his house and furniture (as a sole proprietor or partners might still have to do today) in order to pay off some of a company's debts. Most private companies are family businesses where the investment is divided between the members of a family. The shares are held privately by a minimum to two shareholders, and there is no maximum number. If the company makes a profit, it is divided among the shareholders according to how much they have invested. The person with the largest share (the most money invested) receives a greater proportion of the profit, known as a *dividend*. It is in this way that shareholders benefit from being investors in a private company. A private company must put the word 'Limited' or the abbreviation 'Ltd' after its trading name so that people who lend money to the company are aware that if it goes into liquidation they might not be repaid.

Fig 6.8   The trading floor of the Stock Exchange
(Source: the Stock Exchange Council)

Public joint-stock company

Modern methods of production need vast amounts of money. This can only be obtained by the public joint-stock companies like Chore Products PLC in Fig. 6.7. A public company may have come about by a private company wishing to expand and *go public*. Like a private company, a public company can be formed by a minimum of two people with no upper limit, but a public company must have a certain minimum amount of share capital (at present £50 000). The company attracts a larger number of investors by offering shares for sale on the Stock Exchange (see Fig. 6.8). Many thousands of people may invest money in a public company and thus have a *share* in it. For these people there are two main types of investment: debentures and shares.

Debentures represent a loan to the company at a fixed rate of interest. These provide a safe form of investment because the debenture holders must be paid even if the company makes a loss and has to borrow from the bank in order to meet its obligations.

Shares may be of two main types:

1. *Preference shares*: These earn a fixed dividend which is paid after the debenture holders have been paid, but before the ordinary shareholders receive anything.

2. *Ordinary shares*: These earn a variable dividend according to the profits made by the company and the decision of the Board of Directors about what proportion of the profit should be distributed. Ordinary shareholders may receive a very high return on their capital invested or they may receive nothing for years. They carry most risk, but stand to reap the greatest reward if the company prospers. Investors in public joint-stock companies are still only liable for the amount they have invested should the company fall on hard times. A public company must have the words 'Public Limited Company' or the abbreviation 'PLC' after its trading name.

Conclusion

Business undertakings vary in size, usually depending upon who owns them. The one-man business is usually small; he has only a small amount of money to use in the firm.

In a large company, many thousands of shareholders are the true owners. It is easier for the large public company to attract more money for expansion by offering more shares for sale. It is in this way that large public companies continue to grow although the business may have been started by one man. Can you name 10 of the largest public companies?

TOPIC 6.4   Activities

1. Study the table below and answer the questions:

Table Four   Shareholders in Unilever PLC in 1981

	Number of holdings	Amount of holdings £	%
Banks and discount companies	4 883	1 068 750	2
Financial trusts	112	310 499	1
Insurance companies	843	8 118 631	18
Investment trusts	180	577 000	1
Pension funds	236	2 484 055	6
Nominee companies	3 585	12 989 658	28
Other companies	1 235	2 234 728	5
	11 074	27 783 321	61
Leverhulme Trust*	1	8 443 887	18
Individuals	61 831	9 539 607	21
	72 906	45 766 815	100

Source: Unilever Report and Accounts 1981

* Set up under the will of the first Lord Leverhulme (d. 1925). Much of the Trust's income is used to support scholarly research.

(Source: *Business and Society*, Unilever Educational Publications)

(a) What does the abbreviation 'PLC' mean?
(b) What abbreviation is used to denote a private company?
(c) Unilever is a multinational company. Explain the meaning of the phrase 'multinational company'.
(d) From the table, find three examples of 'institutional investors'.
(e) In your own words, explain how a large part of the income from the Leverhulme Trust's investment is used.

2. Draw a diagram of your nearest local shopping centre, showing the various shops and offices. Colour this diagram according to the ownership of these shops (one-man businesses, partnerships, and companies).

3. In your notebook draw up plans to expand your school tuck shop.
(a) How could you expand?
(b) How would you raise the extra money?
(c) How large should the organization be?

4. Using your library, find out all the legal procedures that must be completed before a public joint-stock company can offer shares for sale for the first time.

5. Cut out the prices of shares from a newspaper. Compare these with those in the same newspaper a month later.
(a) In your notebook write down the names of the five share prices which have changed the most.
(b) Why do you think these prices have changed?

6. Find out what work is carried out by the following large companies.
(a) Bowater.
(b) BP.
(c) Colvilles.
(d) Courtaulds.
(e) GEC.
(f) Guest, Keen and Nettlefolds.
(g) Hawker Siddeley.
(h) ICI.
(i) RTZ.
(j) Unilever.

Unit 7

Advertising

TOPIC 7.1   An advertising campaign

Why advertise?

When a product is advertised, the seller's aim is to persuade consumers to buy it. He often does this by stressing one particular feature, e.g., how economical 'Super Wash' is to use. In the case of a new product an *advertising campaign* is generally launched to promote the product by informing the public of its qualities and usefulness. Such campaigns are carefully thought out since a great deal of money is spent in the hope that the public will buy the new product.

The advertising agency

An advertising agency is a specialist firm employed by a manufacturer to create ideas for advertising a product. The agency may advise the manufacturer that the product should create a certain image to the public. For example, the agency may hardly mention how well a new washing-up liquid washes plates, but stress the softness it gives to the hands. You should be able to think of examples of images created by certain products.

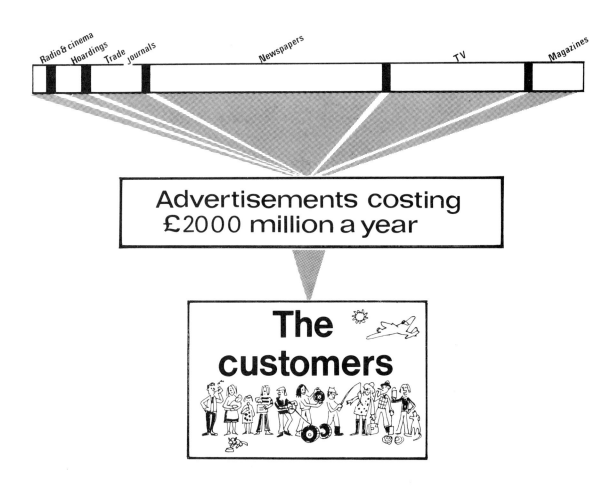

Fig 7.1   Advertising media

Launching the campaign

Once the agency has devised an image for a product, it must organize the promotion of the product. First, it will have to decide on the best media for advertising the product, e.g., television, the national press, women's magazines, etc. (see Fig. 7.1). The agency must also decide whether these advertisements should be backed up by special 'gimmicks', for example:

1. A special offer for one month, e.g., 10p off.
2. A free gift with every purchase.
3. A competition offering a prize of £5000.
4. Money-saving coupons with every purchase.

In the case of a household product, the campaign is then launched in the press, on television, and in the shops where the product is sold. Printed posters may appear in shop windows, while large displays attract customers' attention. The agency may organize a competition for shop managers to see who can arrange the most effective display of the product. By undertaking these tasks, the agency allows the manufacturer to concentrate on production while the shops get on with the job of selling. Table 7.1 summarizes the sequence of selling.

Table 7.1   The sequence of selling

Manufacturer	Production
Agency	Image/Promotion
Shop	Display/Selling
Customer	Buying

Sales

Imagine that an advertising campaign has been launched for 'Super Wash Liquid'. If the campaign was successful, the graph of total sales might look similar to the one shown in Fig. 7.2. During the month of the campaign, many people were attracted to the product and sales increased. The increased sales have more than made up for the large sums spent on the campaign. It would be

hoped that if the product was as good as the advertisers claimed, consumers would continue to purchase it and sales would increase even more. People get to know the product and recommend it to their friends. The success of the campaign can only be judged by the sales of the product concerned.

Fig 7.2   A sales graph for 'Super Wash'

Conclusion

Many advertising campaigns are very lively and increase the sales of a product very quickly. By stressing one or two points about a product over and over again, the advertiser makes us remember his claims.

123

TOPIC 7.1 Activities

1. Look at and read the advertisement below and answer the questions:

ATS   STERLING REMOULDS

TWO FOR THE PRICE OF ONE

Plus! The Sterling Written Road Damage GUARANTEE

Here's your written guarantee of Sterling performance . . . If an ATS Sterling remould
fitted to your vehicle becomes unserviceable as a result of accidental road damage,
we will replace it without question at any ATS depot. All you pay for is the tread you
have used (down to the 1 mm tread depth required by Law).

Now there's even better news & value —
buy a Sterling Remould at current ATS list
price, and we'll supply and fit a second
remould of the same size absolutely
free.

RADIAL OR CROSSPLY TO FIT ALL POPULAR
MAKES OF CAR You can drive with confidence
on ATS Sterling Remoulds, which are manufactured in the
UK to the highest standards, and are available in sizes
to fit all popular makes of car including
imported cars.

HURRY WHILST STOCKS LAST

(Source: *Eastern Evening News,* 26 March 1981)

(a) How does the advertisement persuade the buyer?
(b) What is the guarantee worth?
(c) Does the advert help the potential buyer to compare prices? Are there any ways in which you think the advertisement could be improved?
(d) What additional information would you want if you were going to purchase car tyres from this firm?

2. What 'image' would you try to promote if you were responsible for running an advertising campaign for the following products?
(a) Beer.
(b) Cigars.
(c) Pet food.
(d) Soap.
(e) Washing powder.

3. Design an advertising poster aimed at making an impact for 'Super Wash Liquid'.

4. In your notebook write down the names of five products and the 'gimmicks' which are used to help to sell them.

5. List five products advertised on television which make a *romantic* appeal to the customer.

6. As a class, attempt to invent a new product which would be useful in every household. Plan a campaign to make the public aware of this new product.

TOPIC 7.2   Informing and persuading

Persuasion

When your mother goes shopping for washing powder, does she always choose the same brand or does she choose whichever brand is on offer? Many washing powders are essentially similar; differing only in their *brand name* and the *image* which has been created for them. As a consumer, your mother has to choose which of the brands she is going to buy.

Advertisers try to *persuade* consumers to choose their brand. They may stress certain qualities about their brand and offer various inducements in an attempt to persuade consumers to buy this brand. Over £2000 million is spent on advertising every year and most of it goes on *persuasive advertising*. Advertising 'wars' take place and millions of pounds are spent on boosting the sales of one brand against very similar ones.

Information

Some advertisements are simply informative and do not try to persuade you to choose between products. The advertisement in Fig. 7.3 makes no attempt to persuade you to buy the drill. It just gives you various facts about it; of course these facts may influence your choice when you are selecting a drill. This advertisement is an example of *informative* advertising; far less of the total spent on advertising is spent on this type of advertising. The advertiser must, however, avoid being too informative; if he gives too many facts, people may be bored by the advertisement and stop looking at it or even be put off the product itself.

Competition

Some advertising is designed to combat competition from rival firms which produce similar articles. In this type of advertising a firm concentrates attention on the shortcomings of a rival firm's product rather than making special claims for the one made by itself. This is known as combative advertising.

Communication

As you saw in Topic 7.1, the advertiser has to reach as many possible customers as he can. He does this by placing advertisements where they are likely to be seen by as many people as possible. For example, one advertisement for 30 seconds on ITV may be seen by as many as 20 million viewers.

Fig 7.3   Informative advertising

Advantages and disadvantages of advertising

Can you add to the list below? Do you disagree with any of the points made?

Some advantages of advertising

1. Informs the public about products and prices.
2. Helps people to choose wisely.
3. Increases sales and may lower production costs.
4. Supports newspapers, TV, and radio.
5. Gives employment.

125

Some disadvantages of advertising

1. Persuades people to buy things they do not really want.
2. Wastes money, and thus may put prices up.
3. Aims at weak-minded people who cannot make up their own minds.
4. Causes social problems by being unsightly and repetitive.
5. Misleads consumers.

Advertising standards

The British Code of Advertising Practice which is administered by the Advertising Standards Authority attempts to ensure that all advertising is truthful, legal, decent, and honest. Consumers can complain to the authority if they consider any advertisement is not in keeping with these standards and their complaint will be investigated and action taken by the Advertising Standards Authority if necessary. Many newspapers which do not wish to break the law relating to advertising or the Code of Practice may publish an extract in a prominent place among adverts in the paper. In this way they attempt to cover themselves against criticism of unfair or misleading advertising practices.

Conclusion

Advertising influences *all* of us. You can probably recite several advertising slogans although you have made no effort to learn them. We see and hear so many advertisements that they stay in our mind. This is all the more reason why we should be aware of the methods by which advertising agents attempt to persuade us to purchase a particular brand. Shopping requires careful thought by the buyers so that they are not over-persuaded by sellers.

TOPIC 7.2   Activities

1. Read the passage and answer the questions:

'Legal, Decent, Honest, and Truthful'
In March 1976 a new and stricter code for advertising cigarettes was introduced — it is a voluntary code of practice and the following are extracts taken from the code.

> Advertisements should not seek to establish that to smoke is associated with a luxurious way of life. However, it is acceptable to indicate the appeal of a particular brand by presenting it in an appropriate fashion.
>   Care requires to be exercised in the use of outdoor settings so as to avoid any implications of health that would be inappropriate being conveyed.

(Source: *Which?*, June 1976)

(a) What is a voluntary code of practice?
(b) In what respect is the first paragraph of this new code confusing?
(c) Can you think of an example where a cigarette advertisement suggests a 'luxurious way of life'?
(d) Explain in your own words the second paragraph of the Code of Practice.
(e) All packets of cigarettes now have a health warning printed on them. Suggest ways in which this could be made more effective in persuading young people not to smoke.
(f) In the March 1981 Budget, Sir Geoffrey Howe increased the price of cigarettes by 14 pence for twenty. Give reasons why this may not necessarily lead to a marked decrease in the sales of cigarettes.

2. List five branded products you would expect to find advertised in each of the following magazines:
(a) *Woman's Own.*
(b) *Amateur Gardener.*

3. Name magazines in which you would advertise in order to reach the following groups:
(a) Teenage girls.
(b) Wealthy, fashion-conscious women.
(c) Men interested in decorating and home improvement.
(d) Anglers.
(e) Radio enthusiasts.

4. Write a *persuasive* advertisement for the house in which you live. Stress the favourable aspects, and cut out the unfavourable.

5. If everyone in Great Britain gave you 2½p, you would have over £1 million for any cause you support. You have three minutes of television time to persuade them to give you this sum. Write the script.

6. Open out the cardboard carton from a tube of toothpaste. Describe the advertising features shown in this carton.

Unit 8

Insurance

TOPIC 8.1   What is insurance?

The purpose of insurance

Imagine that you have a new bicycle. What would you do if it were stolen and not returned? It is unlikely that you would be able to afford a new one from your savings. If you had to save from your part-time earnings or pocket-money, it would take a long time before you could afford a new bicycle. Perhaps one of your parents would loan you the money. However, it would not be necessary to consider any of these ways of raising the money if your bicycle was *insured*. If you had paid a *premium* to an insurance company, then your premium would have gone into an *insurance fund* from which you could claim a sum sufficient to enable you to replace your bicycle. Look at Fig. 8.1. You will see that many people pay premiums into the fund, while only some draw money out in the form of insurance claims.

Money goes *in* as *premiums*.
Money comes *out* as *claims*.

Insurance is the sharing of risks

As we have seen, the premiums go into an insurance fund from which the insured may claim if the mishap against which he has insured occurs. However, not everyone who is insured will need to make a claim; the mishap against which they have insured may never occur. In such cases, their premiums go towards compensating those who have to make claims. In other words, the cost of compensation is shared by all of the policyholders. The first Elizabethans summed up this principle: 'The loss lighteth rather easily upon many, than heavily upon a few.'

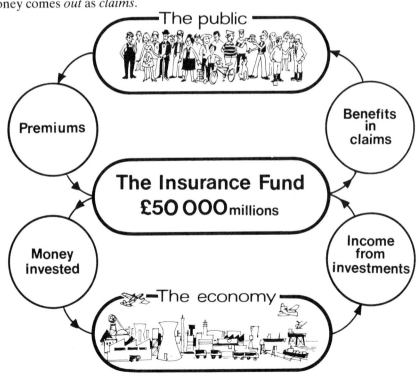

Fig 8.1   How insurance works

129

The principles of insurance

Certain basic principles have to be observed if the insurance system is to operate properly and fairly. These are:

1. *Insurable interest*: You may not insure something unless you would suffer financial loss if the risk against which you are insuring occurs. This usually means that you may only insure your own property or the life of a member of your immediate family. To allow people to insure someone else's property would be to encourage crime: for example, if you insured a farmer's haystack you might be tempted to burn it down if you were short of money.
2. *Utmost good faith*: When you take out insurance it is most unlikely that the insurance company will know you personally, so it relies entirely on the information you put on the forms relating to your insurance. These must therefore be completed observing the *utmost good faith*, that is, you must answer truthfully the questions on the forms, and also disclose any other relevant information.
3. *Indemnity*: The purpose of insurance is to replace the insured person in the same position financially after the loss or damage as he was in before it. This means that neither a loss nor a profit should be made as a result of being insured: for example, if you insured jewellery worth £20 000 and it was stolen and not recovered, the insurance company would pay you £20 000 — you would be indemnified.

There are two sub-principles dependent of indemnity. One is *contribution*, whereby, if an item is insured by more than one company, all the companies involved will contribute towards meeting a claim, in proportion to the terms of the original policies. In the above example, if the jewellery was stolen and was insured with two companies, each company would contribute £10 000, assuming that equal premiums had been paid to both companies. If the two companies each paid out £20 000, the owner of the jewellery would receive double its value and this would obviously be against the principle of indemnity. The other sub-principle is *subrogation*, whereby, when an insurance company meets a claim, it takes over any rights connected with that claim. For example, if a motorist 'wrote off' his car in an accident, the insurance company would pay him the market value of the car, but it would be entitled to claim the wreck, sell it for scrap and return the money thus raised to the pool. If the motorist were to retain the wreck and sell it for scrap himself, he would be receiving more than the true indemnity to which he was entitled.

How does insurance help the economy?

Vast sums of money are paid annually into insurance funds. The insurance companies do not allow this money to remain idle. They invest it in industry and commerce (see Fig. 8.1) to provide:

1. Buildings for factories, warehouses, and offices.
2. Work for people employed in industry and commerce.
3. Goods for use at home and abroad.

In return, the insurance companies receive interest on their investment which allows them to keep premiums relatively low and offer bonuses to their customers. British insurance companies also earn a great deal of money abroad. This money helps with our balance of payments problems.

TOPIC 8.1   Activities

1. Read the passage and answer the questions:

'Pipelines'
The construction of pipelines poses many problems, not only for the engineers who design them and for the contractors who construct them but also for the insurers who are concerned with the provision of insurance against risks of loss or damage of almost every kind, a cover invariably needed not only by the contractor undertaking what can be a very hazardous operation, but also by the principles for whom the work is undertaken.

The pipeline from the Ninian field in the North Sea to the Shetlands which was laid in 1974 cost £200m. It costs approximately as much to lay one kilometre of pipeline in the North Sea as to construct one kilometre of a four-lane motorway. Pipelines also run between offshore oil platforms such as the 24 mile long line which connects two rigs off Melbourne in Australia. This one cost $50m. Pipelines are laid in the Arctic — there is one that crosses Alaska — and in the desert to transport oil. It took 6 weeks to lay 18 miles of pipeline in the Gulf of Suez recently at a cost of £10m.

Insurances on such projects are often required not only while the pipeline is in construction, but also while it is in operation. There are the material-damage risks to the equipment and pipes inseparable from any major construction job, and in addition many and varied third-party risks. These risks vary according to the route followed, whether it passes through thickly populated areas and whether it has to be buried along main roads close to valuable property where foundations might be damaged. In some situations blasting operations may be necessary with their attendant risks. Off shore pipelines may be damaged by heavy weather or even by ships' anchors. The pipeline which runs from the Norwegian Ekofisk field to the shore was struck by an anchor and sustained over $5m worth of damage. Extreme weather conditions are hazardous in the Arctic areas. Nevertheless, wherever in the world the necessary insurance covers are required, British insurance can give them.

(Source: *The Many Faces of Insurance* — Chartered Insurance Institute)

(a) What sort of risks may be involved in the construction of pipelines?
(b) How do the risks vary according to the route of the pipeline?
(c) Give *three* examples of pipelines which are now covered by insurance.
(d) Why did insurance companies have to pay out on the Norwegian Ekofisk pipeline?
(e) How do British insurance companies join to cover the expensive risks involved in this industry?
(f) What risks may an individual worker wish to insure against when working in this construction industry?

2. List the things *which might be worth insuring* that are owned by:
(a) Yourself.
(b) Your family.
(c) Your school.
(d) Your town.

3. Use dictionaries or reference books to find out the meaning of these insurance terms:
(a) Assurance.
(b) Indemnity.
(c) Underwriter.
(d) Surrender value.

4. Much insurance is voluntary. What is meant by the following types of insurance, and why are they compulsory?
(a) Third party motor vehicle insurance.
(b) National Insurance.

5. Suggest some reasons why you cannot insure your neighbour's house. What principle of insurance is involved?

6. Imagine that you are employed by an insurance company as an actuary who works out insurance premiums. If you knew that usually about 1 in 60 bicycles is stolen in a year, and that the average value of a bicycle is £70, then which one of the following annual premiums would have to be charged so that the company does not make a loss?
(a) 50p
(b) £1
(c) £5
(d) £10

TOPIC 8.2 Taking out an insurance policy

Where to go

Your parents probably have several insurance policies. Where did they get them from? If you look at Fig. 8.2, you will see that there are two possible places. Can you spot the main difference between them?

The insurance company

This is probably the first place which comes to mind if you are thinking of taking out an insurance policy. Large insurance companies have offices in most towns and cities. They are able to offer a wide variety of policies covering most of the misfortunes you would want to insure against.

The insurance broker

An insurance broker acts for several insurance companies and offers customers a choice of policies from any of the companies he represents (see Fig. 8.3). He acts as a 'middleman' between the insurance company and the customer. For this service, he receives payment by way of commission from the insurance companies. The advantage you get as the customer is that you are able to *select* a policy which is best suited to cover the risks which you wish to insure against.

Fig 8.2   Effecting insurance

133

What do you have to do?

Obtain a prospectus	From broker or company
↓	
Fill out a proposal form	From broker or company
↓	
Check the cover note	Sent to you by the company
↓	
Pay the premium	Paid to the insurance company
↓	
Retain the policy	Sent to you by the company

These are the five main stages which must be undertaken before the risk you wish to insure against is covered.

Prospectus

The prospectus of an insurance company gives you details of the different types of policies available to cover the risks you may wish to insure against. You should study as many prospectuses as you can, and select the policy best suited to your requirements.

The proposal form

A proposal form must be filled in by everybody wishing to take out any kind of insurance (see Fig. 8.4). Very often the form is attached to the prospectus. On the form, you are required to answer questions about the type of insurance you wish to take out. The insurance company can then calculate the *risk* it is undertaking. For instance, if your house has a thatched roof, you would have to pay more because the fire risk is greater. It is up to you to answer all the questions on the form honestly. Any dishonesty could lead to the cancellation of the insurance.

Cover note

A cover note is issued to you while the insurance company is calculating how much you will have to pay. It means that the company accepts the risk while the premiums are being worked out and the policy drawn up. Cover notes are common in the case of motor insurance, because the person must be insured before he is allowed to take his car on to the road.

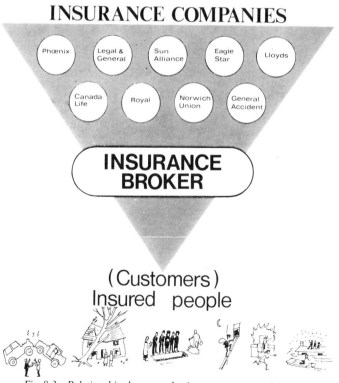

INSURANCE COMPANIES

Phœnix • Legal & General • Sun Alliance • Eagle Star • Lloyds • Canada Life • Royal • Norwich Union • General Accident

INSURANCE BROKER

(Customers)
Insured people

Fig 8.3 Relationship between the insurance companies, an insurance broker, and their customers

134

AGENT (Block letters) NAME: TOWN:	AGENCY REFERENCE	Inspector's Code	POLICY NO.

MOTOR CYCLE PROPOSAL
IMRORTANT—PLEASE ANSWER ALL QUESTIONS

THE INSURER: (tick appropriate box)　　**NORWICH UNION** ☐　　**SCOTTISH UNION** ☐
Fire Insurance Society Ltd.　　　　　and National Insurance Co.

BLOCK LETTERS

First Name(s).. Surname, Mr./Mrs./Miss..

Address ....

County.. Postal Code.................................... Age next birthday....................

Cover operates in respect of :—

(a) **ANY MOTOR CYCLE,** up to the cubic capacity limit selected, owned by the Insured or hired to him under a hire purchase agreement.

(b) **ANY OTHER MOTOR CYCLE** up to the cubic capacity limit selected which is being driven by the Insured with the owner's permission provided such driving is not covered under any other policy. (See "5 Use" overleaf).

Under (b) the cubic capacity limit only operates in respect of loss of or damage to the machine.

Tick appropriate box for cubic capacity limit selected.

Up to 100 c.c. ☐　　　Up to 350 c.c. ☐　　　Unlimited c.c. ☐　　　**NOTE. Driving is permitted by the Insured only.**

	Tick appropriate box
	YES　NO

1. Has any Insurer (a) declined a proposal from you or (b) cancelled or not invited renewal of your policy? If "Yes" give full details　☐ ☐

2. Do you suffer from defective vision or hearing or from any physical or mental infirmity or fits of any kind? If "Yes" give details　☐ ☐

3. Have you been convicted during the past 5 years of any offence in connection with any motor vehicle or is any prosecution or police enquiry pending? If "Yes" give full details—date, conviction, fine, period of disqualification, circumstances, etc.　☐ ☐

4. If you have been involved in an accident or loss in the past 3 years complete the following panel
IF NOT STATE "NONE" HERE.........................

Past 3 years	Total number of cars vehicles or cycles owned by you each year	Total number of accidents or losses in connection with cars, vehicles or cycles OWNED or DRIVEN by you	Damage to Proposer's cars, vehicles or cycles	Third Party	
			Amount	Amount	**OFFICE USE ONLY**
19　to 19					**PREMIUM**
19　to 19					Basic....................
19　to 19					Passenger Risk ....

Tick cover required Comprehensive ☐　　Third Party Fire & Theft ☐

Tick if Passenger Cover required ☐

Total ....

I hereby declare　(i)　the truth and correctness of the above statements and particulars,
　　　　　　　　(ii)　**that I hold a current licence to drive Motor Cycles,**
　　　　　　　　(iii)　that this proposal and declaration shall be held to be promissory and the basis of the contract between me and the Insurer,
　　　　　　　　(iv)　**that I am not a Motor Trader or Motor Dealer and that in the event of undertaking such occupations
　　　　　　　　　　I shall immediately advise the Insurer**

Proposer's Signature.. Date.. 19............

No liability (except for the period stated in the Insurer's Official Cover Note) is undertaken until the proposal is accepted by the Insurer and the premium paid.

The Insurer reserves the right to ask for special terms or to decline the proposal　　　　M19—139—11.70

Fig 8.4　An insurance proposal form (Reproduced by permission of the Norwich Union Insurance Group)

135

ANNUAL PREM.	**MOTOR CYCLE RIDER POLICY**	POLICY NUMBER
£		

REBATE/ ALLOWANCE

FIRST PREMIUM

N.B.—(1) No alteration in the terms of this Policy or of its conditions will be held valid unless signed or initialled by an Authorised Official of the Company.

(2) In this Policy the expression "Motor Cycle" means a mechanically propelled two wheeled vehicle with or without a sidecar attached. For this purpose a three wheeled vehicle having two wheels on one axle where the centres of the points of contact of such wheels and the road are less than 18 inches apart shall be deemed to be a two wheeled vehicle.

(3) This Policy should be examined and returned immediately if any error be found therein.

In consideration of the premium having been paid by the Insured the Company will indemnify the Insured in accordance with the policy cover indicated in the schedule of this Policy in respect of accident injury loss or damage occurring in Great Britain Northern Ireland the Republic of Ireland the Isle of Man or the Channel Islands or in the course of transit by sea between any ports therein during the period of insurance specified in the Schedule or any subsequent period for which the Company may accept payment for renewal of this Policy. The proposal and declaration made by the Insured is the basis of the contract and deemed incorporated herein.

SECTION 1—LOSS OR DAMAGE

The Company will indemnify the Insured against loss of or damage to any motor cycle described in the Schedule and its accessories and spare parts while thereon.

The Company may at its own option repair reinstate or replace such motor cycle or any part thereof or its accessories or spare parts or may pay in cash the amount of the loss or damage. If to the knowledge of the Company the motor cycle is the subject of a hire purchase agreement such payment shall be made to the owner described therein whose receipt shall be a full and final discharge to the Company in respect of such loss or damage. The maximum amount payable by the Company in respect of any claim for loss or damage shall be the market value of such motor cycle immediately prior to such loss or damage.

If such motor cycle is disabled by reason of loss or damage insured under this Policy the Company will bear the reasonable cost of protection and removal to the nearest repairers. The Company will also pay the reasonable cost of delivery to the Insured after repair of such loss or damage not exceeding the reasonable cost of transport to the address of the Insured in Great Britain Ireland and Northern Ireland the Isle of Man or the Channel Islands stated herein.

EXCEPTIONS TO SECTION 1

The Company shall not be liable to pay for

(a) loss of use depreciation wear and tear mechanical or electrical breakdowns failures or breakages or damage by frost

(b) damage to tyres by application of brakes or by road punctures cuts or bursts

(c) loss of or damage to accessories and spare parts by theft if the motor cycle is not stolen at the same time

(d) The first £10 of any amount otherwise payable in respect of each and every occurrence of loss or damage to any motor cycle described in the Schedule. If at the time of the occurrence of loss or damage other than by Fire Self Ignition Lightning or Explosion or by Theft or attempt thereat the Insured:—

  (i) does not hold a full United Kingdom licence to drive the motor cycle the sum specified shall be increased to £15

  (ii) is under 25 years of age the sum specified shall be increased to £20

  (iii) does not hold a full United Kingdom licence to drive the motor cycle and is under 25 years of age the sum specified shall be increased to £25

Notwithstanding anything contained in this Exception if the motor cycle has an engine capacity not exceeding 50 cubic centimetres and is fitted with pedals as a means of propulsion the Insured shall not be liable for a greater amount in all than £5

(e) loss or damage directly occasioned by pressure waves caused by aircraft or other aerial devices travelling at sonic or supersonic speed.

IF YOU HAVE AN ACCIDENT:—

We have a nationwide staff of experienced engineers who will arrange for repairs to be carried out competently and efficiently where the damage is covered by your policy and you wish to claim for it

We would like you to have the benefit of this service. To do so please contact as quickly as possible the motor claims department of the nearest Norwich Union Group branch.

FOR PROCEDURE IN CASE OF ACCIDENT—SEE CONDITIONS 1 AND 2

M123-15-5.71

IN ALL COMMUNICATIONS WITH THE COMPANY PLEASE QUOTE THE POLICY NUMBER.

Fig 8.5   An insurance policy (Reproduced by permission of the Norwich Union Insurance Group)

The premium

This is the sum of money you pay for your insurance. The premium is related to the *risk*; the bigger the risk, the bigger the premium. On payment of the first premium, you usually have full insurance cover.

The policy

This is often a long document setting out the risks the insurance company is covering (see Fig. 8.5). It is as well to read all the *small print* so that you will know the exact extent of your insurance cover.

Conclusion

At first sight, obtaining an insurance policy may seem complicated, but in most cases it is fairly simple in practice. You may only be required to fill in the proposal form and the insurance company or broker will do the rest for you.

TOPIC 8.2   Activities

1. Read the passage and answer the questions:

'The Shock of his Life'

'I just didn't know what hit me', said 43-year-old Alun Armstrong, whose work-mates now call him 'The luckiest man alive'. Alun, a construction worker, drove a pneumatic drill through a 27 000 volt power cable — and WALKED AWAY UNHURT!

'We were digging foundations for a new office block in the City. Of course the Corporation have maps of all the wires and pipes and tunnels under the ground, and we always use them. But this time the map must have been wrong. I'd been told to dig out a three-foot trench in a corner of the site, and I was really pushing on the drill. Then WHAM! There was this huge blue flash, and I picked myself up ten feet away.'

Unscheduled stop

In fact Alun came out of it better than travellers on the nearby Tube line. The cable carried current from a London Transport power station. Trains stopped dead in the tunnels and seven stations were plunged into darkness. Emergency power had to be switched in from another zone to get things moving again. The construction company Alun works for was presented with a hefty bill, itemising not only the replacement of the ruptured cable but also the loss of power and traffic sustained.

Of course the company was insured against this type of accident. It isn't merely bulldozers and cranes that have to be covered, but the workmen and members of the public who might be injured or suffer loss through the company's actions. If Alun had been injured, or killed, it would have been the company's responsibility. It's an increasingly important area of insurance as technology advances and the law relating to damages becomes more complex. The possibility of claims for liability must be considered when the contract is drawn up and the premium decided.

(Source: *Inside Insurance* Convention Edition. The Chartered Insurance Institute)

(a) In what respect was Alun's accident an unforeseen disaster?
(b) Why was the construction company presented with a hefty bill as a result of the accident?
(c) How does the insurance company 'cover' its workmen and the general public?
(d) Why would it have been the company's responsibility if Alun had been injured or killed in the above accident?
(e) Explain the last sentence in your own words.

2. Write down the names of three large insurance companies and three insurance brokers in your nearest town.

3. A friend says: 'All insurance is a waste of money'. Write a letter to him and explain why you think insurance is useful.

4. Write down in your notebook 10 questions which you think should appear on a proposal form for insuring a motor scooter.

5. Obtain a proposal form from a local broker or insurance company. Stick it in your notebook and underneath explain why the insurance company asks the questions on this form.

6. All questions on a proposal form must be answered in 'the utmost good faith', i.e., honestly, or the policy will not be valid. Explain why you think this should be so.

7. Explain why it is more expensive to insure your life if you are in a dangerous occupation. Write down examples of five such occupations.

TOPIC 8.3 What should you insure against?

Responsibilities

Mr Worker is a married man with two children. He is concerned about his house, his furniture, his car, and his family. He will want several types of insurance. In particular, Mr Worker wants his family to be provided for in the event of any misfortune happening to him (see Fig. 8.6).

Motor

Motor insurance differs from every other type of insurance because it is compulsory. Before taking any motor vehicle on to the road, a driver is required by law to have insurance cover. There are three types of motor insurance.

Fig 8.6 What should I insure against?

Third party

This is the legal minimum motor insurance and it is the cheapest. It does not cover the driver or the vehicle he is driving. It covers other people and their property, e.g., other vehicles, in the event of the driver having an accident. It would be wrong for anybody to suffer financially as a result of somebody else driving carelessly. This is why all drivers are required to have third party insurance.

Third party, fire, and theft

This policy provides slightly more cover than the third party only policy. It covers the motorist against the risks of his vehicle catching fire, being stolen, or having anything stolen from it.

Fully comprehensive

This is the most expensive type of motor insurance and covers the driver and the driver's car, as well as any 'third party' who may be hurt in an accident. As far more risks are covered, the premium is higher.

If a driver does not have to claim on his insurance company in one year, he may be offered a 10 per cent reduction in his premium for the next year. This is known as a *no claims bonus*. After the second year free from claims, the premium may be reduced by 20 per cent. This continues usually up to a maximum of 60 per cent. It is worth while, therefore, to be a careful driver.

Possessions

You may have insured your bicycle while still at school. As you grow older, there are likely to be more risks that you will want to cover by insurance. If you are renting a house, for example, you will want to insure your furniture against fire and theft. Most insurance companies offer a *household insurance* which covers the insured's house and the items in the house against fire, theft, flooding, etc.

In addition to a house it is possible to insure at a price (premium) almost all a person's possessions against a variety of risks, e.g.,

1. A TV against breaking down.
2. A valuable item of jewellery against loss or theft.
3. A pedigree cat against being run over.

However, claims for the above may be relatively small when considered in comparison with the amount of money insurance companies pay out for losses as a result of fire each year.

Life assurance

Insuring people's lives in known as *assurance,* because death is an assured fact — we all have to die sooner or later. A married man will probably want to insure his own life. He wants his family to be provided for after his death. The premium for life assurance varies according to your age and state of health. Most insurance companies demand a medical examination before a person is granted life assurance. The insurance company always has to pay out on life assurance policies, in the end.

Endowment

You can insure your life *and* have the benefit of a lump sum of money if you do not die within a certain number of years. This is known as an endowment insurance and it allows a person to insure his life for a certain sum of money over a fixed number of years. For example, to insure your life for 15 years for £5000 might cost you a monthly premium of about £15. If you died within that 15 years, the company would pay out, but if you survived for 15 years you would receive the sum plus bonuses earned by your premiums being invested. An endowment insurance provides a profitable investment as well as life assurance cover.

Conclusion

It is worth while for you to have some type of insurance especially as you take on extra responsibilities and have to provide for your family. All insurance is a bit of a gamble. However, it is better to be safe than sorry. Few people could afford to replace their house and furniture lost as a result of fire. Insurance helps to provide in the case of misfortunes.

TOPIC 8.3 Activities

1. Read the passage and answer the questions:

Life Assurance

The most popular form of long-term saving in Britain is endowment assurance. This is hardly surprising since endowment assurances afford much the surest way of saving profitably for long-term purposes. The risks of loss — short of national economic disaster — are negligible while the prospect of gain is as nearly certain as human ingenuity can make it.

This is because the 'funding' system which makes life assurance practicable is scientifically designed to minimize risk. Life offices (the life assurance companies or societies) guarantee to pay pre-agreed money claims far away into the future. In order to be sure that they can meet these obligations, their funds have to be managed with great skill, care, and judgement.

Some people think of life assurance as a scheme which only pays out when you die. But this is only true for a 'whole life' or 'term' policy (an effective way of providing for your wife and family). It is not true of an 'endowment' policy.

(Source: *Saving and Spending* The Life Offices Association)

(a) Explain how a person insuring his life can also be saving money for the future.
(b) Why are the 'risks of loss negligible' while the prospect of gain is as 'nearly certain as human ingenuity can make it'?
(c) How are insurance company funds managed (or used) to guarantee a pre-agreed money claim far away into the future?
(d) What is the difference between a 'whole life' or 'term' policy compared with an 'endowment policy'?
(e) Explain the difference between 'assurance' and 'insurance'.

2. Write down a list of the furniture and possessions in one room of your house. Try to add up their total value for insurance purposes.

3. A man pays £90 for his first year's fully comprehensive insurance premium.
(a) How much will he have had to pay after three years, if he gets a 'no claims bonus' of 40 per cent?
(b) How much will he pay with a maximum 60 per cent no claims bonus?

4. Mr X carelessly drives his car into his neighbour's brick wall.
(a) Who pays for the damage to the wall?
(b) Who pays for the damage to Mr X's car if he has only third party insurance?
(c) Who pays for the damage to the car if he has a fully comprehensive insurance?

5.

Name	Age	Occupation	Health
B. Quick	21	Racing driver	good
A. Pen	45	Clerk	fair
O. L. D. Man	70	Pensioner	poor

Look at the table.
(a) Who do you think is likely to die first?
(b) Who is least likely to die?
(c) Who is the greatest risk to the insurance company?
Give reasons.

6. Make a list of five occupations which you would consider to be high risks to any life assurance company.

TOPIC 8.4 Making a claim

The protection of insurance

What would you do if your house was destroyed like the one in Fig. 8.7? You could probably find a temporary home, but in the end you would have to find another house and buy new furniture and other things. One of the main principles of insurance is that the insured person should not lose financially as a result of bad luck. The insurance company will pay the *value* of the things which have been lost, but remember that a suite of furniture which is 10 years old is not worth so much as when it was new. You could not claim the full price you paid for it. You must not expect to make a profit from the insurance as the result of your bad luck.

Fig 8.7   Buildings ought to be insured against fire

Examples of insurance claims

Read the following stories:

1. Mr Ladder, a window cleaner, carelessly misses a rung on his ladder, falls, and breaks his ankle. He is away from work for eight weeks and unable to earn any money.
2. Because he had not left on the handbrake, Mr Austin's car runs down his drive, and crashes through a neighbour's brick wall.
3. Mrs Hot burns her husband's trousers while pressing them. Although not ruined, the trousers will have to be invisibly repaired at the local cleaners.

All the above examples could result in a sum of money being claimed from an insurance company. In the first case, Mr Ladder had *personal accident insurance* which will provide him with either a sum of money or a weekly payment to cover his loss of earnings. Mr Austin's neighbour is likely to want some money for the repair of his wall. As Mr Austin does not wish to pay the money out of his own pocket, he will have to go to his insurance company to claim the cost of repairing the wall on his *third party policy*. Mrs Hot will make a claim on her *fire insurance* policy to cover the cost of repairing her husband's trousers.

Paying out the money

The insurance company accepts a risk and may be liable to pay out a sum of money (according to the wording of the policy) at any time after the first premium has been paid. The company would probably require some proof that the window cleaner was unable to work for eight weeks. Mr Ladder would have to show the insurance company a doctor's certificate stating that he is unable to work.

With complicated claims, some of them involving thousands of pounds, an insurance company employs assessors to decide how much actual damage has been done and how much should be paid out. In a similar way the company may employ its own investigators who might look into the cause of a fire, particularly if someone is suspected of starting it deliberately in the hope that he would make a profit by getting a lump sum of money from the insurance company.

Claims on insurance are made by the minority of people insured. Otherwise the insurance company would go broke. Such claims can vary from £3 for the repair of burned trousers to as much as £25 million in respect of the giant chemical plant at Flixborough which was wrecked by an explosion in 1974.

Conclusion

Some people seem to think 'it could never happen to me'. Although the chances of a misfortune may be slim, it is as well to know that you will not lose financially as a result. You might think that a very rich man could afford to manage without insurance, but in fact the richer you are the more insurance cover you are likely to need.

TOPIC 8.4   Activities

1. Study the diagram of a motor accident (Fig. 8.8) and answer the following questions:
(a) What is the difference between a fully comprehensive and a third party, fire and theft motor insurance policy?
(b) Write an eye witness account of the accident as if you were in a car involved in the accident.
(c) Has one of the drivers broken the Highway Code?
(d) Who will pay for the damage (£1,250) for Car B? Why?
(e) Who will pay for the damage (£75) for Car C? Why?
(f) Which drivers are likely to lose their 'no claims bonus'?

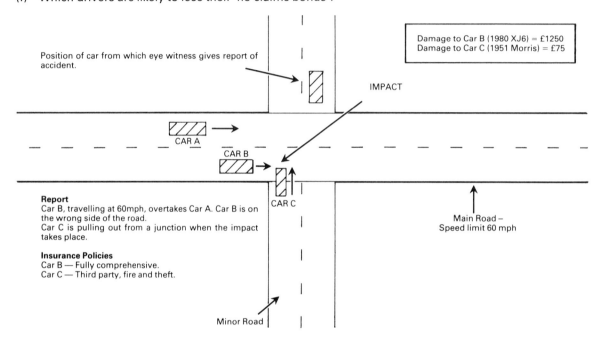

Fig 8.8   Plan of accident

2. Imagine you are the owner of a small confectionery shop. Make a list of the things you want to cover by insurance.

3. Mrs Morris, driving along the high street at 30 m.p.h., hits another car as it comes out of a side road.
(a) Draw a diagram to show the accident and the positions of two people who witnessed it.
(b) Write Mrs Morris's description of how the accident happened.
(c) Whose insurance company would have to pay for the damage to both vehicles and why?

4. What type of person do you think would be able to claim money on the following types of insurance policies?
(a) Mortgage protection policy.
(b) Life assurance policy.
(c) Personal accident policy.
(d) Employer's liability policy.
(e) An endowment policy.

5. For what reasons might the owner of a car *not* wish to claim on his motor insurance policy?

6. Study the table

Type of cycle	Type of claim	Age of insured	Full UK Licence Holder	Others
Mopeds not exceeding 50cc	All accidental damage claims including fire and theft	All ages	£5	£5
Other motor cycles	Fire and theft claims only	All ages	£10	£10
	Other accidental damage claim	25 and over	£10	£15
		under 25	£20	£25

(a) Give reasons why an insurance company might make a driver bear the first portion of any claim according to the amount printed in the last two columns of the table above.

(b) Explain why the amounts vary in the way they do.

Unit 9

Social services

TOPIC 9.1   The welfare state

Looking after people

You will see from Fig. 9.1 that there are still many needy people about. Old people have to live on a small pension, the sick must be cared for, while some people do not have a decent house to live in. Nowadays the State takes much more responsibility for the needy than it used to. Both the central government and local authorities run services to improve our welfare. Great Britain today is often called a *welfare state,* i.e., a country which provides social services for the benefit of all its citizens instead of leaving them to fend for themselves.

The welfare state, as shown in Fig. 9.2, looks after us from the cradle to the grave. For example, before you were born your mother was able to receive special care and was given a maternity grant, and when you die your next of kin will get a death grant to cover funeral expenses.

All workers are compelled to pay National Insurance contributions; the money collected from such contributions is used to pay certain social security benefits. Some benefits available depend on the number of National Insurance contributions a person has made, others are available without any contribution conditions (see Fig. 9.3).

Fig 9.1   People's needs

Fig 9.2   From the cradle to the grave

Contributory social security benefits

1. *Retirement pensions* are for men over 65 and women over 60 who have retired from work.
2. *Unemployment benefit* is paid to people who normally work for an employer but who are at present out of work. A person must be fit and available for work to qualify.
3. *Sickness benefit* is paid to people who are normally employed or self-employed but who cannot work because of illness.
4. *Maternity benefits* include a lump sum maternity grant and maternity allowance for 18 weeks.
5. *Death grant* is paid on the death of the contributor.
6. *Widows' benefits* include an allowance payable for the first 26 weeks of widowhood followed by a widowed mother's allowance or widow's pensions.

Non-contributory social security benefits

1. *Child benefit* is a weekly tax-free cash benefit paid for all children under 16 years of age, and also children up to 18 years old in full-time education.
2. *Guardian's allowance* is payable to a person who takes an orphan child into his or her family.
3. *War pensions* include payments for disablement, war widows, and war orphans.
4. *Injury benefits*: Each year there are about 1 million claims for injury benefit and 130 000 claims for disablement benefits.
5. *Family income supplement* helps families with low incomes. It is paid when the head of the household is in full-time employment, but the family income falls below a prescribed amount. The FIS is half the difference between the family income and the prescribed amount.

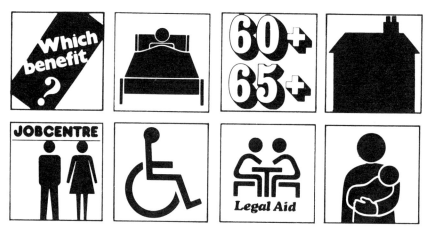

Fig 9.3 Which benefit? (Source: FB2 Which Benefit? Reproduced with the permission of the Controller of HMSO. © Crown copyright)

Table 9.1 Welfare services organized by central government

Government department	Service
Ministry of Social Security	Sickness benefits
Ministry of Health	Hospitals
Department of Employment	Employment exchanges
Department of Education and Science	Schools and colleges
Home Office	Probation and prisons
Department of the Environment	Housing
Ministry of Transport	Roads

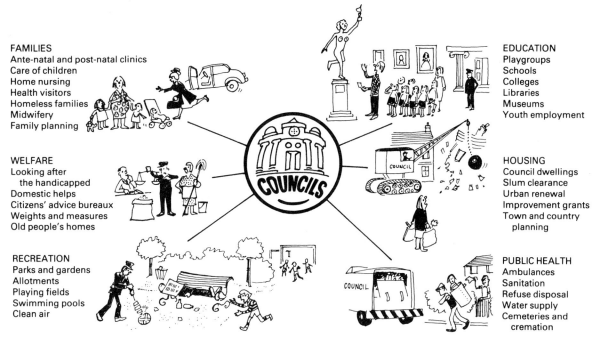

FAMILIES
Ante-natal and post-natal clinics
Care of children
Home nursing
Health visitors
Homeless families
Midwifery
Family planning

WELFARE
Looking after
    the handicapped
Domestic helps
Citizens' advice bureaux
Weights and measures
Old people's homes

RECREATION
Parks and gardens
Allotments
Playing fields
Swimming pools
Clean air

EDUCATION
Playgroups
Schools
Colleges
Libraries
Museums
Youth employment

HOUSING
Council dwellings
Slum clearance
Urban renewal
Improvement grants
Town and country
    planning

PUBLIC HEALTH
Ambulances
Sanitation
Refuse disposal
Water supply
Cemeteries and
    cremation

Fig 9.4   Social services provided by local authorities

Table 9.2   Where to go for help and advice

Your problem	Where to go	To find the address look in a telephone book under
Social security	Social security office	Health and Social Security, Department of
Unemployment	1. Employment office or Job centre 2. Unemployment benefit office 3. Careers office (for young people)	Employment Service Agency, *and* Job centres Careers Service, *or* name of your local council
Education	Local authority education department	Name of your local council
Social services	Social services department of your local council (social work department in Scotland)	Name of your county, district or London borough council (regional council in Scotland)
Welfare rights	Welfare rights officer (usually in the social services department)	
Rent and rates	Housing department of your local council	
Tax	1. Tax office 2. PAYE enquiry office	Inland Revenue
Anything, including those listed above	Citizens' Advice Bureau	Citizens' Advice Bureau

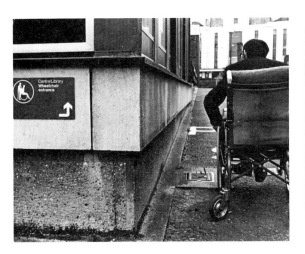

Fig 9.5   The disabled are looked after in many specialized ways (Reproduced by permission of Norwich Corporation)

Fig 9.6   An old people's home (Reproduced by permission of
Norwich Social Services Committee)

Who is responsible for the welfare state?

Central government

The Government has the main job of providing welfare services. The Secretary of State for Health and Social Security has responsibility for all welfare services although different government departments look after certain aspects (see Table 9.1).

The National Insurance scheme is a social service which is run by the Department of Health and Social Security on behalf of the central government.

Local government

Although local authorities may seek the help of government ministries, they carry out much of their work with a great deal of independence. For instance, in 1981 some local authorities refused to sell council houses. Although central government must be obeyed in the end, a local authority has a lot of power to decide what services it will provide for people living in the area (see Fig. 9.4 and Table 9.2).

Voluntary help

Governments do a great deal, but they do not give enough help to everyone. Many people would be in a bad way without charities and voluntary workers. The National Society for the Prevention of Cruelty to Children cares for less fortunate youngsters. An organization such as Shelter helps homeless people or those living in very poor conditions. It attempts to put pressure on the Government to improve housing conditions. Charitable organizations fill the gaps left by the welfare state.

Conclusion

There are many services and benefits available to all of us should we ever need them. You may think that you will never be desperate enough to have to worry about where your next meal is coming from. But you never know. A caring community tries to provide a minimum standard of living for all its citizens (see Figs. 9.5 and 9.6).

TOPIC 9.1   Activities

1. Read the following extract and answer the questions:

Pay levels affect jobseekers' chances
The chances of young people finding work are affected by the level of pay they receive compared to adults. This link between pay and jobs, which relates to young people under 18 during the period from the end of the sixties, is the main finding in a research paper, *The Relative Pay and Employment of Young People,* published by the Department of Employment.

The report shows that increases in the earnings of young people seem to have reduced their job prospects, at the same time their levels of employment were also suffering disproportionately from losses in total employment.

The study, which looked at earnings up to 1982, also found the level of relative average earnings of young people has not risen since the mid-1970s and in recent years has fallen slightly.

The level of the mid-1970s was an historical peak following a substantial upward shift which coincided with the raising of the school-leaving age. Before this the relative earnings of young men rose in the post-war period but those of young women remained roughly constant.

(Source: *Employment News,* January 1984)

(a)   Explain the link between pay and jobs referred to in the extract.
(b)   Explain the meaning of the second paragraph in your own words.
(c)   What has been the trend regarding young people's earnings since the mid-1970s?
(d)   How did the raising of the school leaving age affect the availability of jobs for young people?
(e)   Would you accept a low wage simply to get a permanent job? Give your reasons.

2. Write in your notebook the addresses of the following places nearest to your home:
(a)   Office of the Department of Social Security.
(b)   Hospital.
(c)   Job centre.
(d)   Probation office.
(e)   Technical college.

3. Draw a diagram showing how a decision taken by your local planning committee has changed living conditions in your area.

4. Make a list of the charities which raise money in your area. Describe how they try to persuade people to give money to their causes.

5. Design a poster to attract the public's attention to the plight of homeless people.

TOPIC 9.2　Education

Fig 9.7　Schools yesterday (Reproduced by permission of Norwich Public Libraries)

The two schools in Figs. 9.7 and 9.8 help to remind us of the progress made in education. The State did not provide any schools until 1870, when it was decided that every child should receive some education. Before that, most of the youngsters who had any education had to have parents rich enough to pay for their schooling. Nowadays all young people can be educated without payment.

The organization of education in England and Wales

The Secretary of State for Education and Science is responsible for all aspects of education in England (see Table 9.3). However, local education authorities are responsible for the provision of schools and most post-school education except universities. In this way the Secretary of State decides matters of general policy to be carried out by the local education authorities. Her Majesty's Inspectors for Schools may visit individual schools and report back on the content and value of the education pupils receive in them. In all schools courses should help the individual to take his/her place in modern Britain as a member of the adult population.

In England and Wales no fees are charged to parents of children attending maintained schools and books and equipment are free. About 10 million children attend Britain's 38 000 schools financed mainly by tax and ratepayers. Only a small proportion of children, about 4 per cent, attend schools where their parents choose to pay directly for their education.

Table 9.3

Secretary of State for Education and Science

Department of Education and Science

Local Education Authorities

Directors of Education

· School Governors

Headmistresses/
Headmasters

Parents' –
Teachers'
Meetings

Teachers

Pupils

Fig 9.8 Schools today (Reproduced by permission of the Principal, North Warwickshire College of Technology and Art. Photograph by Graham Bird)

The stages of education

It has been said that children cannot wait to begin school at 5 and cannot wait to leave when they are 16. However, it is possible to go to school before the age of 5 and continue full-time education up to the age of 21 or over. As pupils or students become older, their education becomes more specialized. A large city may provide the following types of education:

1. *Primary* (ages 2 to 11):
   (a) Nursery 2 to 5 years.
   (b) Infant 5 to 7 years.
   (c) Middle 7 to 11/12 years.
2. *Secondary* (ages 11/12 to 16+):
   (a) Modern, Grammar, Technical.
   Or
   (b) Comprehensive.
3. *Further* (ages 16 onwards):
   (a) Technical colleges.
   (b) Art schools.
4. *Higher* (ages 18 onwards):
   (a) Colleges of education.
   (b) Universities, polytechnics, etc.
   (c) Open University.

As you saw in Topic 2.4, the Government spends a great deal of money on education. As well as catering for those who wish to carry on their education beyond the age of 16, it has to look after those who cannot cope with life in an ordinary school. Some children who are physically handicapped are able to reach a high educational standard in special schools geared to their needs. In 1974 there were about 12 000 handicapped children who needed to attend such schools.

Education after school

Education continues right through a person's life. You are never too old to learn. In many jobs workers attend part-time day-release or evening classes. These classes usually take place in technical colleges. There are also colleges of education for training teachers and polytechnics or universities for degree courses. In 1971, the Open University was started and people of all ages and from all walks of life enrolled to improve their educational standards. It is likely that when you leave school, you will take a part-time course for the sake of your chosen career.

Conclusion

Education is important because the country needs skilled workers to produce goods and thus raise our living standards. We also need conscientious citizens to stand for Parliament or for the local council. Everyone must be encouraged to develop his or her skills to the utmost.

TOPIC 9.2   Activities

1. Read the following passage and answer the questions:

Videos are top of the form
Videodiscs have such enormous potential for schools that the government should consider funding them on the lines of its microcomputer scheme, according to the interim report of an experiment covering four London primary schools.

The discs — carrying 'interactive video programmes' — can 'bring distant, complex, dramatic, real-life happenings into the classroom in a way quite impossible through any other medium', say the report from Colin Mably of the school of education at North-East London Polytechnic.

Mably has been monitoring a three-month trial involving programmes on whales, electricity and air which have been developed by Thorn EMI. Previously, 'interactive videos' have been used only in industrial training.

The discs comprise 25 sections which can be watched continuously like a normal schools' broadcast programme. Each is followed by a 20 minute reference section of additional information, divided into short sub sections. Children can dip into either section just as they would with reference books, stopping at any point. A control panel gives them immediate access to any part of the disc, which is divided into 100 chapters, 3600 time check points, and 45 000 'pages'.

The video can be frozen, played at half normal speed or run backwards. Two alternative stereo sound-tracks are available: these can be varied according to the age, ability or even mother tongue of the child.

'The great thing about a book', says Mably 'is that you can flick through it, go to a particular page, use it as a tool. The interactive video can do precisely that, in sound and vision, and the quality is much higher. In one of the schools, the library has just two arid books on whales; the disc provided lots of hard information, vividly. The child could watch a whale spouting in the middle of the ocean.'

(Source: *Sunday Times* Business News, 27 May 1984)

(a) What advantages do videodiscs have over video cassettes?
(b) Where have interactive videos previously been used?
(c) What similar features do videodiscs and books have?
(d) What educational value do you think the use of videodiscs might have for pupils, apart from their actual content?
(e) Make a list of the topics you think would be particularly useful on videodiscs, for the use of 14–18-year-olds?

2. Make a list of some of the decisions which you think ought to be taken in the near future by the education committee in your area.

3. Draw a sketch map of your local area. Mark on it all the different types of schools and colleges.

4. What special consideration would you take into account if you were designing a school for the physically handicapped?

5. Make a list of the types of job in your area which would require you to attend further education courses after you leave school.

6. Describe how you think your school life would be different if you attended a public school as a boarder.

TOPIC 9.3 The National Health Service

Free for you

You have most likely made use of a doctor's services. You should have visited the dentist within the last six months (Fig. 9.9 shows a hygienist at work). Everybody in Great Britain under the age of 18 is entitled to *free* medical care under the National Health Service. However, as you saw in Unit 2, people pay indirectly towards the NHS when they pay taxes and buy National Insurance stamps. The 'free' health service is one of the most important aspects of the welfare state. Since its introduction the National Health Service has been the 'backbone' of the welfare state and most people are pleased to be able to visit their local doctor 'free' of charge. However, there is much more to the National Health Service than your local doctor and, in all, in 1982-83 the cost of the service was about £14 500 million. Health services may be divided into three main groups (see Table 9.4):

1. *Hospitals*: These are administered through regional hospital boards and hospital management committees.
2. *Doctors, dentists, and pharmacists*: These are organized by family practitioner committees.
3. *Local authority and welfare services*: These are administered by local authorities.

Your local doctor

You can choose the doctor you want to go to, although most people go to their nearest doctor. Doctors as well can choose the patients they want to have on their books, although they are unlikely to refuse you unless they have too many patients already. Before you can be accepted you must obtain a medical card issued by the Family Practitioner Committee (see Fig. 9.10). (You can find the address in a telephone directory under the National Health Service.)

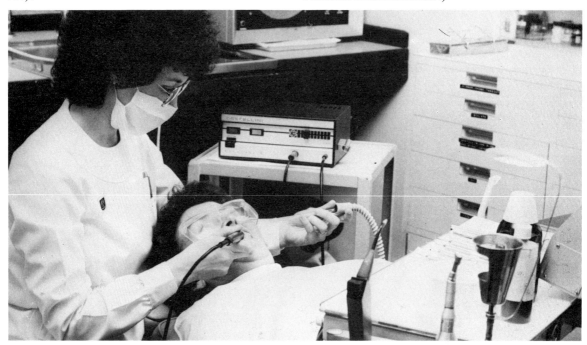

Fig 9.9   A dental hygienist at work

There are over 23 000 family doctors or general practitioners as they are known, in Great Britain. They each see an average of about 2300 patients and are paid a fixed amount for each of the patients 'on their books'. Between them these doctors see each member of the population about four times per year on average and prescribe about 300 million prescriptions. There are fewer family doctors working on their own today.

Many doctors like to be part of a group practice so that they can share surgeries and night calls. Dentists also often work with partners.

Hospitals

Britain has about 3000 hospitals. If you have to go to hospital it is likely that you will be sent by your doctor. On your first visit to hospital (unless you are an emergency case), you will probably see a specialist depending upon what is wrong with you. Specialized services include:

1. Artificial limbs.
2. Drug dependence treatment.
3. Physiotherapy.
4. Psychiatric treatment.
5. Radiography.

Local authority welfare services

Your local council does much for the welfare of all its citizens; these services are described in detail in Topic 9.4.

Conclusion

During your school life, you will have seen the National Health Service in action. How often have you had a medical examination or a dental check-up at school? The object of such examinations and check-ups is to *prevent* illness. The National Health Service has helped to bring down the death rate. Nearly all children born today have a good chance of living to draw their retirement pension. If you are a male, you can expect to live until you are 69; if you are a female until 75. Yours is the healthiest generation that this country has ever known.

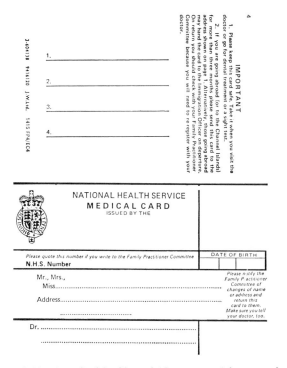

Fig 9.10 A medical health card (Crown copyright reserved. Reproduced by permission of the Controller of HMSO)

Table 9.4 The National Health Service

General medical services	Hospital and specialist services	Local authority services
Your local doctor	Consultations	Mother and baby clinics
Your local dentist	Operations	Help for those ill at home
Your local chemist	Convalescence	Disease prevention
Your local optician	Specialists	Care of the physically handicapped
	Therapy	Care of the mentally handicapped
		Care of the elderly

TOPIC 9.3   Activities

1. Read the passage and answer the questions:

Free NHS Glasses
Who qualified? People on supplementary benefit or FIS have an automatic right to free glasses. So also
do:
* people already getting free milk or prescriptions *because of low income.*
* Children under 16.
* Young people over 16 still at school full-time.
Even if you do not have an automatic right you could get help if you do not have much money coming in;
for example, if you are a pensioner, unemployed, or in a low-paid job.
Type of benefit: Means-tested except for children.
How much? Covers standard NHS lenses, some NHS frames, and repairs and replacement to these. If
you have an automatic right, they are free. If you have a low income, the amount of help depends on how
much money you have coming in, and the charge for the glasses.
How to claim: If you have an automatic right, tell your optician. If you have a low income, ask him for form
F.1. *BUT make sure you are getting NHS glasses; you cannot get help with the cost of private ones.* If you
want to know more get leaflet NHS 6 from an optician (or, if you have a low income, M.11 from a post
office or social security office), or either from the DHSS Leaflets Unit (see page 32).
> (Source: *Which Benefit?* Leaflet issued by Dept. Health and Social Security, November 1979)

(a) Why do people on supplementary benefit or FIS have an automatic right to free glasses?
(b) Which group in the dependent population also qualifies for free glasses?
(c) What is a 'means-tested' benefit?
(d) What type of glasses do you get free?
(e) How could an individual make an initial claim for free glasses?

2. Write in your notebook:
(a) The name(s) and address of your local doctor(s).
(b) The hours of the surgery.
(c) How many doctors are in the practice.
(d) The number on your medical card.
(e) The address of your Family Practitioner Committee.

3. Plot a bar diagram to show the following:
(a) How many of your class have had to stay in hospital at any time.
(b) How many have had an operation.
(c) How many have seen a specialist.
(d) How many have a full set of teeth.
(e) The numbers of visits made to doctors, by all the members, in the past 12 months.

4. Describe the type of help which is offered by the following:
(a) Alcoholics Anonymous.
(b) The Samaritans.
(c) Narcotics Anonymous.

5. Make a list of children's diseases and the ages at which children should be vaccinated or inoculated against
them.

6. Give three reasons why you think men can expect to live until 69 while women live until 75 on the average.

158

TOPIC 9.4 Local authorities and voluntary workers

Services in your local area

If you study Fig. 9.11 closely, you will see that we all benefit in some way from the services provided by local authorities. We expect the roads to be maintained, and we should find life difficult if our dustbins were not emptied. Local authorities make money available, provide suitable premises, and employ men and women to keep these services going. All the services shown in Fig. 9.11 play an important part in promoting the welfare of the local community.

	District Council	County Council
Large-scale planning		
Roads and traffic		
Fire service		
Education		
Youth employment		
Old people's homes		
Libraries		
Housing		
Rates		
Rents		
Rent rebates and allowances		
Improvement grants		
Public health		
Refuse collection		
Planning applications		
Parks, playing fields, open spaces		
Museums and art galleries		

Fig 9.11 Services provided by local authorities

The organization of the services

Local authorities employ a wide range of people: from school teachers to road sweepers, from librarians to park keepers. All help to look after our welfare. The following senior officials are responsible for the smooth running of local government services:

1. *Chief executive*: He is the 'general manager' who sees that things run according to the dictates of the council.
2. *Treasurer*: He keeps a record of finances, supervises the collection of rates, and tells the council what can be afforded from the money available.
3. *Surveyor*: He is responsible for roads, sewers, refuse disposal, building works, and street lights.
4. *Medical Officer of Health*: He is in charge of public health, sanitation, health centres, the ambulance service and disease prevention. He reports to the council about nuisances and bad housing.

Health and welfare in the local community

Four groups of people are looked after by local government health services:

1. *Mothers and young children*: Midwives, home-helps, and health visitors look after the welfare of mothers and the young.

2. *The mentally handicapped*: Training centres and special schools are provided for the benefit of the mentally handicapped.
3. *The physically handicapped*: The blind, deaf, and others permanently handicapped are given special help; for example, the provision of special ramps for wheelchairs in public buildings.
4. *The elderly*: Old people living at home are helped by nurses and home-helps; old people who are unable to look after themselves are often cared for in old people's homes.

Fig 9.12 Voluntary organizations (Reproduced by permission of Royal National Lifeboat Institution, Royal National Institute for the Blind, and St John Ambulance Association and Brigade)

Voluntary workers

A local council cannot do everything it would like to do to help its citizens. Many 'gaps' in the welfare services are filled by voluntary workers (see Fig. 9.12). You probably have given money to a charitable organization and received a small flag in return. Or you may have already joined a voluntary organization as a way of putting something back into the community.

Local authorities know the value of the work carried out by volunteers and often work very closely with them. For example, 'Meals on Wheels' are delivered by the Women's Royal Voluntary Service, who thus back up the help given by the council (see Fig. 9.13). The Samaritans help people with personal problems and look after many people who would rather not seek aid from local authorities.

Fig 9.13 Meals on wheels (Reproduced by permission of the Women's Royal Voluntary Service)

Conclusion

In many countries, your welfare and your standard of living would be your concern and not that of the central or local government. You would be left largely to look after yourself. But in Great Britain those who do not enjoy a reasonable standard of health and welfare can get help from the Government, the local authority, or the voluntary services.

TOPIC 9.4 Activities

1. Read the passage and answer the questions:

Pavements Plea for the Blind
The National Federation of the Blind has declared 6 June as 'Pavement Day' as part of its contribution towards the International Year for the Disabled Person.

A supporting campaign aims to draw attention to the need to repair pavements which are broken and dangerous and to encourage schools to design posters and write stories on the subject of pavements and the disabled.

(Source: *Eastern Evening News,* 6 April 1981)

(a) How does the National Federation of the Blind propose to make local councils and the public aware of the problems encountered by blind people?
(b) In what ways do local councils provide specialized facilities for disabled people?
(c) How do you think more could be done by local councils for these people?
(d) How can pavements maintained by local councils be especially dangerous?

2. Make a survey of some of your local services by finding answers to these questions. (You can add some questions of your own.)
(a) How often are the dustbins emptied?
(b) How often are the roads swept?
(c) How many road improvements have been carried out recently?
(d) How far away is your nearest fire and ambulance station?

3. Under which department of the local council would the following workers be employed?
(a) Accountants.
(b) Architects.
(c) Librarians.
(d) Park keepers.
(e) Refuse collectors.
(f) Rent collectors.
(g) Road sweepers.
(h) Swimming bath attendants.
(i) Teachers.
(j) Welfare workers.

4. What special considerations would you take into account if you were designing a place where blind people could work safely?

5. What plans would you make if you were asked to run a fund-raising scheme for a charity?

6. List some of the problems which face elderly people living alone. How do you think members of your class could help old people?

Unit 10

Population

TOPIC 10.1   Population growth

Who keeps count?

Figure 10.1 shows how the population of Great Britain has increased since 1911. Accurate figures of births and deaths are kept by registrars employed by local authorities. In England and Wales there are nearly 500 superintendent registrars in charge of registration districts and some 1200 registrars in charge of sub-districts. They act under the instruction of the Registrar General who is in charge of a central government department called the Office of Population Censuses and Surveys. Every birth, every marriage, and every death must be recorded by the local registrar. In this way, an attempt is made to keep accurate records of the number of people living in the land, and to note population changes that are taking place.

Britain's total population in 1981 was, according to the census, 56 252 000. This is compared with 53 million people in 1961. There are two main causes for the continuing increase in population.

1. The progressive reduction in the death rate, i.e., people live longer. In 1982 the expectation of life for a man was 69 years and for a woman 75 years.
2. The birth rate, although it has fallen by 30 per cent, has remained higher than the death rate.

Look at Fig. 10.2. You will see that by the 1930s, the birth rate had fallen to less than half the nineteenth-century rate, yet the population continued to increase slowly, mainly because of the decrease in the death rate. Can you add to the following reasons why people live longer today?

1. Better food.
2. Rising standards of living.
3. The advance of medical science.
4. Improved health and welfare.

In 1900, 142 babies out of every 1000 died before they reached their first birthday. By 1980 this figure had been reduced to 14 per 1000 (see Fig. 10.3).

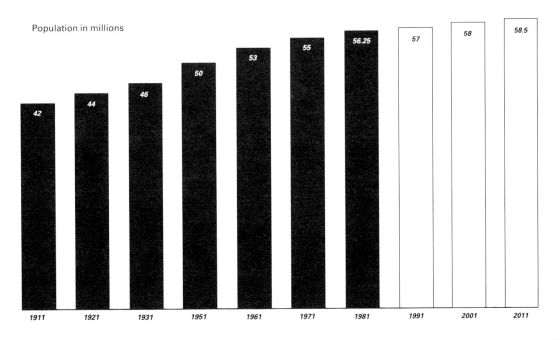

Population in millions

| 1911 | 1921 | 1931 | 1951 | 1961 | 1971 | 1981 | 1991 | 2001 | 2011 |
| 42 | 44 | 46 | 50 | 53 | 55 | 56.25 | 57 | 58 | 58.5 |

Fig 10.1   Population increases in the UK, 1911 to 1981, and projected increases to 2011 (Source: Annual Abstract of Statistics 1984)

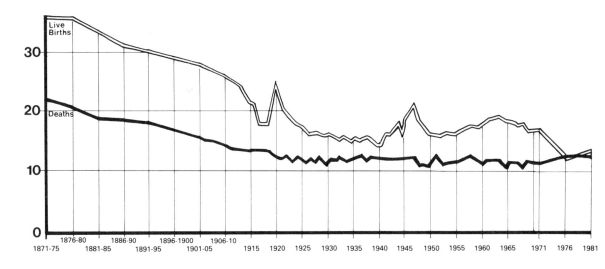

Fig 10.2   Changes in birth rates and death rates in Great Britain (per 1000 population) (Reproduced by permission of HMSO)

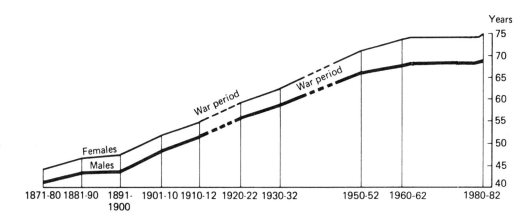

Fig 10.3   Expectation of life at birth in England and Wales 1871 to 1982

People coming to live in Great Britain from foreign countries have helped to increase the population. After the Second World War, a large number of immigrants came from the new Commonwealth countries such as the West Indies, Pakistan, and India. From 1960 to 1962 the total number of immigrants amounted to 388 000. In 1962, the Commonwealth Immigrants Act was passed in an effort to check the number of new settlers coming from abroad. In 1972, many thousands of Ugandan Asian refugees, who were British passport holders, were allowed to settle in Great Britain, but this was an exceptional measure. The tendency for immigrants to have large families means that they are likely to have an 'above average effect' upon population growth in Great Britain.

164

In strict confidence

1981 Census England

H Form for Private Households

*A household comprises **either** one person living alone **or** a group of persons (who may or may not be related) living at the same address with common housekeeping. Persons staying temporarily with the household are included.*

To the Head or Joint Heads or members of the Household

Please complete this census form and have it ready to be collected by the census enumerator for your area. He or she will call for the form on **Monday 6 April 1981** or soon after. If you are not sure how to complete any of the entries on the form, the enumerator will be glad to help you when he calls. He will also need to check that you have filled in all the entries.

This census is being held in accordance with a decision made by Parliament. The leaflet headed 'Census 1981' describes why it is necessary and how the information will be used. Completion of this form is compulsory under the Census Act 1920. If you refuse to complete it, or if you give false information, you may have to pay a fine of up to £50.

Your replies will be treated in STRICT CONFIDENCE. They will be used to produce statistics but your name and address will NOT be fed into the census computer. After the census, the forms will be locked away for 100 years before they are passed to the Public Record Office.

If any member of the household who is age 16 or over does not wish you or other members of the household to see his or her personal information, then please ask the enumerator for an extra form and an envelope. The enumerator will then explain how to proceed.

When you have completed the form, please sign the declaration in Panel C on the last page.

A R THATCHER
Registrar General

Office of Population Censuses and Surveys
PO Box 200 Portsmouth PO2 8HH
Telephone 0329-42511

Please answer questions H1 - H5 about your household's accommodation, check the answer in Panel A, answer questions 1-16 overleaf and Panel B on the back page. Where boxes are provided please answer by putting a tick against the answer which applies. For example, if the answer to the marital status question is 'Single', tick box 1 thus:

1 ☑ Single

Please use ink or ballpoint pen.

To be completed by the Enumerator

Census District	Enumeration District	Form Number

Name . . . .

Address . . . .

. . . .

. . . . Postcode ☐☐☐☐▨☐☐☐

Panel A
To be completed by the Enumerator and amended, if necessary, by the person(s) signing this form.

This household's accommodation is:

- In a caravan   ☐ 20
- In any other mobile or temporary structure   ☐ 30
- In a purpose-built block of flats or maisonettes   ☐ 12
- In any other permanent building in which the entrance from **outside** the building is:

  NOT SHARED with another household   ☐ 10

  SHARED with another household   ☐ 11 ◄

H1   Rooms

Please count the rooms in your household's accommodation.
Do not count:

small kitchens, that is those under 2 metres (6ft 6ins) wide, bathrooms, WCs.

Number of rooms . . . .

Note
Rooms divided by curtains or portable screens count as one; those divided by a fixed or sliding partition count as two.
Rooms used solely for business, professional or trade purposes should be excluded.

H2   Tenure

How do you and your household occupy your accommodation? Please tick the appropriate box.

As an owner occupier (including purchase by mortgage):

1 ☐ of freehold property

2 ☐ of leasehold property

By renting, rent free or by lease:

3 ☐ from a local authority (council or New Town)

4 ☐ with a job, shop, farm or other business

5 ☐ from a housing association or charitable trust

6 ☐ furnished from a private landlord, company or other organisation

7 ☐ unfurnished from a private landlord, company or other organisation

In some other way:

☐ Please give details

. . . .

Note
a If the accommodation is occupied by lease originally granted for, or since extended to, more than 21 years, tick box 2.

b If a share in the property is being bought under an arrangement with a local authority, New Town corporation or housing association, *for example, shared ownership (equity sharing), a co-ownership scheme*, tick box 1 or 2 as appropriate.

H3   Amenities

Has your household the use of the following amenities on these premises? Please tick the appropriate boxes.

- A fixed bath or shower permanently connected to a water supply and a waste pipe

1 ☐ YES – for use only by this household

2 ☐ YES – for use also by another household

3 ☐ NO fixed bath or shower

- A flush toilet (WC) with entrance inside the building

1 ☐ YES – for use only by this household

2 ☐ YES – for use also by another household

3 ☐ NO inside flush toilet (WC)

- A flush toilet (WC) with entrance outside the building

1 ☐ YES – for use only by this household

2 ☐ YES – for use also by another household

3 ☐ NO outside flush toilet (WC)

►H4   Please answer this question if box 11 in Panel A is ticked.

Are your rooms (not counting a bathroom or WC) enclosed behind your own front door **inside** the building?

1 ☐ YES   2 ☐ NO

If your household has only one room (not including a bathroom or WC) please answer 'YES'.

H5   Cars and vans

Please tick the appropriate box to indicate the number of cars and vans normally available for use by you or members of your household (other than visitors).

0 ☐ None
1 ☐ One
2 ☐ Two
3 ☐ Three or more

Include any car or van provided by employers if normally available for use by you or members of your household but **exclude** vans used solely for the carriage of goods.

PLEASE TURN OVER ➡

Fig 10.4   Part of the 1981 Census form (Reproduced with the permission of the Controller of HMSO. © Crown copyright)

Planning for an expanding population

The Government needs to plot future population trends in order to spend its money wisely and plan sensibly for the future. It does this with the aid of a 'census', held every 10 years, and organized by the Office of Population Censuses and Surveys. The first census or 'count' was held in 1801. When a census is held, each householder in Great Britain is asked to complete a form similar to the one, shown in part, in Fig. 10.4. Refusal to fill in the form can lead to a heavy fine or even imprisonment. The questions on the form cover more than simply how many people live at a certain address. For example, the householder must answer questions about:

1. The age of each member of the household.
2. The date of birth of each member.
3. The country of birth of each member.
4. The family's address one year ago and the family's address five years ago.

Distributing and collecting the census forms is a large-scale operation requiring the help of thousands of people. In the 1981 census 22 million forms were filled in and collected by nearly 100 000 enumerators. The completed forms were taken to the office block at Bootle where they were stored on 12½ miles of racks! After all the figures have been fed into a computer the census forms will be stored for 100 years before being placed in the Public Records Office. In all the 1981 census is estimated to have cost £50 million. With such an expensive and large-scale operation the information collected in the census helps the Government in several ways.

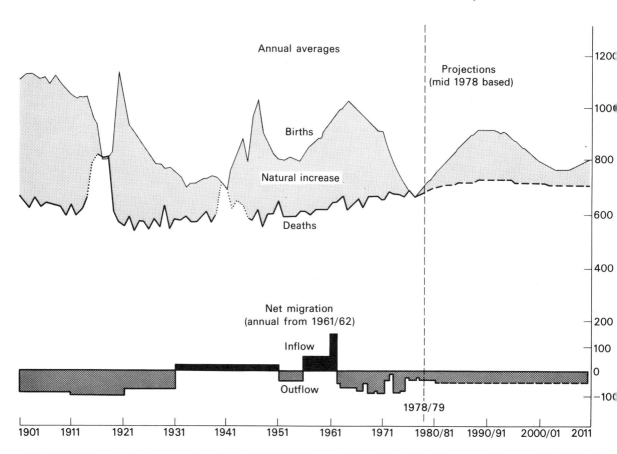

Fig 10.5   UK population changes and projections 1901-2011 (Source: Office of Population Censuses and Surveys, 'Social Trends', 1980. Reproduced with permission of the Controller of HMSO. © Crown copyright)

1. *Housing*: How many people are living in substandard conditions? Which areas have problems of overcrowding?
2. *Education*: Are there sufficient schools in a certain area?
3. *Towns*: Is there overcrowding in certain towns?
4. *Health*: Are hospital facilities adequate for the sick and disabled?
5. *Work*: How many people are unemployed in an area? Which areas need government assistance to encourage industry to be sited there?
6. *Sanitation and drainage*: Is there a flush toilet and good paving?
7. *Power*: Are houses supplied with sufficient gas and electricity, and what are the needs of the future?
8. *Transport*: How do people travel to work and are public transport facilities adequate?
9. *Migration*: Which people have moved since the last census and to which areas have they moved?
10. *Development areas*: How are these special areas faring and what are their future needs?

UK population changes and projections 1901–2011 are recorded in Fig. 10.5.

Conclusion

All information collected in a census is considered essential by the Government for planning further expenditure on the needs of the population. Every 10 years it provides the main method of collecting accurate statistics. An expanding population demands more food, more houses, etc. But it also provides a larger workforce which is an advantage to a country wishing to increase production and play its role in world affairs.

TOPIC 10.1   Activities

1. Read the passage and answer the questions:

1981 Census — Why is it Needed

Today's census of 22 million households is a compromise between inquiring social scientists and the British passion for privacy. The British seem to be winning, writes Laurence Marks.

Its primary purpose is to gather information on a geographical basis that will enable civil servants to distribute national resources fairly — notably the £22 000 million a year that goes to local government and regional health authorities.

Sydney Boxer, head of the Government's census division, said: 'Ever since we began consulting the research interests four years ago, they have been wanting to hang additional questions of their own on it like glass baubles on a Christmas tree: what languages people speak, what kind of aerials they have, what disabilities they suffer from, and so forth'.

The census is the biggest event in the demographic world, but there are conflicting thoughts about what it should be doing.

(Source: *Observer,* 5 April 1981)

(a) What was the primary purpose of the 1981 census?
(b) How did the census provide a guide for the spending of £22 000 million?
(c) Why did many researchers want to include additional questions on the 1981 census form?
(d) How could questions asked be an invasion of individual privacy?

2. Using your local newspapers, conduct a survey of the number of births, deaths, and marriages in one week. Plot the daily totals on a graph in your notebook.

3. Make a list of some of the important advances which have taken place in medical science during the last 100 years. What benefit have these discoveries brought?

4. Give five reasons why you think that women live longer than men.

5. Give five reasons why large numbers of immigrants have come to Great Britain in the twentieth century.

6. Imagine you are a West Indian coming to settle in Great Britain. Describe some of the problems which you might meet during your first six months.

TOPIC 10.2 Modern trends

Where do people live?

Look at Fig. 10.6. Did you know that about one-third of the total population of Great Britain lives in seven large towns? Yet less than 200 years ago, most people lived in the country. It was only with the development of factories that people began to move from the countryside to the towns. The seven very large towns are known as *conurbations*. Today many people live outside large towns and travel to them for their work.

The most crowded area is a 65-mile-wide belt which runs north-west to south-east from Liverpool to London. About one-third of our population lives in seven conurbations: London, Birmingham, Glasgow, Liverpool, Leeds, Manchester, and Newcastle. A large number of city workers choose to live in the country although the opportunities for local employment continue to decrease. Since few people work on farms today, villages are often dormitory suburbs.

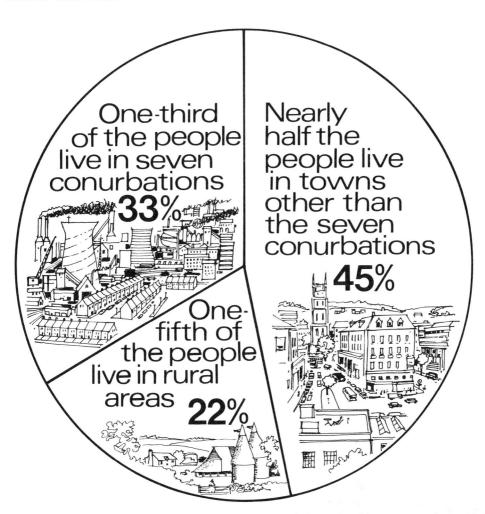

One-third of the people live in seven conurbations 33%

Nearly half the people live in towns other than the seven conurbations 45%

One-fifth of the people live in rural areas 22%

Fig 10.6 Population distribution in conurbations, towns, and the countryside (Reproduced from correspondence with the Office of Population Censuses and Surveys)

Population movements

People usually live in or around an area where they can find work. As a result, nearly half of the population of Great Britain lives within a 30-mile rectangle stretching across England from the mouth of the River Mersey to the mouth of the River Thames. In the centre are the large industrial towns of the Midlands. The central lowlands of Scotland and south-east Wales also have fairly high densities of population. Can you account for this? London has always been a centre for commerce and trade in Great Britain. Historically, it has always had a high density of population.

Many people living in London and other large cities have been encouraged to move elsewhere since the Second World War attracted by better housing and jobs provided in new towns and 'overspill' towns.

Large numbers of people have moved from other areas where industry has declined. The eastern fringes of England, the far south-west, and the mountainous areas have always been sparsely populated. Figure 10.7 shows an aerial view of East Kilbride New Town.

Fig 10.7   Aerial view of East Kilbride New Town

Age and sex distribution

The number of boys born is greater than the number of girls by about 6 per cent, but the number of people dying at all ages is higher among males. You see far more old women than old men; for every 29 women over the age of 70 there are only 15 men.

Figure 10.8 shows the distribution of the population of Great Britain by age. The first column represents the number of the population taking part in full-time education. The second column includes most of the working population, while retired people make up the third column.

Figure 10.8 also shows the 'ageing' of the population — the proportion of older people in the population is increasing. It is obviously easier to predict the retired population in 10 years' time than it is the number of children.

A greater number of old people mean increased demands on health and social benefits. Old age pensions have to be financed from government revenue, and as the proportion of old people increases, so the burden of paying pensions increases. Fewer workers means less revenue unless tax rates are raised.

Population movements in the future

Population movements can never be predicted with complete accuracy. Census figures are used to obtain a picture of where people are likely to be living in the next 10 years. Examples of three areas where population increases were expected to take place in the 10 years following the 1971 census are given in Table 10.1. The right-hand column gives the actual figures recorded in the 1981 census, showing that in one of the areas, the South-East, the population actually decreased significantly.

Estimates of this type are useful when it comes to planning housing sites. The forecasts may also influence industrialists in their choice of location for new factories.

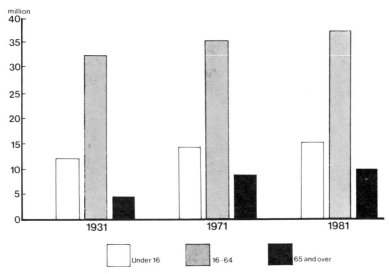

Fig 10.8   Age distribution of the population (Reproduced by permission of HMSO)

Table 10.1

Area	1971 (census figures)	1981 (estimate)	1981 (census figures)
East Anglia	1 669 000	1 941 000	1 872 000
South-East	17 230 000	18 281 000	16 796 000
South-West	3 781 000	4 099 000	4 349 000

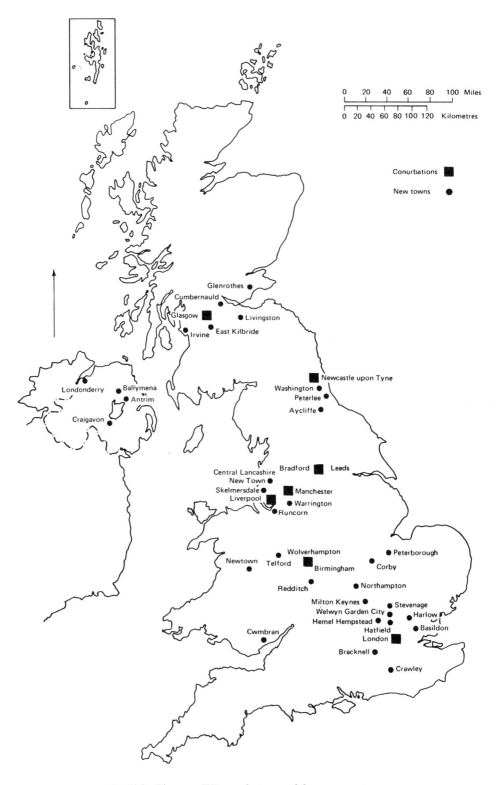

Fig 10.9   The seven UK conurbations and the many new towns

Conurbations

Future population movements are likely to lead to the further development of conurbations. These occur when large cities spread outwards so that they join up with neighbouring smaller towns and villages (see Fig. 10.9). You would find it difficult to draw boundary lines between Manchester, Salford, and Stretford. Conurbations are usually centred around one large town (see Table 10.2). Figure 10.10 shows the conurbation around Birmingham.

Table 10.2   Conurbations and their main towns

Conurbation	Main town
(a) Greater London	London
(b) West Midlands	Birmingham
(c) Merseyside	Liverpool
(d) South-east Lancashire	Manchester
(e) West Yorkshire	Leeds
(f) Tyneside	Newcastle
(g) Clydeside	Glasgow

You have learnt that the population of Greater London has decreased, so you might think that this conurbation is getting smaller. But this is not so. What has happened is that it has spread out even further and taken up more of the surrounding countryside. Many people who work in London travel 20 to 30 miles to and from work each day. More houses will mean that market towns and villages will spread outwards and ugly 'sprawls' may take place unless great care is taken over planning. Some towns are protected by a 'Green Belt' so that it is forbidden to build on the land which surrounds them.

Conclusion

The population of Great Britain is likely to increase steadily so that there will be about 58 million of us in AD 2001. As people strive for better standards of living, they will demand more building land, more roads, and other facilities. These are the trends of the future. Your generation must make sure that the countryside is preserved and not ruined by people who want a shortcut to a higher standard of living at the expense of everything else.

Fig 10.10   The city of Birmingham 1980 (Courtesy of the City of Birmingham Press and PR Unit)

TOPIC 10.2   Activities

1. Read the passage and answer the questions:

Housing standards

The latest English House Condition Survey showed that in 1981 there were 18.1 million dwellings in England of which 1.1 million were considered unfit for human habitation, 0.9 million lacked basic amenities, and 1 million required repairs costing more than £7000. (Definitions of unfitness, basic amenities, and cost of repairs are contained in the Appendix to this chapter.) These categories of dwellings are not mutually exclusive; many dwellings are, for example, both physically unfit and lacking basic amenities. The total number of dwellings with one or more of the three types of deficiency was 2 million in 1981, about 1.1 per cent of the total dwelling stock.

   The character of the 1981 housing stock is the result of a variety of trends over past decades. Since 1971 the number of dwellings lacking amenities has fallen by about two-thirds, from 2.8 million in 1971 to 1.5 million in 1978, and 0.9 million in 1981. There has also been a reduction in the number of dwellings in the worst condition, i.e., jointly lacking amenities, being unfit, and in serious disrepair — 145 thousand between 1971 and 1976 and 45 thousand between 1976 and 1981. However, the net effect of these reductions and of additions as a result of other dwellings becoming unfit with the passage of time, has been to leave the total numbers of unfit dwellings, 1.1 million, relatively constant between 1971 and 1981. In 1971, the lack of amenities in otherwise sound dwellings accounted for over a half of all dwellings in an unsatisfactory condition but by 1981 the number of these sound dwellings lacking amenities had fallen by four-fifths. On the other hand, dwellings which were unfit or in serious disrepair increased from 1.5 million in 1971 to 1.7 million in 1981, accounting for 84 per cent of all unsatisfactory dwellings.

(Source: *Social Trends 1984,* HMSO)

(a)   How many dwellings in England in 1981 were fit for human habitation?
(b)   Make a list of what you would consider to be basic amenities.
(c)   What does the phrase 'These categories of dwelling are not mutually exclusive' mean?
(d)   Describe in your own words the trends in the quality of housing between 1971 and 1981.
(e)   Why do you think there are so many dwellings in England classified as unfit for human habitation?

2 Draw a rough sketch map of the area within five miles of your home. Show places where:
(a)   A large number of houses have been built in the past five years.
(b)   People can spend their leisure time.
(c)   Farming and horticulture are still carried out.

3. Describe how your district has grown in the past 100 years.

4. Imagine that a village of 500 people expands to house a further 1000 people. What new services do you think should be available for these people?

5. Give three reasons why you think that certain areas of Great Britain should remain as National Parks.

6. Give three examples of ways in which our crowded country is being polluted. Now choose *one* example and suggest some ways in which pollution might be checked.

Unit 11

Housing

TOPIC 11.1   Renting a home

Where are you going to live?

You are probably living at home with your parents. When you begin work you may wish to leave home, and certainly when you get married you will want a home of your own. When you look for somewhere to live you will be faced with several choices:

1. Living in a hostel. The YMCA and local councils sometimes provide hostels where you can live with a group of people.
2. Renting a bedsitter or a flat from a private landlord (see Fig. 11.1).
3. Renting a house or flat owned by a local authority.
4. Living in lodgings with another family.
5. Buying or renting a caravan.
6. Buying a house of your own.

Accommodation

TO LET fully furnished, Single BEDSITTER. – Tel. 33042 –

ACCOMMODATION urgently required by young married couple with baby, three/four months only, anything considered. – Tel. 591. –

GROVE ESTATE AGENCY. – For all types of ACCOMMODATION, consult us. – Tel. 20979. –

YOUNG Executive shortly taking up a management position seeks small FLAT or Bed-sitter, central area. – Tel. 56431. –

STUDENT or Professional Person required to share flat in city area; own room. – Write Box F834 .–

YOUNG Mechanic seeks FLAT or Flatlet, city centre. – Box A358.–

RETIRED Man requires ACCOMMODATION: anything considered. – Box F1049. –

WANTED, FLAT or House to rent, Furnished/Unfurnished, for married couple: no children or pets; repairs or modernisation done free if materials are provided. – Tel. 24535 after 6 p.m. –

RICHARDSONS AGENCY deals with Furnished/Unfurnished ACCOMMODATION: no charge to landlords for immediate introductions; references supplied; management services available. – Contact 23084. –

TO LET, 2-bedroomed detached BUNGALOW, for approx. 12 months. – Box H1164. –

Fig 11.1   Accommodation wanted and to rent

The 21 million dwellings in the UK can be divided into the three main groups shown in Fig. 11.2. Although over 10 million new dwellings have been built since 1945, there are still millions of people who are inadequately housed. A 1976 survey revealed that 5 per cent of dwellings were unfit for human habitation and 920 000 lacked basic amenities.

Improvements have been made (especially by way of slum clearance, urban renewal, and better standards of living) but there is still much to be done before all the people in the UK are properly housed.

Private rented accommodation

Nearly half the people in Great Britain live in rented accommodation. It may be cheaper in the short run to rent a house rather than buy one, but the rent has to be paid for a dwelling that you will *never own*. The first place to look if you want to rent *private* accommodation is in the classified section of your local paper. Or you could advertise in the paper for a suitable place to rent, or make use of the services of a rental agency. All of these methods are illustrated in Fig. 11.1. If you choose to use the services of an agency, you will be charged a fee. You could also contact the Citizens' Advice Bureau which will advise you of the type of rented accommodation available in the area and how much you might expect to pay for it.

If you rent from a private landlord, you will be expected to obey certain rules and regulations. But you have certain protections under the law. The landlord must provide you with a rent book if you pay the rent weekly. It should contain the following information:

1. A brief description of the rooms, house, or flat you are renting.
2. Any facilities which you are expected to share with others.
3. The address of the landlord or his agent.
4. The amount of rent to be paid and any extras which have to be paid for.

If you pay rent monthly, the law does not insist that you are provided with a rent book. You should, however, make sure that you get a receipt for each monthly payment. Keep these receipts because they are evidence that you have paid. If you consider that your rent is too high you can appeal to the Rent Tribunal. The Tribunal will hear the views of both the tenant and the landlord and fix a *fair rent*. The 1972 Housing Finance Act allowed tenants renting unfurnished accommodation from private landlords (or local councils) to receive rent rebates according to their means.

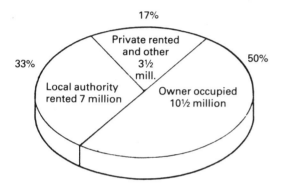

Fig 11.2   Housing stock, Great Britain, 1980

Renting a council house or flat

Renting a house or flat from your local authority is probably the best value for money if you cannot afford to buy a house of your own. If you want to apply for a council house you should go along to the Housing Department of your local authority. You may be placed on a 'waiting list' because council houses are usually in short supply and those available are allocated to people with the most urgent needs. Most councils require applicants to have lived in the area for a certain period. Today the tendency is for local authorities to build flats rather than houses. These flats are likely to be more modern and have more amenities than privately rented property. Three out of four dwellings in Great Britain were built before 1919, but only one in four *council* dwellings was built before this date. Most council houses have been built within the last 25 years and many of those

Fig 11.3   Modernization: before and after (Reproduced by permission of Norwich District Council)

built today have central heating. The amount of rent you pay for a council house will depend on the age of the house, its amenities, and size. People in council houses may be entitled to a rent rebate, according to their income.

Local councils also spend a great deal on improvements in order to provide tenants with modernized dwellings (see Fig. 11.3). A 1980 Act allowed council tenants to buy their council dwellings.

Conclusion

Although a large number of houses are provided for rent by councils and private landlords, there are still not enough to go round. There is a serious housing problem in Great Britain, so you ought to start thinking early about where you are going to live when you leave home.

TOPIC 11.1   Activities

1. Read the passage and answer the questions:

Housing changes

Girls today, when they get married, will not necessarily lead the same sort of lives as their mothers and grandmothers. For one thing, more and more girls expect to combine home and family with a job of their own.

It is a lot easier for them to do this today, because families are a great deal smaller than they once were. In Grandma's time, families of six or seven children were not unusual. This, naturally, affected the sort of homes people lived in, and also the way they lived. Either homes had to be big enough to contain a large family adequately, or they were overcrowded. Today, the average family, with two children, can move into a three-bedroomed house where parents and both children can have rooms of their own. Grandma's family would have filled such a house to bursting point and the privacy which members of smaller families can enjoy today was something they hardly dreamed of.

We have other new expectations, too. We expect, for instance, to have a family car or at least we intend to acquire one at some time. This means that housebuilders today have to think in terms of providing garages on the new estates they build. Grandparents and perhaps parents, too, had no such expectations unless they were very lucky. With no cars, they had no need of garages attached to their homes, and so, living in terraced houses or houses built close to one another was no inconvenience to them. However, since they expected to get about by using public transport, it could be very inconvenient if home was too far from a bus stop or railway station.

You can find even greater differences in the home lives of the various generations if you take a look at what we expect homes to contain today, and what they had, or did not have, in previous years. Take the business of doing the family washing as an example.

Thirty or forty years ago, a housewife thought she was well off if she had a glass scrubbing board on which to wash the family's clothes instead of a wooden one. Nowadays, an automatic washing machine is nothing unusual in homes, and most newly wed wives envisage having one. Their mothers, when just married, probably expected to use the local launderette. Grandma, at the same stage in her life, expected to do the washing mainly by hand.

Similarly, it is only a few years since an appreciable number of households acquired fridge-freezers, or automatic driers or central heating.

All these new or different factors in everyday life have changed the sort of homes we live in, the way they look, the sort of facilities we expect them to have and the size and number of labour-saving devices they contain.

(Source: 'One day . . .', Building Societies Association)

(a) How have changes in family life influenced housing?
(b) What new expectations do young people have today as far as housing is concerned?
(c) In what respects have household durables changed in the past 50 years?
(d) What items would you consider to be *essential* when furnishing your first home?
(e) List the labour-saving devices in a modern home which would not have been available for your grandparents.

2. In your notebook set out the advantages and disadvantages of living in the following types of accommodation:
(a) A caravan.
(b) A hostel.
(c) Lodgings.
(d) A privately rented flat.
(e) A council house.

3. From your local paper cut out some advertisements for rented accommodation. Stick them in your book. What is the average rent you would have to pay for:

(a) A bedsitter?

(b) A flat?

(c) A house?

4. Write out an advertisement for the type of rented accommodation you are likely to require in a few years' time.

5. Write a letter of application to your local housing department, requesting local authority accommodation. Give as many points *in your favour* as possible.

6. Imagine you are a private landlord owning a house which is let out as bedsitters. What rules and regulations would you impose upon the people who rented these rooms?

TOPIC 11.2   Buying a house

Why buy when you can rent?

Many people, who live in rented accommodation, could never save enough money to buy a house similar to the one advertised in Fig. 11.4. In recent years, house prices have increased so much that it is very difficult for a young married couple to buy their own house. As you get older, your earnings increase, so that one day you may be able to afford a house of your own. You may well think that buying a house is the most sensible thing to do if you can afford it, especially as the money you would pay out in rent never allows you to own the house. If you buy your house your money is going towards something which is increasing in value. Many people look upon house purchase as a good investment. About 56 per cent of all householders own, or are in the process of buying, their houses.

How much will it cost to buy a house?

The price of houses today runs into thousands of pounds. Very few people have that amount of money with which to purchase the property outright. They have to borrow money through a *mortgage* lasting for anything from 10 to 30 years. There are various ways by which a person can borrow a large sum for house purchase:

1. Through a building society. This is the most popular way.
2. Through a government option mortgage scheme linked to a building society.
3. Through a local authority.
4. Through an insurance company.
5. Through a private loan.

Before you can borrow any money in order to buy a house, you will need enough cash for a *deposit*. This usually has to be a minimum of 10 per cent of the price of the house. The remainder of the money has to be borrowed and repaid with interest. The interest rate seems high, but the burden is decreased by income tax allowances.

BENNING CLOSE South Road

3 bedroomed town houses each with garage and central heating. Landscaped gardens.

Probably the cheapest new houses available today

from only   **£24 950**

Fig 11.4   House for sale

Most mortgage loans granted in the UK are made by one or other of the 280 building societies. House mortgages as a loan are repayable over 10, 15, 20, 25, 30, and even 35 years.

People on low incomes, who are not liable for taxation, can take advantage of the option mortgage scheme. Under this scheme borrowers receive a subsidy (instead of tax relief) that reduces the rate of interest by 3 per cent. However, whichever type of mortgage you require it would still be necessary to have a 10 per cent deposit and thus saving for a house is usually the first step before you decide to apply for a mortgage. In addition, you would also need enough money to pay the fees of the building society and your solicitor. Today most building societies will also take into account the earnings of a wife, when they decide how much they should lend to an applicant. As you can see from Fig. 11.5 the amount of money loaned by Britain's building societies has steadily increased and loans to first-time buyers account for approximately 50 per cent of all money lent.

The stages in purchasing a house

Looking around

You will be wise to spend plenty of time looking around and comparing the types and prices of

181

property. Look in the local newspaper or visit estate agents in your area to see what property they have on their books. As the *buyer* you will not have to pay fees to estate agents. They make their money by charging the people who *sell* their houses.

Finding a solicitor

Though it is no longer strictly necessary, most people who purchase property prefer to engage the services of a solicitor. Once you have found a property and wish to make an offer for it, the solicitor begins his job. He makes careful enquiries about the house and the area in which it is situated, and finds out if there are any snags, such as planning permission for further building developments, which might spoil the outlook. Your solicitor will make a very careful check about the ownership of the land. He will let you know about your new obligations, e.g., you may become legally responsible for the upkeep of the fence on the north side of your garden.

Having the house surveyed

When buying a house, you will need to employ the services of a surveyor. His job is to examine the house to see if it is structurally sound and that it will not subside. He will check for such things as rising damp or dry rot. He sees that you get value for your money. Building societies will not loan money for a property which is not sound, so they insist on the house being properly surveyed. If you are buying a new house it is likely to be covered by a National Housebuilders' Registration Council Certificate which gives a 10-year guarantee and shows that the house has been built in accordance with standards laid down by the NHRC.

The contract

The solicitors of both the buyer and the seller draw up contracts. When these contracts are exchanged, you will have to pay the deposit. If you are planning to buy a house that has not yet been built, your solicitor will advise you that it is cheaper to

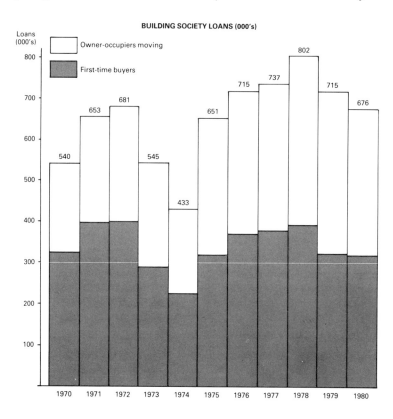

Fig 11.5   Building society loans

contract to buy the land first. So the initial deposit will not be large compared with what you will have to pay when the house is completed according to contract. For instance, if the land is valued at £5000 you will only have to pay £500 before the builders start to build the house. The contract will probably state that the payments will have to be made in stages, but the building society will take care of that, for example:

First stage, when roofed, one-third the cost of the house

Second stage, when plastered, one-third the cost of the house

Third stage, when completed, one-third the cost of the house

When the sale has been made according to the contracts, you will be given the key of *your house*.

Conclusion

More and more people want to buy their own homes. If you own your house you have more freedom since the same restrictions are not placed on you as in rented accommodation. Also it is likely that your home will rise in value after you have bought it. If you can save enough money, you will probably decide to own your home (see Fig. 11.6).

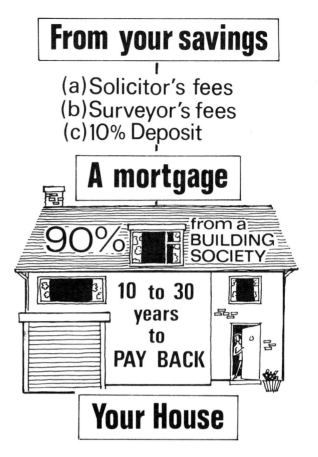

Fig 11.6   Buying a house

TOPIC 11.2 Activities

1. Read the following passage and answer the questions:

Rise in house prices
A very active housing market with steady price rises is reported by the Royal Institution of Chartered Surveyors in its latest survey of prices in England and Wales.

Record numbers of inquiries from buyers in some parts of the country are resulting in a shortage of property, particularly at the top end of the market and many agents in the south have reported that demand is beginning to exceed supply and drive prices up.

In the new houses market, over two-thirds of those agents who contributed said that prices were higher than three months ago, with more than one-fifth of them reporting price increases of 5 per cent and more.

Some agents say that houses needing modernisation or repair are selling more slowly following the Government's measures to curb improvement grants and the VAT charge of alterations and extensions that applies from tomorrow. Buyers are cautious about investing in neglected pre-1919 terraced houses in areas such as Wales, where a special survey was carried out.

Commenting on the latest figures, John Thomas, the RICS spokesman on the housing market, said: 'At last the market has really shaken free from the doldrums which it has experienced during the past two to three years. The better than average weather conditions combined with the lowering of interest rates and availability of money have been contributory factors, but there is a greater sense of future confidence in homes as secure investments.

'Price increases are higher than the annual rate of inflation, but the market could tail off in the second half of the year if external factors force up the cost of borrowing.'

(Source: *Building Trades Journal,* 31 May 1984)

(a) Explain in your own words the phrase 'demand is beginning to exceed supply and drive prices up'.
(b) Which types of property are selling more slowly?
(c) What effect has the new VAT charge on alterations and extensions had on buyers of this type of property?
(d) List the factors which might have contributed to the rise in house prices.
(e) What 'external factors' might force up the cost of borrowing?

2. From your local paper cut out advertisements for a selection of properties and stick them in your notebook. What is the average price of the following:
(a) A two-bedroomed bungalow?
(b) A three-bedroomed bungalow?
(c) A three-bedroomed house?
(d) A four-bedroomed house?

3. In your opinion what are the advantages and disadvantages of:
(a) Living in rented accommodation?
(b) Buying a house of your own?

4. Write down the names of the following in your local area:
(a) Three solicitors.
(b) Three building societies.
(c) Three surveyors.
(d) Three architects.
(e) Three estate agents.
Find out their scales of charges.

5. What different types of accounts are offered by a building society for people who want to save money? What interest rate is offered on each account? Why do the rates differ?

6. Describe some of the important points which you think should be included in a contract drawn up by a solicitor. What is conveyancing? What do you think a surveyor will look for when he surveys a house for a client?

Unit 12

Communications

TOPIC 12.1   The Post Office and British Telecom

The importance of postal and telecommunications services

Before 1981 the Post Office was responsible for all postal and telecommunications services but in 1981 a new public corporation, British Telecom, was formed to take over responsibility for telephone and related services, leaving the Post Office to concentrate on postal services (Fig. 12.1). The Post Office and British Telecom are vitally important to commerce, trade, and industry. Without the essential services provided by these organizations, the business world could not work smoothly.

Fig 12.1   Post Office and British Telecom services (Telephone by courtesy of British Telecom)

187

Royal Mail
East Midlands and 'Spokes from Speke' Air Networks

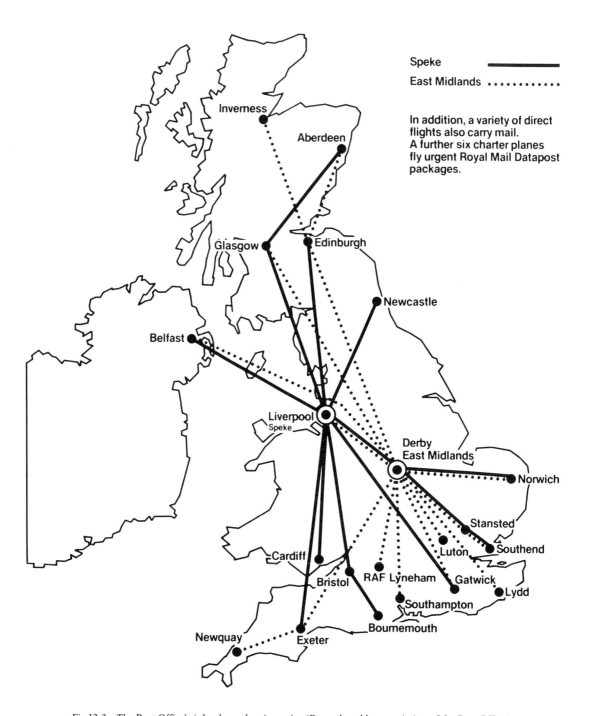

Speke   ━━━━━━

East Midlands ....

In addition, a variety of direct
flights also carry mail.
A further six charter planes
fly urgent Royal Mail Datapost
packages.

Fig 12.2   The Post Office's inland post by air service (Reproduced by permission of the Post Office)

The Post Office

The Post Office handles an enormous amount of mail. On an average day in 1983 40 million letters and over half a million parcels were dealt with, while the inland post by air service carried nearly 2 million letters nightly. This service is centred on the East Midlands Airport and Speke Airport, Liverpool (see Fig. 12.2). The amount of mail handled by the Post Office and the efficiency of its services have increased greatly in recent years.

Modern methods of handling the mail

The machine shown in Fig. 12.3 is typical of modern methods of handling mail. Letter sorting and facing machines are at work in more than 60 centres throughout Great Britain. Most areas have their own postal coding system to speed the sorting of mail. A two-tier letter service provides a fast delivery for first-class letters and a cheaper second-class service for less urgent items. The ordinary postal service ran at a loss for many years, though in recent years it has begun to show a profit to add to that of other profitable services, in particular the parcels service, in spite of the fact that it has to compete with many private parcel-delivery firms.

In an effort to improve its services, the Post Office has introduced the following:

1. Highly mechanized sorting offices with letter segregating and sorting machines.
2. Datapost, which is a package collection and delivery service with guaranteed overnight delivery to addresses throughout Britain.
3. A post code system which is one of the most sophisticated in the world.
4. Expresspost, which guarantees same-day delivery across a city or between cities.
5. Electronic post, a computer-based service which enables businesses to have mass mailings electronically transmitted for printing and delivery to distant parts of the world.
6. Intelpost, a high-speed electronic mail service which can copy letters, contracts, drawings, etc., and transmit them from London to New York, Hong Kong and many other major cities of the world.

Fig 12.3   Sorter feeding letters into an automatic letter facer (Reproduced by permission of the Post Office)

189

National Giro

This banking service was started by the Post Office in 1968, mainly to attract the many thousands of wage earners who did not have accounts with commercial banks. It has developed and increased its services over the years and at the present time offers virtually all the banking services which a commercial bank can provide. The most recent National Girobank service is Freepay, which enables the public to order and pay for goods advertised in the press or on television at post offices.

Service to rural communities

Half of the 22 000 post offices in the United Kingdom are in rural areas. Most of these are part of, and therefore help to support, village shops. The National Girobank may be the only local banking service for many country people, who are enabled by the Transcash service to pay a wide range of bills, such as gas, electricity, and payments to mail-order companies. In very remote areas the Post Office operates fleets of post-buses, which not only collect and deliver the mail but transport villagers to and from town. Without the Post Office, the quality of life in rural areas would be so much worse.

Not all of the many services of the Post Office have been described. A detailed description of *every* service the Post Office provides can be found in the *Post Office Guide*.

British Telecom

After becoming a public corporation in its own right, British Telecom became extremely profitable, making it an ideal organization for 'privatization', the Government's policy of selling state-owned concerns to private buyers. In 1984 the Telecommunications Act was passed which converted British Telecom to a public limited company, with private investors holding 51 per cent of the shares and the Government retaining the rest.

Fig 12.4   The London Telecom Tower
(Source: British Telecom)

Telephone services

The telephone provides a cheap and rapid means of communication for both the businessman and the private individual. Although there is often a waiting period before a telephone is installed, by 1980 about 18 million people had their own phone. The telephone service is continually being improved. All London's exchanges are automatic and in 1983 the most advanced electronic exchange in the world opened in Coventry. It was planned to open twelve similar exchanges in 1984 and by 1988 the number should have increased to 60. In 1958 a Subscriber Trunk Dialling (STD) system was introduced and today there are over 3000 exchanges linked to this system. The British Telecom telephone service is not confined to Great Britain. The London International Exchange has direct links via cable networks to more than 70 foreign countries. The Telecom Tower in London (Fig. 12.4) provides a microwave link for carrying long-distance telephone and television circuits. There are more than 100 communication masts and towers in use: the one in London is 189 metres high.

Other communications services

1. *Telegrams and telemessages*: Telegram messages to countries overseas are sent from Electra House in London: this is the world's largest overseas telegraph office. Telemessages were introduced by British Telecom in 1981 to replace inland telegrams. These have to be phoned in instead of filling in a form in a post office, and the message is delivered by post the next working day. In 1982 the Queen's traditional greetings telegram for hundredth birthdays and diamond weddings was replaced by the Royal Telemessage. In 1983 transatlantic telemessages were launched.
2. *Telex*: This business service enables messages to be sent by a machine similar to a typewriter, with the great advantage that the message is recorded at the receiving end even if no operator is present. There are more than 32 000 telex subscribers in Great Britain. Telex messages can be sent to ships hundreds of miles out to sea.

3. *Cardphones*: These are specially made to take plastic cards similar to credit cards instead of cash: 8600 of them are being installed in busy public locations between August 1983 and spring 1985.
4. *Telephone conferencing system*: Introduced in 1982, this system now enables up to 20 people to hold a meeting over the phone by pre-booking a date and time and giving a list of the people taking part. Participants join the conference from the nearest phone wherever they are, even from a public kiosk. At the present time, tests are being carried out for transatlantic video-conferencing.
5. *Teletext and viewdata*: Television viewers with suitable sets can call up up-to-date information on a wide variety of topics, from politics to the weather. Britain leads the world in the number of sets in use — 1 033 800 in mid-1983.
6. *Satstream*: This, the world's first satellite business service for transmitting telephone messages and electronic mail, came into operation between Britain and Canada in 1984.
7. *Submarine cables*: Many of these have been laid over recent years for providing telephone links between countries, such as the COMPAC cable, 8130 nautical miles long, connecting Canada, Hawaii, Fiji, New Zealand, and Australia. There are more than 350 underwater cables providing vital links for world-wide business. The most recent is TAT-7, a new £100 million submarine transatlantic cable which commenced operation in late 1983. It can carry more than 4200 simultaneous phone calls. British Telecom contributed 22 per cent of the cost, the rest being provided by other European countries and the United States.

Conclusion

Even though only the main services of British Telecom have been described, it can readily be seen that Britain is among the world leaders in communications technology. The services provided by the Post Office and British Telecom help both national and international trade to work smoothly.

TOPIC 12.1   Activities

1. Read the passage and answer the questions:

Britain Leads in Viewdata, Teletext Standards

British standards are being used in 98 per cent of viewdata and teletext sets throughout the world. This is shown by a survey undertaken for British Telecom, Mullard Ltd, and the Department of Trade and Industry.

The survey, which identified more than 2¼ million viewdata and teletext sets in 26 countries, was carried out by the US-based consultancy, CSP International Inc.

After Britain, which has about 1 033 800 teletext and viewdata sets in use — more than any other country — come the Netherlands, West Germany, and Sweden. These countries each have about 250 000 sets in operation — all on the British standard.

Britain's international competitors in viewdata and teletext technology, France and Canada, have 1.2 per cent and 0.2 per cent of the world market respectively.

Most of the microchips for British standard teletext and viewdata sets are manufactured by Mullard Ltd at their Southampton plant. The production of these chips was one million in 1980, four million in 1982, and this year will total seven million, half being exported to countries including the US, Japan, the Far East, and Europe.

(Source: British Telecom, Corporate Relations Department)

(a) What is the viewdata and teletext service provided by British Telecom?
(b) What percentage of viewdata and teletext sets throughout the world do not use British standards?
(c) What is the total of viewdata/teletext sets used in Britain, the Netherlands, West Germany, and Sweden?
(d) Draw a bar-chart to illustrate the number of microchips produced from 1980 to 1983, estimating the figure for 1981.
(e) Find out and list the topics on which teletext provides information. If you have a teletext set at home, which do you use most?

2. Draw a rough sketch map and mark:
(a) The three nearest telephone boxes to your school.
(b) The three nearest post boxes to your home.
(How many collections per day are there from these post boxes?)

3. Find out the following information:
(a) The cost of installation of a telephone in a private house.
(b) The cost of a local call from (i) a house, (ii) a telephone box.
(c) The cost of a six-minute STD call to London or Birmingham from your home.

4. List 10 things which can be obtained over a post office counter, e.g., a dog licence.

5. Draw a diagram showing how many times a letter might be handled if it had a Glasgow address and was posted in London.

6. What number would you dial if you wanted to:
(a) Know the time?
(b) Check some motoring information?
(c) Get a recipe?
(d) Request a record?
(e) Find a test match score?

TOPIC 12.2   Road transport

The increasing number of vehicles

In March 1904 there were only 8500 cars in use in Great Britain. By 1910, there were 50 000. Today there are over 19 million motor vehicles. Future estimates are given in Table 12.1.

Table 12.1   Estimates of the probable number of motor vehicles in Britain, 1980 – 2000

Year	Probable number of vehicles (million)
1980	19.25 (Actual)
1990	25.50
2000	29

These may prove to be underestimates. Even today, Great Britain has one of the highest densities of road traffic in the world with about 65 vehicles per mile.

In 1978 motor vehicle traffic in Great Britain rose by a record 41 per cent of which private cars and taxis accounted for 80 per cent.

The roads

Road transport offers advantages over other means of transport and has been the main cause of the decline in rail transport. The increase in the number of motor vehicles has led to a huge programme of road construction. Trunk roads and motorways provide a national network of routes for through traffic. Altogether Great Britain has over 200 000 miles of public highway which may be divided up into the sectors shown in Table 12.2.

In future we are likely to see further improvements in roads and a steady increase in motorway mileage.

Table 12.2   Road mileage (Source: *Britain 1983,* HMSO)

	Public roads[a]	Trunk roads[a] (including motorways)	Trunk motorways[b]	
			in use[c]	under construction
England	161 649	6360	1472	71
Scotland	31 049	1971	153	—
Wales	19 803	1086	74	—
Northern Ireland	14 652	409	70	—
Britain	227 153	9826	1769	71

Sources: Department of Transport Northern Ireland, Department of the Environment, Scottish Development Department, Welsh Office.
[a] As at April 1981.
[b] As at April 1982.
[c] In addition, there were 48 miles (77 kilometres) of local authority motorway in use in England and 21 miles (33 kilometres) in Scotland.

193

Fig 12.5   A juggernaut lorry

Fig 12.6   Traffic congestion

Road haulage

Huge juggernaut lorries are becoming familiar sights on many of Britain's roads and motorways (see Fig. 12.5). A large quantity of manufactured goods and raw materials can be transported in these huge lorries. Many big firms have their own fleets of lorries. The main advantage is that goods can be transported to their exact destination at any time. The transport manager of a large firm must abide by the Transport Act of 1969; lorries can be stopped at any time for a roadside safety check. There are nearly 2 million haulage vehicles on the road; the type of goods they carry depends on the class of Ministry of Transport licence that they hold. Under the 1969 Transport Act all road hauliers must have an operator's licence enabling them to carry *any* kind of goods for *anyone*. To obtain this licence they have to prove to the Department of the Environment that their vehicles are serviced properly and regularly. In 1970 new regulations came into force limiting the number of hours drivers are allowed to work, and compelling all drivers of lorries to keep a log book showing how many miles they have driven in a certain period. A tired driver is a safety hazard on the roads.

The growth of road haulage has been concentrated on long distance traffic, particularly international road haulage, and British hauliers are increasingly running goods vehicles to the rest of Europe and as far afield as North and West Africa and the Middle East. The Minister of Transport has set up an independent inquiry to consider the growth in road haulage, especially its impact on people and the environment, and the best way of ensuring that future developments meet the public interest.

Congestion

Figure 12.6 shows some of the chaos caused by the motor vehicle. Some people feel that our cities and towns are dominated by motor cars, so that pedestrians have very little space and are forced to live dangerously. We must have careful town planning designed to look after the interests of both pedestrians and motorists. Such planning was recommended by the Buchanan Report, *Traffic in Towns*. Some measures have already been carried out in several large cities:

1. The number of car parks has been increased, especially on the outskirts.
2. Restricted parking has been introduced in the centre of cities and towns.
3. Pedestrian shopping areas have been created.
4. One-way systems have been designed to help the traffic flow.

It is beginning to be more accepted that shopping precincts in towns should be left to pedestrians, and that cars should be prohibited from the innermost parts. Ring roads will take traffic round towns so it does not have to pass through the centres. At Coventry, Plymouth, and the City of London, attempts have been made to rebuild, using pedestrian walkways and platforms. In these places one feels that the people, not cars, are in charge. Similarly, the new towns of Cumbernauld and Basildon have been designed to solve the problem of the car.

Noise and accidents are two other problems created by motor vehicles. Some large lorries even disturb the foundations of buildings. About 7000 people are killed every year in motor accidents. But we must not look just on the black side. The motor vehicle has brought benefit to us all: we are able to move about quickly and conveniently, while our standard of living has been vastly improved by the movement of goods by road.

Conclusion

It is very likely that you will want to have a car when you are old enough and can afford it. As the number of vehicles on Britain's roads increases, we shall have to adjust our lives. We must make sure that the motor vehicle does not dominate our way of life so that everything gives way to it, but rather see that it is used for the benefit of the community as a whole.

TOPIC 12.2   Activities

1. Read the passage and answer the questions:

City Plague of Take-Home Lorries
The symptoms are: churned-up grass verges, cracked pavements and noise late at night and early in the mornings.

At yesterday's City Council meeting Mrs Lila Cooper complained that heavy lorries were being parked throughout the night outside more and more people's homes.

'This sort of thing is happening all over the city. I don't know what we can do about it, but we should make our feelings known,' she said.

'To bring your lorry home with you seems to me to be absolutely shocking and very bad treatment of neighbours,' she went on.

The lorries were noisy late at night and early in the mornings when the drivers wanted an early start. 'It is up to the employers to see employees do not bring these things home with them,' she said.

Mr Bob Symonds thought the damage caused by the heavy lorries on footways could easily extend to water and gas mains and other services underground.

The whole of the British transport system, which was so heavily in favour of heavy lorries, was stupid, said Mr Len Stevenson.

'It isn't the motor vehicle that's the source of the trouble, it's the person behind the wheel,' said Mr Richard Phelan. He hoped the introduction of tachographs could help employers find out if employees took vehicles home.

(Source: *Eastern Evening News,* 8 April 1981)

(a) Why should lorry drivers wish to take their lorries home with them?
(b) What problems result when these lorries are taken into residential areas at night?
(c) What additional problems could result if lorry drivers continue this action?
(d) Explain the statement made by Mr Len Stevenson.
(e) What is a *tachograph* and how could this help to solve the problem outlined above?

2. Conduct a survey on one of your local trunk roads counting the following types of vehicles which pass in one hour:
(a) Private cars.
(b) Lorries transporting goods.
(c) Public transport (buses).
(d) Cyclists.

3. Draw a diagram to show one road improvement in your area. Underneath describe how this improvement has helped the flow of traffic.

4. Draw a sketch map to show the route taken by your nearest local bus. Are there any points in the journey where the bus causes congestion? If so, how could this congestion be cut down?

5. Write the names of five brands of four star petrol with their various prices. If you had a car that did 30 miles to the gallon, how much would you pay out on petrol if you used the cheapest petrol and travelled 150 miles a week?

6. Describe some of the recommendations you would make in order to avoid the increasing number of accidents caused by motor vehicles.

TOPIC 12.3   British Rail

The decline of the railways

The invention of the steam locomotive led to a great railway boom in nineteenth-century England. The railways enabled people to move about a lot more and goods to be transported in bulk. However, the ever-increasing popularity of the motor vehicle in the twentieth century has meant the rapid decline of the railways. After the Beeching Report of 1963, it was decided to close many railway lines that did not pay their way.

The railway network has been cut from about 25 000 miles at its peak to about 11 000 miles today, and the following have been successfully adopted:

1. Discontinuance of many stopping passenger services.
2. Closure of small stations to passenger traffic.
3. Selective improvements of inter-city passenger services and rationalization of routes.
4. Development of network of 'liner-train' services.

British Rail services

Passenger services

The passenger network comprises a fast inter-city network, linking the main centres of Britain, local shopping services and commuter services in and around the large conurbations, especially London and the South-East (see Fig. 12.7). British Rail introduced the world's fastest diesel rail service, known as the Inter-City 125. These services are operated by high speed trains which travel at maximum speeds of 125 m.p.h.

Electrification of British Rail is continuing in the 1980s. An £80 million scheme to electrify the line between London and Bedford was completed in 1982, and a £30 million scheme to extend electrified services to Ipswich, Norwich, and Harwich is in progress. With government approval, further electrification projects will follow.

Freight Services

You can imagine the traffic jams there would be if all our coal had to be moved by road. Much of the railway's future lies in transporting bulky goods. The first freightliner train ran in 1965 and there are now over 20 freightliner terminals throughout England, some of them with vital links to the Continent. British Rail has longterm contracts to move oil from refineries, while coal is fed by rail direct to power stations on 'merry-go-round-trains' on which coal is loaded and discharged automatically. Other important goods moved by rail include cars, china clay, milk, grain, mail, and newspapers.

British Rail Hovercraft Ltd

This organization was set up by British Rail in 1966 and is the world's largest commercial operator of hovercrafts. It runs regular services across the English Channel between Dover and Boulogne using a 165-tonne hovercraft carrying both passengers and cars (see Fig. 12.8).

National Freight Corporation

British Rail also owns and is responsible for about 100 ships. They provide passenger and freight services on most of the main routes between Britain and Europe.

A network of about 80 'Speedlink' high speed freight services using high capacity new wagons has been established between the major industrial centres. Freight traffic is being concentrated at fewer and better equipped marshalling yards and terminals. Operations are controlled by computer which reduces costs and allows a more intensive use of rolling stock and the withdrawal of many obsolete freight vehicles.

The Channel Tunnel

The British and French Governments have said that they intend to develop a twin-rail tunnel underneath the Channel between Britain and

197

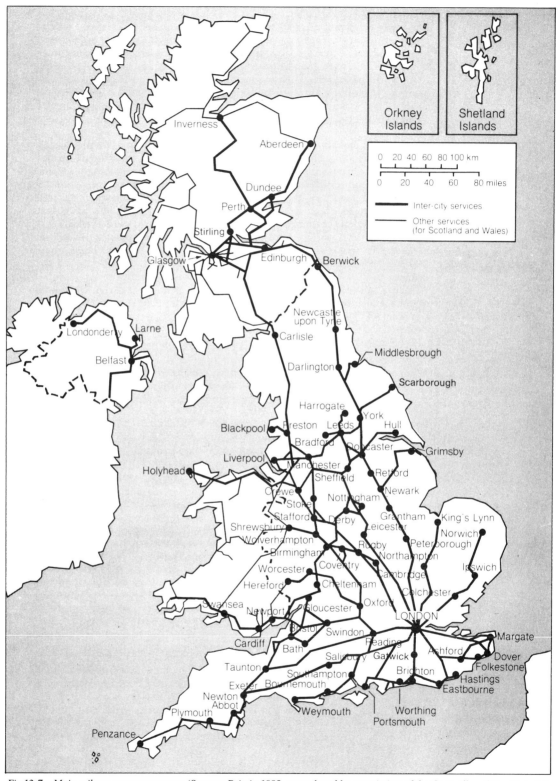

Fig 12.7   Main railway passenger routes (Source: Britain 1985, reproduced by permission of the Controller of Her Majesty's Stationery Office. ©Crown copyright)

France. It is aimed that the tunnel should provide ferry-train services for passengers and cars. The advantages of a rail tunnel over a road tunnel include:

1. Only one locomotive is required to pull many coaches and car ferries.
2. Ventilation is easier. Cars give off poisonous fumes.
3. The rail tunnel is less likely to be troubled by accidents (if a car broke down in a road tunnel, there would be many problems).

It is hoped that a tunnel might be profitable for the British and French state-owned railways, both of which run at a loss. There is renewed speculation in the 1980s that this project may be started, even though the idea was first thought of in the nineteenth century.

Conclusion

The railways were once our most important means of inland transport, but they now have to compete with the popularity of road transport. The railways have had to change their image. The whole system has been modernized and wasteful services cut out. Future modernization is still essential and in 1981 British Rail received £810 million from the Government, much of it to continue essential modernization programmes. A large passenger railway system can no longer be run for profit. The future of the railways lies in fast inter-city services and carrying heavy goods which would otherwise clutter up the roads.

Fig 12.8   A hovercraft

TOPIC 12.3   Activities

1. Read the passage and answer the questions:

Operations
British Rail's operating statistics are shown in Table 24. In 1981 the Board's turnover, including financial support and income from other activities but excluding internal transactions, was £2899 million and there was a net deficit of £37.2 million. Financial support for British Rail includes compensation for the financial burden of operating the rail passenger system as a public service and grants for level crossings. In 1981 the British Railways Board received £810 million from the Government and the passenger transport executives in respect of the public service obligation. At the end of 1981 the British Railways Board employed 227 300 people.

Table 24   Railway statistics

	1976	1979	1980	1981
Passenger journeys (million)	707	748	760	718
Passenger-miles (million)	17 700	19 900	19 700	19 100
Freight train traffic (million tonnes)	176	169	153	154
Freight train traffic (million net tonne-miles)	12 794	12 361	10 961	10 877
Assets (at end of year):				
Locomotives	3689	3571	3379	3131
HST power cars and passenger carriages	193	669	772	845
APT power cars and passenger carriages	—	20	36	36
Other coaching vehicles	22 222	20 963	20 408	18 268
Freight vehicles	187 000	137 589	119 507	87 955
Stations	2865	2821	2787	2739
Route open for traffic (miles)	11 189	11 020	10 964	10 831

(Source: *Britain 1983,* HMSO)

(a) What does the phrase 'there was a net deficit of £37.2 million' mean?

(b) Why should operating the rail passenger system as a public service be a financial burden?

(c) Plot graphs to illustrate (i) freight traffic (million tonnes) and (ii) freight vehicles. Compare your graphs — do you find the results surprising in any way?

(d) Why do you think the numbers of HST power cars and passenger carriages have increased, while numbers of other coaching vehicles have decreased?

(e) Do you think the railway system should be smaller, more efficient and profitable, or should it be extended to provide a better service for the public?

2. In your notebook write five advantages and five disadvantages of using the railways as a means of transport.

3. Draw a sketch map to show the nearest railway station to your home and the routes served by the main lines from this station.

4. Imagine you were given a free railway pass that lasted for one week. Plan an interesting holiday using this free ticket to see as much of Great Britain as you can. (Use a train timetable.)

5. Draw a plan to show what a section of the Channel tunnel might look like.

6. Design a poster to encourage more people to travel by rail.

TOPIC 12.4 Sea and air

Sea transport

The tramp ship shown in Fig. 12.9 is capable of crossing the world's ocean and carrying large quantities of cargo in each of its five holds. Britain has a large fleet of merchant ships which act as carriers of the world's trade. She has the second largest oil tanker fleet and the fourth largest ore and bulk carrier fleet.

Larger and faster ships are always being constructed. Specially designed vessels carry ore, cement, wine, chemicals, etc. (see Fig. 12.10). Many ships have been built to carry fully loaded road vehicles, pallets, and containers. The use of enormous storage containers means that door-to-door journeys can be made. There is no need for unloading individual items, because the container is simply lifted off the ship on to a lorry to make the remainder of its journey. This results in speedier, safer, and cheaper carriage of a wide range of goods.

Lloyd's Register of Shipping

Lloyd's Register classifies ships according to their safety and efficiency. Ships can be insured against damage or total loss. Much of the world's shipping is insured through Lloyd's of London. The Lloyd's insurance dealers are known as underwriters because at one time they used to accept the risk of insurance by writing their name or initials *underneath* the policy. Today, an underwriter, who thinks that it would be unwise to accept a very large risk on his own, will insure himself with another underwriter to cover some of the heavy payments he would have to make if the ship were lost. The register kept at Lloyd's helps the underwriters to get the information they need about the ship and the risks involved.

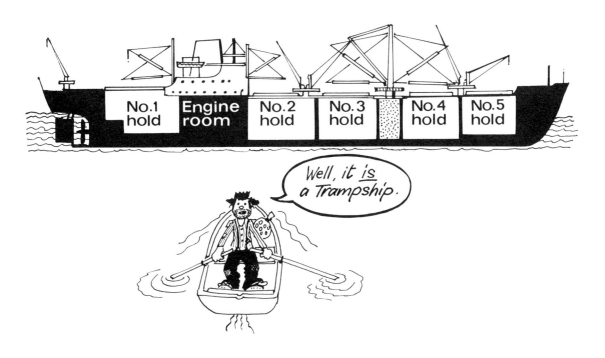

Fig 12.9   A trampsteamer

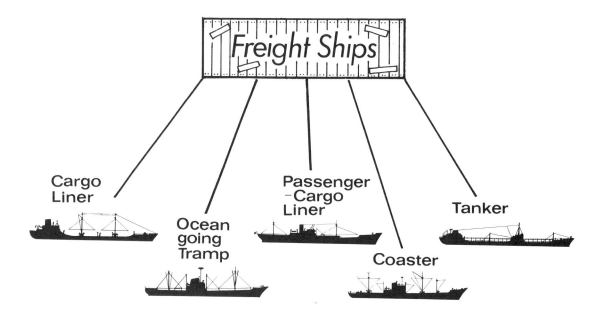

Fig 12.10   *Different types of ships*

Fig 12.11   *Heathrow Airport (Reproduced by permission of*
British Airways)

Air transport

The London Airport of Heathrow is one of the busiest in the world (see Fig. 12.11). Aircraft take off or land at the rate of about one a minute. A large number of these flights are operated by the state-owned airline, British Airways, and some by independent airlines.

State-owned airline

The British Airways route network covers some 359 200 miles and is among the largest in the world. The airline serves 140 destinations in 70 countries and in 1981/82 carried some 15.3 million passengers on scheduled services. In 1985 the Government plans to privatize British Airways by selling shares to private investors. Air transport is growing in importance both for the movement of passengers and relatively expensive goods (see Fig. 12.12).

Independent airlines

In recent years there has been an increase in the passengers and freight carried by independent airlines. In 1970, British Caledonian Airways was formed as the main independent commercial airline. It is a 'second force airline' with a fleet of 30 aircraft carrying annually about a million passengers, plus freight, on chartered and scheduled services. Independent airlines play a vital part in the provision of vehicle ferry services, specialized air-cargo facilities, and package holidays abroad. Their routes throughout the British Isles compete with those of British Airways. Airports such as Manchester and Luton are kept busy in the summer with holiday makers journeying to and from the Continent.

Conclusion

As Great Britain is an island we must rely on sea and air transport to link us with the outside world. People in Great Britain cannot exist without trade: we must sell goods abroad to get the money to buy much of our food and raw materials. Roads and railways provide our best methods of inland transport, but we need ships and aircraft to move goods and people between Great Britain and the rest of the world.

Fig 12.12 A British Airways jumbo jet (Reproduced by permission of British Airways)

TOPIC 12.4   Activities

1. Read the passage and answer the questions:

Air Traffic
In 1981 a total of some 43.7 million passengers travelled by air (international terminal passengers) to or from Britain, 2.1 per cent more than in 1980. Total capacity offered on all services by British airlines amounted to 13 087 million capacity-tonne-kilometres in 1981: 9936 million tonne-kilometres on scheduled services and 3151 million tonne-kilometres on non-scheduled services. British Airways accounts for some 80 per cent of scheduled services flown by British airlines, whereas the charter market is dominated by independent companies.

In 1980 the value of Britain's overseas trade carried by air was some £18 200 million and the proportions carried by air amounted to approximately 18 per cent of the value of exports and of imports. Air freight is important for the carriage of goods with a high value-to-weight ratio, especially where speed of movement is essential. Precious stones, live animals, medicinal and pharmaceutical products, clothing, leather and skins, and scientific instruments are major categories where a relatively high proportion of exports is sent by air.

(Source: *Britain 1983,* HMSO)

(a) In 1981 about 20 million passengers travelled to and from Britain by sea. Why do you think the total number of passengers travelling by air compared to sea has increased so dramatically?
(b) What does the extract mean when it says that 'total capacity has increased'?
(c) What is the 'charter market'?
(d) What proportion of Britain's overseas trade is carried by air?
(e) What are goods with a high value-to-weight ratio?
(f) Why are the goods mentioned suitable for export by air freight?

2. Make a list of 10 commodities which come to this country from abroad. Opposite each one write which country they come from and the approximate distance they have travelled.

3. What types of goods are carried by coasters? Why is the sea the best method of transporting these goods?

4. Describe some of the advantages and disadvantages of travelling by air.

5. What types of goods make up the freight traffic of aircraft flying to the highlands and islands of Scotland? Why to you think aircraft are used to transport these goods?

Appendices

APPENDIX 1 CSE Examination questions

Unit 1   Starting work

1. Unemployment.

Table to show regional unemployment in the UK (April 1979)

Regions		Unemployed			
			Of whom:		School-leavers included in total
	% age rate* (per cent)	Total no. (000s)	Males (000s)	Females (000s)	(000s)
South-East	3.7	277.9	208.2	69.7	2.4
East Anglia	4.8	33.6	24.8	8.7	0.3
South-West	5.9	95.3	67.4	27.8	1.2
W. Midlands	5.2	119.3	84.6	34.7	1.9
E. Midlands	4.6	72.1	52.9	19.3	0.7
Yorkshire & Humberside	5.6	115.7	83.5	32.2	1.9
North West	6.8	192.9	137.5	55.5	4.4
North	8.3	113.2	80.9	32.3	2.3

* % age rate = number of unemployed as a percentage of the working population.

Reproduced from *A Working World Topic Book* by Hilary Street published by Macdonald Educational Limited by courtesy of the author and publishers.

(a)   Examine the above table and answer the following questions:
   (i)   Giving the figures, show which regions of the country have the highest and the lowest percentage of unemployed people.
   (ii)   Give a reason for this difference.
   (iii)   Giving the figures, show in which regions of the country the unemployment position for school leavers is at its best and its worst.
   (iv) What is being done to help the unemployed school leaver? (6)
(b)   In a paragraph describe the effects of unemployment on the individual and on society. (5)
(c)   Describe the factors that cause unemployment and say which of these is influencing the situation shown in the table. (9)

------

(20)

(The West Midlands Examinations Board)

2. What factors determine differences in wages and salaries for skilled, unskilled, and professional workers?
(East Anglian Examinations Board for CSE)

3. Using examples explain why certain groups of workers earn more than others.
(East Anglian Examinations Board for CSE, Hewett School, Mode 3)

4. Explain why four of the following people may find their work presents difficulties or gives rise to dissatisfaction.
(a) Night-shift worker.
(b) Assembly-line worker.
(c) Housewife doing part-time work.
(d) Worker being changed from time-rate to piece-rate.
(e) Production worker on being promoted to foreman.
(f) Manager of a firm considering introduction of automation.
(g) Worker in an occupation you have studied.

(East Anglian Examinations Board for CSE, Specimen Paper)

Unit 2   You won't get all you earn

5. Distinguish between direct and indirect taxation. How might a married man with two children benefit from government expenditure?

(East Anglian Examinations Board for CSE, Hewett School, Mode 3)

6. Answer one of the following:
(a) Describe the main items of government expenditure.
(b) Give an account of the main provisions of the Spring Budget of 1985.

(East Anglian Examinations Board for CSE)

7. Describe the sources of income of a local authority.

(East Anglian Examinations Board for CSE)

8. Local councils levy rates on shops, homes, offices, and factories, in order to raise money. Explain the following terms in relation to rates.
(a) Gross value.
(b) Rateable value.
(c) Rate in the pound.
(d) Rate rebate.

(East Anglian Examinations Board for CSE)

Unit 3   Will you join a trade union?

9. What benefits do trade unions offer to their members? What are the disadvantages of membership?

(East Anglian Examinations Board for CSE)

10. Explain the main features of the following types of trade union:
(a) Industrial union.
(b) Craft union.
(c) General union.
(d) White collar union.

(East Anglian Examinations Board for CSE)

11. Explain, in detail, three of the following:
(a) Shop steward.
(b) Collective bargaining.
(c) Craft unions.
(d) Trades Union Congress.

(East Anglian Examinations Board for CSE)

12. Give a detailed account of *three* of the following trade union terms. Credit will be given if you are able to refer to any relevant news items you have studied during the period of your course.
(a) Secondary picketing.
(b) Working to rule.
(c) Official and unofficial strikes.
(d) Closed shop.

(East Anglian Examinations Board for CSE)

Unit 4   Spending your wages

13. Describe the main features of the following retail outlets:
(a)   Unit shop.
(b)   Hypermarket.
(c)   Department store.
(d)   Mail order firm.

(East Anglian Examinations Board for CSE)

14. Describe the organisation of a retail co-operative society mentioning the following points:
(a)   Membership.
(b)   Management.
(c)   Distribution of profits.
(d)   Importance in retailing.

(East Anglian Examinations Board for CSE)

15. What are the differences between buying goods on hire purchase and credit sale. In what ways are buyers on credit protected legally?

(East Anglian Examinations Board for CSE)

16. Describe the work of one major organization for the guidance of the consumer in buying goods. What are your rights in the following circumstances?
(a)   The wellington boots you bought prove not to be waterproof.
(b)   You believe you have been given short weight by the greengrocer.
(c)   You signed a hire purchase agreement and now wish to cancel it.

(East Anglian Examinations Board for CSE, Hewett School, Mode 3)

Unit 5   Banking your money

17. Describe, in detail, an investment you would recommend for each of the following individuals:
(a)   Mrs Jones, a pensioner, wishes to protect her capital from the effects of inflation.
(b)   Mr Smith, a young family man, wishes to protect his dependants financially were he to die at an early age.
(c)   Mrs Roberts, a wealthy widow, is willing to take a gamble on interest but wants her capital to be safe.
(d)   Mr Briggs, a young factory worker, wishes to save a few pounds a week, but would like to be able to draw out these savings within a few days if necessary.

(East Anglian Examinations Board for CSE)

18. Explain the meaning of each of the following banking terms:
(a)   Open cheque.
(b)   Not negotiable.
(c)   Account payee only.
(d)   Stale cheque.
(e)   Drawer.
(f)   Drawee.

(East Anglian Examinations Board for CSE)

19. You are a bank employee and have been asked the following questions by a bank customer. Answer them fully.
(a)   'Is it necessary to cross my cheque when paying a creditor?'
(b)   'How can I get money from a bank outside banking hours?'
(c)   'How can the bank assist my forgetful mother to pay her yearly subscription to her choral society?'

(East Anglian Examinations Board for CSE)

20. Describe *six* of the services a commercial bank might offer you when you leave school.

(East Anglian Examinations Board for CSE)

Unit 6   How goods are produced

21. Explain fully the main factors which affect the location of industry in Britain.

(East Anglian Examinations Board for CSE)

22. Distinguish between primary, secondary, and tertiary workers. How do the characteristics of working in the building industry differ from those in manufacturing industries?

(East Anglian Examinations Board for CSE, Hewett School, Mode 3)

23. What are the advantages and disadvantages of a business run by a sole trader compared with one run by a partnership?

(East Anglian Examinations Board for CSE)

24. Your nephew wishes to know more about your shareholding in the ABC Public Limited Liability Company. Answer his questions:
(a) What is meant by limited liability?
(b) Tell me *two* items of information to be found in your Company's Memorandum of Association.
(c) You refer to ordinary shares as 'risk takers'. What do you mean?
(d) Why does your company issue a prospectus?

(East Anglian Examinations Board for CSE)

Unit 7   Advertising

25.

Reasons for approval of advertising		Reasons for disapproval of advertising	
Number of adults who approve of advertising	Percentage	Number who disapprove of advertising	Percentage
tells about product/prices	32	products should sell on merit	6
tells about new products	13	too much advertising	14
helps people choose products	10	too much repetition	5
helps sell products	19	misleading	23
lower costs	1	puts prices up/wastes money	32
helps business/trade	12	makes people spend more	3
helps employment	4	people buy what they don't	
supports TV	1	want to	10
supports the press	1	makes up your mind for you	2
essential/useful	7	aims at lowest intelligence	5
interesting/educational	7	gets on your nerves	4
amusing	2	spoils TV	7
other reasons	3	other answers	5
ambiguous answers	3	ambiguous answers	5
don't know/not stated	3	don't know/not stated	—

Reproduced from *Sociology* by J. Nobbs, R. Hine and Margaret Flemming, published by Macmillan Education Ltd., by courtesy of the authors and publisher.

(a) From the information provided above choose the *five* most important reasons for people approving of advertising and the *five* most important reasons for disapproving. List these in order of importance and then, in your answer book, display the information in two bar graphs.   (6)
(b) Write a paragraph explaining the meaning of the term 'the affluent society' and the part that advertising plays in such a society.   (4)

(c) Explain, with examples, the part that credit plays in the affluent society and the steps that have been taken to protect the consumer. (10)

(20)

(The West Midlands Examinations Board)

26. For what products is each of the following advertising media best suited? Give full reasons for your answers.
(a) An expensive monthly magazine.
(b) Posters.
(c) A tabloid national daily newspaper.

(East Anglian Examinations Board for CSE)

27. Why do firms advertise? What are the advantages and disadvantages of advertising to the consumer?

(East Anglian Examinations Board for CSE, Hewett School, Mode 3)

28. Advertising, by firms to sell their products has become part of the everyday scene, and many artistic talents are employed at great expense to capture the attention of the general public.
(a) What two factors must the advertiser balance against each other before he can decide whether advertising was worth while?
(b) What benefits might there be to the public?
(c) Why might it be wrong to advertise?
(d) What do you think would make an advertisement effective?

(East Midland Examinations Board for CSE)

Unit 8   Insurance

29. Mr and Mrs Smith have two children at school, own a car, and are buying their house.
(a) Give an account of the types of insurance they might be purchasing.
(b) They also pay National Insurance contributions. What benefits can they obtain from this scheme?

(East Anglian Examinations Board for CSE)

30. Explain the meaning of each of the following insurance principles:
(a) Indemnity.
(b) Utmost good faith.
(c) Insurable interest.

(East Anglian Examinations Board for CSE)

31. Give an account of the kinds of insurance a shop-keeper might be advised to have.

(East Anglian Examinations Board for CSE)

32. Write an essay on the insurance market known as Lloyd's of London, mentioning its organization and functions.

(East Anglian Examinations Board for CSE)

Unit 9   Social Services

33. **The Welfare State**
One hundred years ago the 'Welfare State' did not exist. A man who was out of work or sick and who could not pay his way was sent to the poor house. At the poor house, conditions were deliberately made harsh because it was believed that the unemployed were all lazy and trying to 'scrounge' off the state. However, since 1908, the state has been gradually taking on a greater responsibility. It was just after the Second World War that the Welfare State, as we know it today, emerged. Lord Beveridge, one of the founders of it, wrote in 1942 that there were five main problems:

1 *Want* – which could be conquered by a National Insurance Scheme.
2 *Disease* – which could be overcome by a free national health service.
3 *Ignorance* – which could be attacked by more and better schooling.
4 *Squalor* – which could be avoided by more and better housing.
5 *Idleness* – which could be controlled by greater government control of industry.

Reproduced from *An Introduction to Social Economics* by A. G. Anderton, published by Heinemann Educational Books, by courtesy of the author and publisher.

(a) Read the information provided above and then answer the following questions:
 (i)   Who does the passage say is a founder of the Welfare State?
 (ii) Name any *three* of the problems that he felt needed to be solved.
 (iii) How could the State help solve the problem of disease?
 (iv) What existed before the Welfare State for those who were sick or unemployed?
 (v)   What action was taken to discourage 'scroungers' at this time?
 (vi) In a sentence explain what is meant by a 'National Insurance Scheme'.   (5)
(b) In a paragraph, explain what is meant by the term 'Welfare State' and how it operates in Britain today.   (5)
(c) The Welfare State has now been working for over thirty years; some people argue that it is no longer relevant to people's needs. Outline the main arguments for and against the present Welfare State system.   (10)

                                                                                             (20)

(The West Midlands Examinations Board)

34. Give an account of any community service connected with your school in which you have participated actively. Describe the problems faced by the aged, invalid or handicapped, and outline the provisions made for aiding them.

(East Anglian Examinations Board for CSE, Specimen Paper)

35. In our complex and ever changing society, voluntary organizations (e.g., the Marriage Guidance Council) seem to find more demands for their services than ever. Write briefly about the work of each of the following organizations:
(a) NSPCC.
(b) Shelter.
(c) Samaritans.
(d) What have these organizations in common with each other?

(East Midland Examinations Board for CSE)

36. Describe the social services which you and your parents make use of.

(Middlesex Examinations Board for CSE)

Unit 10 Population

37.

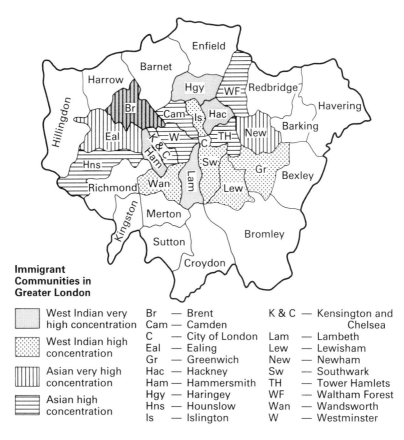

Immigrant Communities in Greater London

West Indian very high concentration	Br — Brent	K & C — Kensington and Chelsea	
West Indian high concentration	Cam — Camden		
	C — City of London	Lam — Lambeth	
	Eal — Ealing	Lew — Lewisham	
	Gr — Greenwich	New — Newham	
Asian very high concentration	Hac — Hackney	Sw — Southwark	
	Ham — Hammersmith	TH — Tower Hamlets	
	Hgy — Haringey	WF — Waltham Forest	
Asian high concentration	Hns — Hounslow	Wan — Wandsworth	
	Is — Islington	W — Westminster	

Reproduced from *The Community, Topic Book,* by Richard Clark and Jennifer Vaughan. Reproduced by permission of the publishers, Macdonald & Company (Publishers) Ltd, copyright Macdonald Educational Limited, 1980.

(a) Examine the information provided above and answer the following questions:
  (i) Name an area of high concentration in
    1 the Asian and
    2 the West Indian communities in London.
  (ii) Name a country of origin for the (1) Asian and (2) West Indian communities.
  (iii) Give a reason for the concentration of immigrant communities.
  (iv) Give *one* example of how immigrants can influence the culture of an area.
  (v) In a sentence, explain what is meant by the term immigration.   (5)
(b) Giving at least *two* examples explain what is meant by the term 'racial discrimination'.   (5)
(c) Describe the pattern of immigration to Britain since 1945, the main areas of settlement, the problems which arise and the action being taken to create an integrated multi-racial society.   (10)

                                                                                    (20)

(The West Midlands Examinations Board)

38. Our population is growing, pollution is increasing and there are more and more cars on the roads. Explain how you think these things are affecting life in our big cities.

(Metropolitan Examinations Board for CSE)

39.
(a) (i)   What is meant by the term 'census'?
    (ii) Who organizes the census?
    (iii) When was the first census carried out in Great Britain?
    (iv) How often does the census take place?
(b) Describe some of the uses that the State may make of the material gathered in the census in social planning.

(East Anglian Examinations Board for CSE, Specimen Paper)

40. In an urban area which is to be redeveloped, what amenities would you provide which would be of benefit to the community?

(Metropolitan Examinations Board for CSE)

Unit 11   Housing

41. You are about to set up home. Giving reasons, answer the following:
(a) Would you choose a house, flat, or some other type of accommodation?
(b) Would you prefer to buy or rent your accommodation?
(c) Would you use Hire Purchase to equip your home?

(East Anglian Examinations Board for CSE, Specimen Paper)

42. Explain how you would set about buying a house, from the very first stage of making up your mind to the day you moved in.

(Metropolitan Examinations Board for CSE)

43.
(a) How can a building society assist John Smith to buy his house?
(b) How does it help Mary Brown to save her money?

(East Anglian Examinations Board for CSE)

44. Describe the part played by each of the following in the purchase of a house: Estate Agent, Surveyor, Solicitor, Building Society, Insurance Company.

(Associated Lancashire Examinations Board for CSE)

Unit 12   Communications

45. Describe the Recorded Delivery Service of the Post Office and compare it with the Registered Letter Service.

(Welsh Joint Education Committee, CSE)

46. Name *three* different methods of inland transport apart from road transport and give *one* advantage and *one* disadvantage for each of them. Write fully on the main advantages and disadvantages of road transport bearing in mind current trends.

(South-East Regional Examinations Board for CSE)

47. What are the advantages and disadvantages of road transport over other methods of moving freight?
(East Anglian Examinations Board for CSE)

48. For what purposes is air transport most suitable? Describe the advantages and disadvantages of air transport. How is air transport keeping in line with the needs of modern times?
(South-East Regional Examinations Board for CSE)

APPENDIX 2   Objective test questions

Select which you think is the correct answer and write the appropriate letter (A, B, C, or D) in the box.

Unit 1   Starting work

1. If you applied for a job with a large firm you would probably be interviewed by the
A   Managing Director.
B   Personnel Officer.
C   Works Manager.
D   Company Secretary

2. An employee's net wage is the pay
A   excluding overtime.
B   before any deductions are made.
C   after income tax has been deducted.
D   when all deductions have been made.

3. When the major part of a manufacturing process is done by machines rather than men, this is known as
A   automation.
B   the division of labour.
C   specialization.
D   standardization.

4. Which of the following offences by an employee would be most likely to result in dismissal on the spot?
A   Being rude to a supervisor.
B   Being rude to a customer.
C   Stealing money from the till.
D   Arriving late for work.

5. Which of the following industries employs the most workers?
A   Distribution.
B   Mining.
C   Farming.
D   Construction.

Unit 2   You won't get all you earn

6. Which of the following is a statutory deduction from an employee's wage packet?
A   Trade union subscription.
B   National Insurance contribution.
C   'Save As You Earn' payment.
D   Donation to charity.

7. Which of the following is a direct tax?
A   Customs duty.
B   Excise duty.
C   Income tax.
D   Value added tax.

8. Which of the following is an indirect tax?
A   Value added tax.
B   Capital gains tax.
C   Capital transfer tax.
D   Income tax.

9. The price of an item excluding value added tax is £7. What would be the price including VAT, assuming a standard rate of 15 per cent?
A   £7.70
B   £7.85
C   £8.05
D   £8.25

10. Which of the following is *not* an example of government expenditure?
A   Defence.
B   Social services.
C   Environmental services.
D   Banking services.

Unit 3   Will you join a trade union?

11. The trade union for shop workers is
A   NUT.
B   USDAW.
C   TGWU.
D   NUM.

12. NALGO is an example of
A   a white-collar union.
B   an industrial union.
C   a general union.
D   a craft union.

13. The process of management and workers getting together to discuss wages and working conditions is known as
A   arbitration.
B   conciliation.
C   restrictive practices.
D   collective bargaining.

14. The organization which is called in to help settle industrial disputes is
A   TUC.
B   CBI.
C   ILO.
D   ACAS.

15. A disagreement between two trade unions regarding 'who does what' is known as
A   an official strike.
B   an unofficial strike.
C   a demarcation dispute.
D   a go-slow.

Unit 4   Spending your wages

16. A trader who supplies goods direct to the general public is known as a
A   wholesaler.
B   retailer.
C   middleman.
D   producer.

17. A working wife is likely to do most of her shopping at
A   several small shops.
B   market stalls.
C   a multiple store.
D   a supermarket.

18. A large store on the outskirts of town, on one level and having a large car park is called a
A   variety chain store.
B   hypermarket.
C   multiple store.
D   supermarket.

19. Which of the following articles would be unsuitable for a hire purchase transaction?
A   A suit of clothes.
B   A refrigerator.
C   A dining suite.
D   A washing machine.

20. In all of the following credit transactions the purchaser of the goods becomes their legal owner except
A   deferred payment.
B   budget account.
C   hire purchase.
D   trading checks.

Unit 5   Banking your money

21. Which of the following forms of saving does *not* earn interest?
A   Commercial bank deposit account.
B   Building society share account.
C   Save As You Earn.
D   Premium bonds.

22. All of the following *must* appear on a cheque before it can be cleared except
A   the date.
B   a crossing.
C   the drawer's signature.
D   the amount in words and figures.

23. The person who signs a cheque is known as the
A   drawer.
B   drawee.
C   payer.
D   payee.

24. The most convenient way of paying variable sums of money at irregular intervals to a creditor is by
A   cash.
B   cheque.
C   direct debit.
D   standing order.

216

25. Which of the following banking services would be particularly useful for a retail business?
A   Cash dispenser.
B   Night safe.
C   Safe deposit box.
D   Budget account.

Unit 6   How goods are produced

26. Which of the following wage payment systems results in more pay for the worker for more work done?
A   Day rates.
B   Time rates.
C   Piecework rates.
D   Hourly rates.

27. Which of the following terms is the most similar in meaning to the term 'division of labour'?
A   Specialization.
B   Simplification.
C   Standardization.
D   Automation.

28. In which of the following types of business do the owners have unlimited liability?
A   Partnership.
B   Private joint-stock company.
C   Public joint-stock company.
D   Co-operative retail society.

29. What is the maximum number of members of a non-professional partnership?
A   2
B   20
C   50
D   No maximum.

30. Which of the following investments is paid interest rather than dividend?
A   Ordinary share.
B   Preference share.
C   Debenture.
D   Government stock.

Unit 7   Advertising

31. All of the following are examples of point-of-sale promotion except
A   a 'money off next purchase' coupon.
B   a free gift with a purchase.
C   an advertisement in a magazine.
D   a competition entry form.

32. Which of the following advertising media would be suitable for publicizing a small hairdressing salon?
A   Local cinema.
B   Television.
C   National newspaper.
D   Women's magazine.

217

33. Which of the following is an example of informative, rather than persuasive, advertising?
A   A fire prevention advertisement issued by the Government.
B   A television advertisement for a new hairspray.
C   An advertisement in a magazine for an expensive perfume.
D   A poster advertising a particular make of car.

34. Which of the following is a disadvantage of advertising?
A   It gives the public information they need.
B   It may persuade people to buy unnecessary things.
C   It increases sales and therefore may create jobs.
D   It supports television, radio, and the press.

35. All of the following impose some sort of legal control on advertising except the
A   Sale of Goods Act 1893.
B   Trade Descriptions Act 1968.
C   Consumer Credit Act 1974.
D   British Code of Advertising Practice.

Unit 8   Insurance

36. Arthur Bloggs, aged 65, applied for life assurance and stated his age as 45 on the proposal form. This illustrates the principle of
A   indemnity.
B   insurable interest.
C   utmost good faith.
D   subrogation.

37. A person employed by an insurance company to work out premiums is known as
A   an actuary.
B   an agent.
C   a broker.
D   an underwriter.

38. The document which sets out the details of an insurance contract is the
A   cover note.
B   proposal.
C   policy.
D   certificate.

39. The most suitable insurance for a young married man who wished to insure his life and save for the future at the same time would be
A   a whole life policy.
B   an endowment policy.
C   a mortgage protection policy.
D   a personal accident policy.

40. Marlene Moneybags had jewellery worth £50 000 insured with two insurance companies. It was stolen and each company paid her £25 000. This illustrates the principle of
A   subrogation.
B   contribution.
C   utmost good faith.
D   insurable interest.

Unit 9 Social Services

41. Which government department is responsible for housing?
A   Department of Health and Social Security.
B   Department of Education and Science.
C   Department of Employment.
D   Department of the Environment.   ☐

42. Which of the following organizations is directly responsible for job centres?
A   MSC.
B   ACAS.
C   NHS.
D   CBI.   ☐

43. If you left school with five GCE 'O' level passes, you could attend a
A   university.
B   polytechnic.
C   college of education.
D   college of further education.   ☐

44. The average life expectancy for a woman in the United Kingdom is approximately
A   65 years.
B   70 years.
C   75 years.
D   80 years.   ☐

45. Which of the following organizations tries to ensure that children are not ill-treated?
A   RSPCA.
B   NSPCC.
C   RNLI.
D   WHO.   ☐

Unit 10 Population

46. A census is held every
A   2 years.
B   5 years.
C   10 years.
D   20 years.   ☐

47. The present population of Great Britain is approximately
A   50 million.
B   53 million.
C   56 million.
D   59 million.   ☐

48. All of the following are reasons why people are living longer today except
A   alcohol and tobacco are cheaper.
B   food is more nutritious.
C   standards of living have risen.
D   health and welfare have improved.   ☐

49. What percentage of the population live in urban areas?
A   58 per cent.
B   68 per cent.
C   78 per cent.
D   88 per cent.   ☐

50. Which of the following is a 'new town'?
A   Cheltenham.
B   Northampton.
C   Kings Lynn.
D   Telford.

□

Unit 11   Housing

51. All of the following have to appear by law in the rent book of a weekly-paying tenant except
A   a description of the accommodation.
B   the address of the landlord or his agent.
C   the amount of rent to be paid.
D   the amount of rates to be paid.

□

52. Approximately how many dwellings in Great Britain are rented from local authorities?
A   6 million.
B   7 million.
C   8 million.
D   9 million.

□

53. Which of the following would be considered a basic amenity in a home?
A   A piped water supply.
B   Central heating.
C   A fitted kitchen.
D   A deep-freeze.

□

54. A couple wished to buy a house for £30 000 and the building society was prepared to grant them an 85 per cent mortgage. How much deposit would they pay?
A   £4000
B   £4500
C   £5000
D   £5500

□

55. Enquiries about a house for sale on behalf of a prospective purchaser would be carried out by
A   an estate agent.
B   a bank manager.
C   a surveyor.
D   a solicitor.

□

Unit 12   Communications

56. The Post Office's package collection and overnight delivery service is known as
A   Express Post.
B   Datapost.
C   Intelpost.
D   Electronic post.

□

57. British Telecom's service for transmitting telephone messages by satellite is known as
A   Telex.
B   Teletext.
C   Viewdata.
D   Satstream.

□

58. All of the following have directly helped to ease the problem of traffic in town and city centres except
A   pedestrian precincts.
B   multistorey car parks.
C   ring-roads.
D   motorways. ☐

59. Disadvantages of transporting goods by rail include
A   a door-to-door service.
B   quick transport for bulky goods.
C   low labour costs.
D   easing congestion on the roads. ☐

60. A ship which transports almost any cargo anywhere in the world is known as a
A   tanker.
B   tramp.
C   coaster.
D   cargo liner. ☐

APPENDIX 2   Answers to Objective test questions

1.	B	21.	D	41.	D
2.	D	22.	B	42.	A
3.	A	23.	A	43.	D
4.	C	24.	C	44.	C
5.	A	25.	B	45.	B
6.	B	26.	C	46.	C
7.	C	27.	A	47.	C
8.	A	28.	A	48.	A
9.	C	29.	B	49.	C
10.	D	30.	C	50.	D
11.	B	31.	C	51.	D
12.	A	32.	A	52.	B
13.	D	33.	A	53.	A
14.	D	34.	B	54.	B
15.	C	35.	D	55.	D
16.	B	36.	C	56.	B
17.	D	37.	A	57.	D
18.	B	38.	C	58.	D
19.	A	39.	B	59.	A
20.	C	40.	B	60.	B

INDEX

Advertising:
  informative, 125–126
  persuasive, 125–126
Advertising agency, 122–123
Advertising campaign, 122–123
Advertising Standards Authority, 126
Advisory, Conciliation and Arbitration Service, 51–52, 57
Amalgamated Union of Engineering Workers, 58
Annual percentage rate, 77
Assurance, life, 140
Automation, 112–114

Bank charges, 95
Bank giro, 100
Bank statement, 95
Bar code, 114
Basic rates, 13
Board of Arbitration, 52
British Airways, 203
British Caledonian Airways, 203
British Code of Advertising Practice, 126
British Rail Hovercraft Ltd, 197
British Standards Institution, 83
British Telecom, 187–191
Budget account, 78
Building society, 90, 181–183
Bulk carrier, 201

Careers Advisory Officer, 5
Careers Advisory Service, 5, 6
Careers Office, 22
Census, 163–167
Chancellor of the Exchequer, 42
Channel tunnel, 197–198
Cheque, 93–95
Cheque card, 99
Citizens' Advice Bureau, 82, 176
Code number, 31–33
Collective bargaining, 50–52
Commercial bank, 89
Commission, 14
Communication services, 191
Community Enterprise Programme, 22
Conditions of employment, 9
Confederation of British Industry, 51, 57, 59
Consumer Credit Act 1974, 77, 85
Consumer protection, 82–85
Consumer Safety Act 1978, 85
Consumers' Association, 83–85
Conurbations, 169–174
Co-operative society, 67
Credit card, 79, 99
Credit sale, 78

Current account, 93–95
Curriculum vitae, 5
Customs and Excise, 37

Datapost, 189
Death grant, 27
Debenture, 118
Deductions, 13, 25
Demarcation dispute, 54
Department of Education and Science, 153–154
Department of the Environment, 195
Department of Health and Social Security, 25, 43, 151
Department store, 65
Deposit account, 100
Development area, 105
Direct debit, 99
Direct tax, 39
Director General of Fair Trading, 77, 84
Discount store, 67
Dividend, 117–118
Division of labour, 10, 109–110

Education, stages of, 154
Electronic post, 189
Employment Act 1980, 59
Employment Protection Act 1975, 59
Enterprise zone, 105
Environmental Health Officer, 83
Environmental services, 44
Equal Pay Act 1970, 51
Expresspost, 189

Fair Trading Act 1973, 84
Family Income Supplement, 27
Flat rate, 13
Food and Drugs Act 1955, 83, 84

General and Municipal Workers Union, 58
Government expenditure, 42–44
Gross pay, 13
Guardian's allowance, 27

Health and Safety at Work Act 1974, 10
Hire purchase, 75–79
Hire Purchase Act 1964, 76
Hospitals, 157
Housing Finance Act 1972, 177
Hypermarket, 66

Immigration, 164
Income tax, 31–34
Indirect tax, 39
Induction programme, 9
Industrial injuries benefit, 26

Industrial Relations Act 1971, 59
Inland Revenue, 31–34
Input tax, 37
Insurance:
  broker, 133
  company, 133
  cover note, 134
  endowment, 140
  fire, 143
  household, 140
  life, 140
  motor, 139–140
  personal accident, 143
  policy, 134, 136–137
  premium, 129, 134, 137
  principles, 130
  proposal form, 134–135
  prospectus, 134
Intelpost, 189
Interest, 99–100
International Labour Organization, 58

Job centre, 6, 18–20
Joint consultation, 50
Joint-stock company:
  private, 116–117
  public, 118

Kitemark, 83–85

Letter of application, 5
Limited liability, 117–118
Lloyd's of London, 201
Lloyd's Register of Shipping, 201
Loan, 98–99
Local authority, 159–160, 177–178
Local education authority, 3, 153–154
London Airport, 203

Mail order, 67–73
Managing agent, 22
Manpower Services Commission, 17–22, 57
Mass production, 109–110
Maternity grant, 27
Microchip, 10
Mortgage, 181
Motorways, 193, 195
Multiple store, 66

National Association of Local Government Officers, 58
National Freight Corporation, 197
National Giro, 93, 190
National Health Service, 26, 43, 156–157
National Housebuilders' Registration Council, 182
National Insurance, 18, 25–28, 43, 147, 151, 156–157
National Savings Bank, 88–89, 93
National Union of Mineworkers, 47
Net pay, 13
Notice of coding, 31–33

Office of Population Censuses and Surveys, 163–167
Oil tanker, 201
Output tax, 37
Overdraft, 98
Overtime ban, 54

P14 form, 33
P45 form, 33–34
Partnership, 116
Partnership, Deed of, 116
Pay As You Earn, 31
Personnel manager, 9
Piecework, 14, 110
Post code, 189
Post Office, 88, 93, 187–191
Post Office Guide, 190
Private pension scheme, 27
Public analyst, 83
Public Records Office, 166

Race Relations Act 1976, 51
Registrar General, 163
Restrictive practices, 54
Retailer, 62–67
Retirement pension, 27

Save As You Earn, 90
Self-selection, 66
Self-service, 66
Sex Discrimination Act 1975, 51
Share, 117–118
Share, ordinary, 118
Share, preference, 118
Shop steward, 48
Sickness benefit, 24
Social security benefits, 148–151
Sole proprietor, 116
Solicitor, 182
Standing order, 99
Stock Exchange, 118
Strike:
  official, 54
  unofficial, 54
Superannuation, 27
Supermarket, 66
Supply of Goods (Implied Terms) Act 1973, 84

Tax allowances, 31, 33
Telecommunications Act 1984, 190
Teleshopping, 114
Trade Descriptions Act 1968, 84
Trade Union and Labour Relations Act 1974, 59
Trades Union Congress, 47–48, 51, 57–59
Trading Standards Department, 82–85
Trading Standards Officer, 82, 84
Training Opportunities Scheme, 19
Tramp ship, 201
Transport Act 1969, 195
Transport and General Workers Union, 47, 58

Travellers' cheque, 99
Trustee Savings Bank, 88–89

Underwriter, 201
Unemployment, 105
Unemployment benefit, 18, 26
Unfair Contract Terms Act 1977, 84
Unit trust, 90

Value added tax, 37–39
Variety chain store, 66
Voluntary organizations, 43–44, 151, 160

Weights and Measures Act 1963, 82
Welfare state, 147–151
Which? magazine, 83–85
Widow's pension, 27
Work to rule, 54

Youth Training Scheme, 5, 20–22